Roberts Unanimous

A collection of unanimous opinions from the Supreme Court of the United States authored by Chief Justice John Roberts

collected by
JOSHUA WARREN

Roberts Unanimous

Copyright © 2018
Joshua Warren
New York, NY
All rights reserved.

ISBN: 1727757386
ISBN-13:   978-1727757385

This book is an original collection of public government works, compiled for the purpose of research, scholarly inquiry, and conceptual art.

Pursuant to Title 17 U.S. Code § 105: "Copyright protection under this title is not available for any work of the United States Government". Therefore, the court texts collected in this compilation are not protected by U.S. copyright.

Additionally, pursuant to Title 17 U.S. Code § 107 the use "for purposes such as criticism, comment, news reporting, teaching (including multiple copies for classroom use), scholarship, or research, is not an infringement of copyright." Therefore, even if there was copyright protection in any of the works included in these government texts (and there isn't, pursuant to § 105), the use in this compilation is a fair use pursuant to § 107.

ACKNOWLEDGMENTS

This book would not be possible without
the continuing support and encouragement of my family.

Thank you to everyone who supports nominal togetherness.

DEDICATION

to consensus seekers

Published as a late commemoration to the start
of October Term 2018

Happy Thanksgiving

INTRODUCTION

Chief Justice John G. Roberts was born January 27, 1955 in Buffalo, New York. He assumed the role of Chief Justice of the Supreme Court of the United States on September 29, 2005. He was nominated by President George W. Bush and confirmed by a Senate vote of 78-22.

Roberts was originally nominated to the Supreme Court for the retirement of Justice Sandra Day O'Connor. However, with the death of Chief Justice William Rehnquist, President Bush withdrew the original nomination and re-nominated Roberts for the Chief position.

At his swearing-in ceremony, the then 50-year-old Roberts became the third youngest Chief Justice in American history. Only John Marshall (age 45 in 1801) and John Jay (age 44 in 1789) were younger.

This book collection is published to commemorate the start of October Term 2018: the 13th term of the Roberts era. This term began in the cloud of hoopla that was kicked up when Justice Kennedy announced his retirement and kept swirling ever more feverishly through multiple Senate hearings and floor votes, and eventual thrice swearing-in of Justice Brett Kavanaugh (confirmed October 6th, 2018 by a vote of 50-48, to joining the Court already in term, one week late).

During the 2005 hearings for Roberts to become Chief, Roberts spoke about judicial restraint and a desire for greater institutional unity. He lamented the partisanship of 5-4 decisions and wanted to strengthen the institutional character of the Court with greater agreement.

This book is a collection of unanimous opinions from the Supreme Court of the United States written by Chief Justice John Roberts. This book collection is intended as conceptual art and political commentary. These court opinions are collected with the hope of encouraging average readers to consider jurisprudential writing. It is hoped that some readers will discover intriguing tidbits of American law in these opinions and that they will later investigate using internet search tools.

Justice Roberts is a powerful figure who has held a position of tremendous influence for over a decade. With the recent appointment of Justice Kavanaugh, and the escalation of post-Scalia partisanship this will be a moment for Justice Roberts to step deeper into his legacy. To turn pun on the title and theme of this book collection, now may be a moment for less judicial animus. With Scalia gone and Kennedy replaced by two of his former clerks, it is presumed that we are continuing an era of Roberts5 (as in 5-4), but readers of this book are intended to remember that there are some broad agreements too.

Reading law, even brief pieces of it, will improve the ability to read law. The legacy of the Roberts Court is barely ripe for critical review and actuarial likelihoods suggest that his tenure is only just getting started. As a lifetime appointee, he could remain in his position for many decades more. This book collection is both commentary on this current state of modern American legal affairs and a research tool to begin that quest. It is not intended as legal advice.

Select quotes from opinions in this book:

"The question presented in this case is whether securities fraud plaintiffs must also prove loss causation in order to obtain class certification. We hold that they need not."
    Erica P. John Fund v. Halliburton

"Bad things happen if you fail to pay federal income taxes when due."
    Hinck v. United States

"President Carter's actions were unpopular among many Alaskans, who were concerned that the new monuments would be subject to restrictive federal regulations."
    Sturgeon v. Frost

"But the meaning of "consolidate" in the present context is ambiguous."
    Hall v. Hall

FOREWORD

What is a majority opinion?

The Supreme Court of the United State is composed of nine justices. This court is the highest appellate court in the United States federal jurisdiction. Decisions of the court are by the majority decision of the nine justices. If at least five justices are willing to sign an opinion then the holding becomes law. The holding is the outcome of the case as for that particular case, with those particular facts. The holding becomes law to be used by the lower courts to apply the law consistent with the principles of stare decisis. In order to apply the holding properly, the lower courts need to understand the holding and so the majority opinion is an explanation of the court's reasoning.

What are unanimous opinions?

There are nine members of the Supreme Court: eight associate justices and the chief. When they all agree it is unanimous. But there are different ways to measure their agreement on a case.

They can agree in judgment but also file their own separate concurring opinion. The concurring opinion might then incorporate the majority reasoning or potentially rewrite some reasoning completely. Some scholars might consider an opinion unanimous even if there are these concurring opinions. However, this book collection includes only opinions in which all nine sitting members signed on and did not file their own separate opinion.

At times during the Roberts Court there has been only eight sitting members. This occurred while awaiting replacements or because of recusals on specific cases. Some scholars might consider an opinion during these periods signed by all eight of the then sitting justices to be unanimous. However, these cases have not been included in this book either. While unanimous consensus of eight is impressive, this editor has decided that those agreements would be a qualitatively different type of negotiated agreement. In hindsight, it would have been interesting to hold those cases in comparison to these within the same volume and motivated readers are encouraged to do that work on their own.

How do they decide who writes which opinion?

The opinions in this book are all authored by Chief Justice Roberts. Sometimes with a unanimous decision they might decide to take the authors name off and release it Per Curiam. Other times the opinion is assigned after a straw vote is taken in closed meeting. Assignment of majority opinion is by the most senior justice in the majority. The process by which they sign on, and make adjustments, and try to sway favor of the other justices, is mostly secretive. We don't know if there were any fault lines in earlier drafts that smoothed out into unanimous opinions.

In terms of the law, there is no difference in effect based on which justice authored the opinion or whether is it unanimous. All that matters for legal effect is that the holding had majority support. Unanimous opinions are not more legally powerful than those of 5-4 majorities. Nevertheless, it speaks to a confidence in that holding and the stability of announced rules for application to future variations of the case facts.

Why does it matter that Chief Justice Roberts is the named author on the opinions in this book, and that they are unanimous opinions?

When justices file concurring and dissenting opinions, they know that all of their language is not law. Only the holding is law. Nevertheless, the justices write separately to explain how they would steer the law in the future. And since these are lifetime appointments, these justices expect to be around in the future. They are signaling disagreements and threads for the future.

Contra-similarly, these unanimous opinions authored by Chief Justice Roberts provide a view into the Chief, assigning himself to hold together group consensus. He found a way to write these opinions in ways that no other justice felt a need to pull away from. These opinions represent pieces of Chief Justice Roberts' vision for the future that are without disagreement (well, except from the losing parties).

Does it make sense for non-lawyers to read Supreme Court opinions?

If you find any of the opinions interesting, go read more about that case on the internet. More information about each of these cases is easily found on the internet by searching the case name and citation. Consider using supremecourt.gov, scotusblog.com, oyez.org, law.cornell.edu, as well as Wikipedia.org, and search engines, like Google (and Google Scholar), to find more information about every case in this book. And don't be afraid to use a dictionary.

It can be hard work to read court opinions but imagine how difficult it is to write one. Often the public thinks the act of being a Supreme Court judge (they're called Justices) is simply to decide which side of the issue they like better. The work of weaving reasoned arguments from textual sources is hard work. The unanimously agreed opinions in this book may make the work seem deceptively simple. Even these unanimous opinions are difficult legal work. The general public should have more exposure to the hard workings within the public decision-making processes. In American democracy, the law is the responsibility of all citizens, not just the lawyers, and the first step to becoming involved in the law is to read it.

Reading law will improve your ability to read law.

As you read you may consider yourself as a law clerk and try to summarize the arguments and holdings of each case. This is good practice and any attempt to write (and re-write) a case summary will promote your thinking. You should look up the words and other cases that are referenced. But if you prefer, just sit under a tree and enjoy the togetherness of a Supreme Court in agreement, as woven together by the legal genius of Chief Justice Roberts.

These are all serious legal texts each with a serious legal purpose but they are also appreciable as the high art of American legal civilization. This collection is gathered with the hope of finding enjoyment in these works of art, brought to us from the team of America's top jurisprudential thinkers, as channeled through its current Chief. Law is for reading.

ROBERTS

UNANIMOUS

CHRONOLOGICAL TABLE OF AUTHORITY

		Page #
1.	Martin v. Franklin Capital Corporation	14
2.	Sereboff v. Mid Atlantic Medical	20
3.	Jones, Williams, & Walton	28
4.	Hinck v. United States	46
5.	CSX Transportation v. Georgia State Board of Equalization	53
6.	William L. Rudkin Testamentary Trust	62
7.	U.S. v. Clintwood Elkhorn Mining Company	72
8.	Erica P. John Fund v. Halliburton	81
9.	Gunn v. Minton	88
10.	Gabelli and Alpert v. U.S.	97
11.	Bullard v. Blue Hills Bank	105
12.	Sturgeon v. Frost	113
13.	Endrew F. v. Douglas County School District	124
14.	Dean v. U.S.	136
15.	Hall v. Hall	142
16.	U.S. v. Sanchez-Gomez	154

GERALD T. MARTIN, et ux., Petitioners
v.
FRANKLIN CAPITAL CORPORATION et al.

04-1140
SUPREME COURT
OF THE UNITED STATES

546 U.S. 132

November 8, 2005, Argued
December 7, 2005, Decided

ON WRIT OF CERTIORARI TO THE UNITED STATES COURT OF APPEALS FOR THE TENTH CIRCUIT.

Chief Justice Roberts delivered the opinion of the Court.

A civil case commenced in state court may, as a general matter, be removed by the defendant to federal district court, if the case could have been brought there originally. 28 U.S.C. § 1441 (2000 ed. and Supp. II). If it appears that the federal court lacks jurisdiction, however, "the case shall be remanded." § 1447(c). An order remanding a removed case to state court "may require payment of just costs and any actual expenses, including attorney fees, incurred as a result of the removal." *Ibid.* Although § 1447(c) expressly permits an award of attorney's fees, it provides little guidance on when such fees are warranted. We granted certiorari to determine the proper standard for awarding attorney's fees when remanding a case to state court.

I

Petitioners Gerald and Juana Martin filed a class-action lawsuit in New Mexico state court against respondents Franklin Capital Corporation and Century-National Insurance Company (collectively, Franklin). Franklin removed the case to Federal District Court on the basis of diversity of citizenship. See §§ 1332, 1441 (2000 ed. and Supp. II). In its removal notice, Franklin acknowledged that the amount in controversy was not clear from the face of the complaint--no reason it should be, since the complaint had been filed in state court--but argued that this requirement for federal diversity jurisdiction was nonetheless satisfied. In so arguing, Franklin relied in part on precedent suggesting that punitive damages and attorney's fees could be aggregated in a class action to meet the amount-in-controversy requirement. See App. 35.

Fifteen months later, the Martins moved to remand to state court on the ground that their claims failed to satisfy the amount-in-controversy requirement. The District Court denied the motion and eventually dismissed the case with prejudice. On appeal, the Court of Appeals for the Tenth Circuit agreed with the Martins that the suit failed to satisfy the amount-in-controversy requirement. The Tenth Circuit rejected Franklin's contention that punitive damages and attorney's fees could be aggregated in calculating the amount in controversy, in part on the basis of decisions issued after the District Court's remand decision. The Court of Appeals reversed and remanded to the District Court with instructions to remand the case to state court. 251 F.3d 1284, 1294 (2001).

Back before the District Court, the Martins moved for attorney's fees under § 1447(c). The District Court reviewed Franklin's basis for removal and concluded that, although the Court of Appeals had determined that removal was improper, Franklin "had legitimate grounds for believing this case fell within th[e] Court's jurisdiction." App. to Pet. for Cert. 20a. Because Franklin "had objectively reasonable grounds to believe the removal was legally proper," the District Court denied the Martins' request for fees. *Ibid.*

The Martins appealed again, arguing that § 1447(c) requires granting attorney's fees on remand as a matter of course. The Tenth Circuit disagreed, noting that awarding fees is left to the "wide discretion" of the district court, subject to review only for abuse of discretion. 393 F.3d 1143, 1146 (2004). Under Tenth Circuit precedent, the "'key factor'" in deciding whether to award fees under § 1447(c) is "'the propriety of defendant's removal.'" *Ibid.* (quoting *Excell, Inc.* v. *Sterling Boiler & Mechanical, Inc.*, 106 F.3d 318, 322 (CA10 1997)). In calculating the amount in controversy when it removed the case, Franklin had relied on case law only subsequently held to be unsound, and therefore Franklin's basis for removal was objectively reasonable. 393 F.3d, at 1148. Because the District Court had not abused its discretion in denying fees, the Tenth Circuit affirmed. *Id.*, at 1151.

We granted certiorari, 544 U.S. 998, 125 S. Ct. 1941, 161 L. Ed. 2d 772 (2005), to resolve a conflict among the Circuits concerning when attorney's fees should be awarded under § 1447(c). Compare, *e.g., Hornbuckle* v. *State Farm Lloyds*, 385 F.3d 538, 541 (CA5 2004) ("Fees should only be awarded if the removing defendant lacked objectively reasonable grounds to believe the removal was legally proper" (internal quotation marks omitted)), with *Sirotzky* v. *New York Stock Exchange*, 347 F.3d 985, 987 (CA7 2003) ("[P]rovided removal was improper, the plaintiff is *presumptively* entitled to an award of fees"), and *Hofler* v. *Aetna U.S. Healthcare of Cal., Inc.*, 296 F.3d 764, 770 (CA9 2002) (affirming fee award even when "the defendant's position may be fairly supportable" (internal quotation marks omitted)). We hold that, absent unusual circumstances, attorney's fees should not be awarded when the removing party has an objectively reasonable basis for removal. We therefore affirm the judgment of the Tenth Circuit.

II

The Martins argue that attorney's fees should be awarded automatically on remand, or that there should at least be a strong presumption in favor of awarding fees. Section 1447(c), however, provides that a remand order "may" require payment of attorney's fees--not "shall" or "should." As Chief Justice Rehnquist explained for the Court in *Fogerty* v. *Fantasy, Inc.,* 510 U.S. 517, 533, 114 S. Ct. 1023, 127 L. Ed. 2d 455 (1994), "[t]he word 'may' clearly connotes discretion. The automatic awarding of attorney's fees to the prevailing party would pretermit the exercise of that discretion." Congress used the word "shall" often enough in § 1447(c) --as when it specified that removed cases apparently outside federal jurisdiction "shall be remanded"--to dissuade us from the conclusion that it meant "shall" when it used "may" in authorizing an award of fees.

The Martins are on somewhat stronger ground in pressing for a presumption in favor of awarding fees. As they explain, we interpreted a statute authorizing a discretionary award of fees to prevailing plaintiffs in civil rights cases to nonetheless give rise to such a presumption. *Newman* v. *Piggie Park Enterprises, Inc.,* 390 U.S. 400, 402, 88 S. Ct. 964, 19 L. Ed. 2d 1263 (1968) *(per curiam).* But this case is not at all like *Piggie Park.* In *Piggie Park*, we concluded that a prevailing plaintiff in a civil rights suit serves as a "'private attorney general,'" helping to ensure compliance with civil rights laws and benefiting the public by "vindicating a policy that Congress considered of the highest priority." *Ibid.* We also later explained that the *Piggie Park* standard was appropriate in that case because the civil rights defendant, who is required to pay the attorney's fees, has violated federal law. See *Flight Attendants* v. *Zipes,* 491 U.S. 754, 762, 109 S. Ct. 2732, 105 L. Ed. 2d 639 (1989) ("Our cases have emphasized the crucial connection between liability for violation of federal law and liability for attorney's fees under federal fee-shifting statutes").

In this case, plaintiffs do not serve as private attorneys general when they secure a remand to state court, nor is it reasonable to view the defendants as violators of federal law. To the contrary, the removal statute grants defendants a right to a federal forum. See 28 U.S.C. § 1441 (2000 ed. and Supp. II). A remand is necessary if a defendant improperly asserts this right, but incorrectly invoking a federal right is not comparable to violating substantive federal law. The reasons for adopting a strong presumption in favor of awarding fees that were present in *Piggie Park* are accordingly absent here. In the absence of such reasons, we are left with no sound basis for a similar presumption. Instead, had Congress intended to award fees as a matter of course to a party that successfully obtains a remand, we think that "[s]uch a bold departure from traditional practice would have surely drawn more explicit statutory language and legislative comment." *Fogerty, supra*, at 534, 114 S. Ct. 1023, 127 L. Ed. 2d 455.

For its part, Franklin begins by arguing that § 1447(c) provides little guidance on when fees should be shifted because it is not a fee-shifting statute at all. According to Franklin, the provision simply grants courts jurisdiction to award costs and attorney's fees when otherwise warranted, for example when Federal Rule of Civil Procedure 11 supports awarding fees. Although Franklin is correct that the predecessor to § 1447(c) was enacted, in part, because courts would otherwise lack jurisdiction to award costs on remand, see *Mansfield, C. & L. M. R. Co.* v. *Swan,* 111 U.S. 379, 386-387, 4 S. Ct. 510, 28 L. Ed. 462 (1884), there is no reason to assume Congress went no further than conferring jurisdiction when it acted. Congress could have determined that the most efficient way to cure this jurisdictional defect was to create a substantive basis for ordering costs. The text supports this view. If the statute were strictly jurisdictional, there would be no need to limit awards to "just" costs; any award authorized by other provisions of law would presumably be "just." We therefore give the statute its natural reading: Section 1447(c) authorizes courts to award costs and fees, but only when such an award is just. The question remains how to define that standard.

The Solicitor General would define the standard narrowly, arguing that fees should be awarded only on a showing that the unsuccessful party's position was "frivolous, unreasonable, or without foundation"--the standard we have adopted for awarding fees against unsuccessful plaintiffs in civil rights cases, see *Christiansburg Garment Co.* v. *EEOC,* 434 U.S. 412, 421, 98 S. Ct. 694, 54 L. Ed. 2d 648 (1978), and unsuccessful intervenors in such cases, see *Zipes, supra*, at 762, 109 S. Ct. 2732, 105 L. Ed. 2d 639. Brief for United States as *Amicus Curiae* 14-16. But just as there is no basis for supposing Congress meant to tilt the exercise of discretion in *favor* of fee awards under § 1447(c), as there was in *Piggie Park*, so too there is no basis here for a strong bias *against* fee awards, as there was in *Christiansburg Garment* and *Zipes*. The statutory language and context strike us as more evenly balanced between a pro-award and anti-award position than was the case in either *Piggie Park* or *Christiansburg Garment* and *Zipes;* we see nothing to persuade us that fees under § 1447(c) should either usually be granted or usually be denied.

The fact that an award of fees under § 1447(c) is left to the district court's discretion, with no heavy congressional thumb on either side of the scales, does not mean that no legal standard governs that discretion. We have it on good authority that "a motion to [a court's] discretion is a motion, not to its inclination, but to its judgment; and its judgment is to be guided by sound legal principles." *United States* v. *Burr*, 25 F. Cas. 30, 35, F. Cas. No. 14692d (No. 14,692d) (CC Va. 1807) (Marshall, C. J.). Discretion is not whim, and limiting discretion according to legal standards helps promote the basic principle of justice that like cases should be decided alike. See Friendly, Indiscretion About Discretion, 31 Emory L. J. 747, 758 (1982). For these reasons, we have often limited courts' discretion to award fees despite the absence of express legislative restrictions. That is, of course, what we did in *Piggie Park,* supra, 390 U.S., at 402, 88 S. Ct. 964, 19 L. Ed. 2d 1263 (A prevailing plaintiff "should ordinarily recover an attorney's fee unless special circumstances would render such an award unjust"), *Christiansburg Garment, supra,* at 422, 98 S. Ct. 694, 54 L. Ed. 2d 648 ("[A] plaintiff should not be assessed his opponent's attorney's fees unless a court finds that his claim was frivolous, unreasonable, or groundless"), and *Zipes,* 491 U.S., at 761, 109 S. Ct. 2732, 105 L. Ed. 2d 639 (Attorney's fees should be awarded against intervenors "only where the intervenors' action was frivolous, unreasonable, or without foundation").

In *Zipes,* we reaffirmed the principle on which these decisions are based: "Although the text of the provision does not specify any limits upon the district courts' discretion to allow or disallow fees, in a system of laws discretion is rarely without limits." *Id.,* at 758, 109 S. Ct. 2732, 105 L. Ed. 2d 639. *Zipes* also explains how to discern the limits on a district court's discretion. When applying fee-shifting statutes, "we have found limits in 'the large objectives' of the relevant Act, which embrace certain 'equitable considerations.'" *Id.,* at 759, 109 S. Ct. 2732, 105 L. Ed. 2d 639 (citation omitted). *

> * In *Fogerty v. Fantasy, Inc.,* 510 U.S. 517, 114 S. Ct. 1023, 127 L. Ed. 2d 455 (1994), we did not identify a standard under which fees should be awarded. But that decision did not depart from *Zipes* because we granted certiorari to decide only whether the same standard applied to prevailing plaintiffs and prevailing defendants. See 510 U.S., at 521, 114 S. Ct. 1023, 127 L. Ed. 2d 455 (1994). Having decided this question and rejected the claim that fee shifting should be automatic, we remanded to the Court of Appeals to consider the appropriate test in the first instance. *Id.,* at 534-535, 114 S. Ct. 1023, 127 L. Ed. 2d 455.

By enacting the removal statute, Congress granted a right to a federal forum to a limited class of state-court defendants. If fee shifting were automatic, defendants might choose to exercise this right only in cases where the right to remove was obvious. See *Christiansburg Garment, supra,* at 422, 98 S. Ct. 694, 54 L. Ed. 2d 648 (awarding fees simply because the party did not prevail "could discourage all but the most airtight claims, for seldom can a [party] be sure of ultimate success"). But there is no reason to suppose Congress meant to confer a right to remove, while at the same time discouraging its exercise in all but obvious cases.

Congress, however, would not have enacted § 1447(c) if its only concern were avoiding deterrence of proper removals. Instead, Congress thought fee shifting appropriate in some cases. The process of removing a case to federal court and then having it remanded back to state court delays resolution of the case, imposes additional costs on both parties, and wastes judicial resources. Assessing costs and fees on remand reduces the attractiveness of removal as a method for delaying litigation and imposing costs on the plaintiff. The appropriate test for awarding fees under § 1447(c) should recognize the desire to deter removals sought for the purpose of prolonging litigation and imposing costs on the opposing party, while not undermining Congress' basic decision to afford defendants a right to remove as a general matter, when the statutory criteria are satisfied.

In light of these "'large objectives,'" *Zipes, supra,* at 759, 109 S. Ct. 2732, 105 L. Ed. 2d 639, the standard for awarding fees should turn on the reasonableness of the removal. Absent unusual circumstances, courts may award attorney's fees under § 1447(c) only where the removing party lacked an objectively reasonable basis for seeking removal. Conversely, when an objectively reasonable basis exists, fees should be denied. See, *e.g., Hornbuckle,* 385 F.3d at 541; *Valdes* v. *Wal-Mart Stores, Inc.,* 199 F.3d 290, 293 (CA5 2000). In applying this rule, district courts retain discretion to consider whether unusual circumstances warrant a departure from the rule in a given case. For instance, a plaintiff's delay in seeking remand or failure to disclose facts necessary to determine jurisdiction may affect the decision to award attorney's fees. When a court exercises its discretion in this manner, however, its reasons for departing from the general rule should be "faithful to the purposes" of awarding fees under § 1447(c). *Fogerty,* 510 U.S., at 534, n. 19, 114 S. Ct. 1023, 127 L. Ed. 2d 455; see also *Milwaukee* v. *Cement Div., National Gypsum Co.,* 515 U.S. 189, 196, n. 8, 115 S. Ct. 2091, 132 L. Ed. 2d 148 (1995) ("[A]s is always the case when an issue is committed to judicial discretion, the judge's decision must be supported by a circumstance that has relevance to the issue at hand").

* * *

The District Court denied the Martins' request for attorney's fees because Franklin had an objectively reasonable basis for removing this case to federal court. The Court of Appeals considered it a "close question," 393 F.3d, at 1148, but agreed that the grounds for removal were reasonable. Because the Martins do not dispute the reasonableness of Franklin's removal arguments, we need not review the lower courts' decision on this point. The judgment of the Court of Appeals is therefore affirmed.

It is so ordered.

JOEL SEREBOFF, et ux., Petitioners
v.
MID ATLANTIC MEDICAL SERVICES, INC.

No. 05-260
SUPREME COURT
OF THE UNITED STATES

547 U.S. 356

March 28, 2006, Argued
May 15, 2006, Decided

ON WRIT OF CERTIORARI TO THE UNITED STATES COURT OF APPEALS FOR THE FOURTH CIRCUIT.

Chief Justice Roberts delivered the opinion of the Court.

In this case we consider again the circumstances in which a fiduciary under the Employee Retirement Income Security Act of 1974 (ERISA) may sue a beneficiary for reimbursement of medical expenses paid by the ERISA plan, when the beneficiary has recovered for its injuries from a third party.

I

Marlene Sereboff's employer sponsors a health insurance plan administered by respondent Mid Atlantic Medical Services, Inc., and covered by ERISA, 88 Stat. 829, as amended, 29 U.S.C. § 1001 *et seq.* (2000 ed. and Supp. III). Marlene Sereboff and her husband Joel are beneficiaries under the plan. The plan provides for payment of certain covered medical expenses and contains an "Acts of Third Parties" provision. This provision "applies when [a beneficiary is] sick or injured as a result of the act or omission of another person or party," and requires a beneficiary who "receives benefits" under the plan for such injuries to "reimburse [Mid Atlantic]" for those benefits from "[a]ll recoveries from a third party (whether by lawsuit, settlement, or otherwise)." App. to Pet. for Cert. 38a. The provision states that "[Mid Atlantic's] share of the recovery will not be reduced because [the beneficiary] has not received the full damages claimed, unless [Mid Atlantic] agrees in writing to a reduction." *Ibid.*

The Sereboffs were involved in an automobile accident in California and suffered injuries. Pursuant to the plan's coverage provisions, the plan paid the couple's medical expenses. The Sereboffs filed a tort action in state court against several third parties, seeking compensatory damages for injuries suffered as a result of the accident. Soon after the suit was commenced, Mid Atlantic sent the Sereboffs' attorney a letter asserting a lien on the anticipated proceeds from the suit, for the medical expenses Mid Atlantic paid on the Sereboffs' behalf. App. 87-90. On several occasions over the next two years, Mid Atlantic sent similar correspondence to the attorney and to the Sereboffs, repeating its claim to a lien on a portion of the Sereboffs' recovery, and detailing the medical expenses as they accrued and were paid by the plan.

The Sereboffs' tort suit eventually settled for $750,000. Neither the Sereboffs nor their attorney sent any money to Mid Atlantic in satisfaction of its claimed lien which, after Mid Atlantic completed its payments on the Sereboffs' behalf, totaled $74,869.37.

Mid Atlantic filed suit in District Court under § 502(a)(3) of ERISA, 29 U.S.C. § 1132(a)(3), seeking to collect from the Sereboffs the medical expenses it had paid on their behalf. Since the Sereboffs' attorney had already distributed the settlement proceeds to them, Mid Atlantic sought a temporary restraining order and preliminary injunction requiring the couple to retain and set aside at least $74,869.37 from the proceeds. The District Court approved a stipulation by the parties, under which the Sereboffs agreed to "preserve $74,869.37 of the settlement funds" in an investment account, "until the [District] Court rules on the merits of this case and all appeals, if any, are exhausted." App. 69.

On the merits, the District Court found in Mid Atlantic's favor and ordered the Sereboffs to pay Mid Atlantic the $74,869.37, plus interest, with a deduction for Mid Atlantic's share of the attorney's fees and court costs the Sereboffs had incurred in state court. See 303 F. Supp. 2d 691, 316 F. Supp. 2d 265 (Md. 2004). The Sereboffs appealed and the Fourth Circuit affirmed in relevant part. 407 F.3d 212 (2005). The Fourth Circuit observed that the Courts of Appeals are divided on the question whether § 502(a)(3) authorizes recovery in these circumstances. See *id.*, at 219-220, n. 7. [1] We granted certiorari to resolve the disagreement. 546 U.S. 1030, 126 S. Ct. 735, 163 L. Ed. 2d 567 (2005).

---

1 Compare *Administrative Comm. of Wal-Mart Assoc. Health & Welfare Plan* v. *Willard*, 393 F.3d 1119 (CA10 2004), *Bombardier Aerospace Employee Welfare Benefits Plan* v. *Ferrer, Poirot & Wansbrough*, 354 F.3d 348 (CA5 2003), and *Administrative Comm. of Wal-Mart Stores, Inc. Assoc. Health & Welfare Plan* v. *Varco*, 338 F.3d 680 (CA7 2003), with *Qualchoice, Inc.* v. *Rowland*, 367 F.3d 638 (CA6 2004), and *Westaff (USA) Inc.* v. *Arce*, 298 F.3d 1164 (CA9 2002).

II

A

A fiduciary may bring a civil action under § 502(a)(3) of ERISA "(A) to enjoin any act or practice which violates any provision of this subchapter or the terms of the plan, or (B) to obtain other appropriate equitable relief (i) to redress such violations or (ii) to enforce any provisions of this subchapter or the terms of the plan." 29 U.S.C. § 1132(a)(3). There is no dispute that Mid Atlantic is a fiduciary under ERISA and that its suit in District Court was to "enforce . . . the terms of" the "Acts of Third Parties" provision in the Sereboffs' plan. The only question is whether the relief Mid Atlantic requested from the District Court was "equitable" under § 502(a)(3)(B).

This is not the first time we have had occasion to clarify the scope of the remedial power conferred on district courts by § 502(a)(3)(B). In *Mertens* v. *Hewitt Associates*, 508 U.S. 248, 113 S. Ct. 2063, 124 L. Ed. 2d 161 (1993), we construed the provision to authorize only "those categories of relief that were *typically* available in equity," and thus rejected a claim that we found sought "nothing other than compensatory *damages*." *Id.*, at 256, 255, 113 S. Ct. 2063, 124 L. Ed. 2d 161. We elaborated on this construction of § 502(a)(3)(B) in *Great-West Life & Annuity Ins. Co.* v. *Knudson*, 534 U.S. 204, 122 S. Ct. 708, 151 L. Ed. 2d 635 (2002), which involved facts similar to those in this case. Much like the "Acts of Third Parties" provision in the Sereboffs' plan, the plan in *Knudson* reserved "'a first lien upon any recovery, whether by settlement, judgment or otherwise,' that the beneficiary receives from [a] third party." *Id.*, at 207, 122 S. Ct. 708, 151 L. Ed. 2d 635. After Knudson was involved in a car accident, Great-West paid medical bills on her behalf and, when she recovered in tort from a third party for her injuries, Great-West sought to collect from her for the medical bills it had paid. *Id.*, at 207-209, 122 S. Ct. 708, 151 L. Ed. 2d 635.

In response to the argument that Great-West's claim in *Knudson* was for "restitution" and thus equitable under § 502(a)(3)(B) and *Mertens*, we noted that "not all relief falling under the rubric of restitution [was] available in equity." 534 U.S. at 212, 122 S. Ct. 708, 151 L. Ed. 2d 635. To decide whether the restitutionary relief sought by Great-West was equitable or legal, we examined cases and secondary legal materials to determine if the relief would have been equitable "[i]n the days of the divided bench." *Ibid.* We explained that one feature of equitable restitution was that it sought to impose a constructive trust or equitable lien on "particular funds or property in the defendant's possession." *Id.*, at 213, 122 S. Ct. 708, 151 L. Ed. 2d 635. That requirement was not met in *Knudson*, because "the funds to which petitioners claim[ed] an entitlement" were not in Knudson's possession, but had instead been placed in a "Special Needs Trust" under California law. *Id.*, at 214, 207,

122 S. Ct. 708, 151 L. Ed. 2d 635. The kind of relief Great-West sought, therefore, was "not equitable--the imposition of a constructive trust or equitable lien on particular property--but legal--the imposition of personal liability for the benefits that [Great-West] conferred upon [Knudson]." *Id.*, at 214, 122 S. Ct. 708, 151 L. Ed. 2d 635. We accordingly determined that the suit could not proceed under § 502(a)(3). *Ibid.*

That impediment to characterizing the relief in *Knudson* as equitable is not present here. As the Fourth Circuit explained below, in this case Mid Atlantic sought "specifically identifiable" funds that were "within the possession and control of the Sereboffs"--that portion of the tort settlement due Mid Atlantic under the terms of the ERISA plan, set aside and "preserved [in the Sereboffs'] investment accounts." 407 F.3d, at 218. Unlike Great-West, Mid Atlantic did not simply seek "to impose personal liability . . . for a contractual obligation to pay money." *Knudson*, 534 U.S., at 210, 122 S. Ct. 708, 151 L. Ed. 2d 635. It alleged breach of contract and sought money, to be sure, but it sought its recovery through a constructive trust or equitable lien on a specifically identified fund, not from the Sereboffs' assets generally, as would be the case with a contract action at law. ERISA provides for equitable remedies *to enforce plan terms*, so the fact that the action involves a breach of contract can hardly be enough to prove relief is not equitable; that would make § 502(a)(3)(B)(ii) an empty promise. This Court in *Knudson* did not reject Great-West's suit out of hand because it alleged a breach of contract and sought money, but because Great-West did not seek to recover a particular fund from the defendant. Mid Atlantic does.

B

While Mid Atlantic's case for characterizing its relief as equitable thus does not falter because of the nature of the recovery it seeks, Mid Atlantic must still establish that the basis for its claim is equitable. See *id.* ,at 213, 122 S. Ct. 708, 151 L. Ed. 2d 635 (whether remedy "is legal or equitable depends on 'the basis for [the plaintiff's] claim' and the nature of the underlying remedies sought"). Our case law from the days of the divided bench confirms that Mid Atlantic's claim is equitable. In *Barnes* v. *Alexander*, 232 U.S. 117, 34 S. Ct. 276, 58 L. Ed. 530 (1914), for instance, attorneys Street and Alexander performed work for Barnes, another attorney, who promised them "one-third of the contingent fee" he expected in the case. *Id.*, at 119, 34 S. Ct. 276, 58 L. Ed. 530. In upholding their equitable claim to this portion of the fee, Justice Holmes recited "the familiar rul[e] of equity that a contract to convey a specific object even before it is acquired will make the contractor a trustee as soon as he gets a title to the thing." *Id.,* at 121, 34 S. Ct. 276, 58 L. Ed. 530. On the basis of this rule, he concluded that Barnes' undertaking "create[d] a lien" upon the portion of the monetary recovery due Barnes from the client, *ibid.*, which Street and Alexander could "follow . . . into the hands of . . .

Barnes," "as soon as [the fund] was identified," *id.*, at 123, 34 S. Ct. 276, 58 L. Ed. 530.

Much like Barnes' promise to Street and Alexander, the "Acts of Third Parties" provision in the Sereboffs' plan specifically identified a particular fund, distinct from the Sereboffs' general assets--"[a]ll recoveries from a third party (whether by lawsuit, settlement, or otherwise)"--and a particular share of that fund to which Mid Atlantic was entitled--"that portion of the total recovery which is due [Mid Atlantic] for benefits paid." App. to Pet. for Cert. 38a. Like Street and Alexander in *Barnes*, therefore, Mid Atlantic could rely on a "familiar rul[e] of equity" to collect for the medical bills it had paid on the Sereboffs' behalf. *Barnes, supra*, at 121, 34 S. Ct. 276, 58 L. Ed. 530. This rule allowed them to "follow" a portion of the recovery "into the [Sereboffs'] hands" "as soon as [the settlement fund] was identified," and impose on that portion a constructive trust or equitable lien. 232 U.S. at 123, 34 S. Ct. 276, 58 L. Ed. 530.

The Sereboffs object that Mid Atlantic's suit would not have satisfied the conditions for "equitable restitution" at common law, particularly the "strict tracing rules" that allegedly accompanied this form of relief. Reply Brief for Petitioners 8. When an equitable lien was imposed as restitutionary relief, it was often the case that an asset belonging to the plaintiff had been improperly acquired by the defendant and exchanged by him for other property. A central requirement of equitable relief in these circumstances, the Sereboffs argue, was the plaintiff's ability to "'trac[e]' the asset into its products or substitutes," or "trace his money or property to some particular funds or assets." 1 D. Dobbs, Law of Remedies § 4.3(2), pp 591, n 10, 592 (2d ed. 1993).

But as the Sereboffs themselves recognize, an equitable lien sought as a matter of restitution, and an equitable lien "by agreement," of the sort at issue in *Barnes*, were different species of relief. See Brief for Petitioners 24-25; Reply Brief for Petitioners 11; see also 1 Dobbs, *supra*, § 4.3(3), at 601; 1 G. Palmer, Law of Restitution § 1.5, p 20 (1978). *Barnes* confirms that no tracing requirement of the sort asserted by the Sereboffs applies to equitable liens by agreement or assignment: The plaintiffs in *Barnes* could not identify an asset they originally possessed, which was improperly acquired and converted into property the defendant held, yet that did not preclude them from securing an equitable lien. To the extent Mid Atlantic's action is proper under *Barnes*, therefore, its asserted inability to satisfy the "strict tracing rules" for "equitable restitution" is of no consequence. Reply Brief for Petitioners 8.

The Sereboffs concede as much, stating that they "do not contend--and have never suggested--that any tracing was historically required when an equitable lien was imposed *by agreement*." *Id.*, at 11. Their argument is that such tracing was required when an equitable lien was "predicated on a theory of *equitable restitution.*" *Ibid.* The Sereboffs appear to assume that *Knudson* endorsed application of all the restitutionary conditions--including restitutionary tracing rules--to every action for an equitable lien under § 502(a)(3). This assumption is inaccurate. *Knudson* simply described in general terms the conditions under which a fiduciary might recover when it was seeking equitable restitution under a provision like that at issue in this case. There was no need in *Knudson* to catalog all the circumstances in which equitable liens were available in equity; Great-West claimed a right to recover in restitution, and the Court concluded only that equitable restitution was unavailable because the funds sought were not in Knudson's possession. 534 U.S. at 214, 122 S. Ct. 708, 151 L. Ed. 2d 635.

The Sereboffs argue that, even under *Barnes,* equitable relief would not have been available to fiduciaries relying on plan provisions like the one at issue here, because when the beneficiary agrees to such a provision "no third-party recovery" exists which the beneficiary can "place . . . beyond his control and grant [the fiduciary] a complete and present right therein." Brief for Petitioners 26, 25 (internal quotation marks omitted). It may be true that, in contract cases, equity originally required identification at the time the contract was made of the fund to which a lien specified in the contract attached. See, *e.g., Trist* v. *Child,* 88 U.S. 441, 21 Wall. 441, 447, 22 L. Ed. 623 (1875) ("[A] mere agreement to pay out of such fund is not sufficient. Something more is necessary. There must be an appropriation of the fund *pro tanto*"). But *Barnes* explicitly disapproved of this rule, observing that *Trist* addressed the issue only in dicta (since the contract containing the lien provision in *Trist* was illegal), and treating the "question as at large," even in light of earlier opinions that had dealt with it head on. *Barnes, supra,* at 120, 34 S. Ct. 276, 58 L. Ed. 530 (citing *Trist, supra; Christmas* v. *Russell,* 81 U.S. 69, 14 Wall. 69, 20 L. Ed. 762 (1872); *Wright* v. *Ellison,* 68 U.S. 16, 1 Wall. 16, 17 L. Ed. 555 (1864)).

Apart from those cases, which *Barnes* discredited, the Sereboffs offer little to undermine the plain indication in *Barnes* that the fund over which a lien is asserted need not be in existence when the contract containing the lien provision is executed. See 4 S. Symons, Pomeroy's Equity Jurisprudence § 1236, pp 699-700 (5th ed. 1941) ("[A]n agreement to charge, or to assign . . . property not yet in existence," although "creat[ing] no legal estate or interest in the things when they afterwards come into existence . . . does constitute an equitable lien upon the property" just as would "a lien upon specific things existing and owned by the contracting party at the date of the contract"); *Peugh* v. *Porter,* 112 U.S. 737, 742, 5 S. Ct. 361, 28 L. Ed. 859 (1885) ("[I]n contemplation of equity, [it] is not material" that the "very fund now in dispute" was "not . . . in existence" when an equitable lien over that fund was created). Indeed, the most they can muster in this regard are several state cases predating *Barnes* and a single decision that rests, contrary to the Sereboffs' characterization, on the simple conclusion that a contractual provision purporting to secure an equitable lien did not properly do so. See Brief for Petitioners 26; Reply Brief for Petitioners 12; *Taylor* v. *Wharton*, 43 App. D.C. 104, 1915 U.S. App. LEXIS 2577 (1915).

The Sereboffs finally fall back on the argument that *Barnes* announced a special rule for attorneys claiming an equitable lien over funds promised under a contingency fee arrangement. Outside of this context, they say, the "typical rules regarding equitable liens by assignment" persisted and would have prevented recovery here. Reply Brief for Petitioners 13.

But *Barnes* did not attach any particular significance to the identity of the parties seeking recovery. See 232 U.S., at 119, 34 S. Ct. 276, 58 L. Ed. 530. And as *Barnes* itself makes clear, other cases of this Court--not involving attorney's contingency fees--apply the same "familiar rul[e] of equity that a contract to convey a specific object even before it is acquired will make the contractor a trustee as soon as he gets a title to the thing." *Id.*, at 121, 34 S. Ct. 276, 58 L. Ed. 530In *Walker* v. *Brown*, 165 U.S. 654, 17 S. Ct. 453, 41 L. Ed. 865 (1897), for instance, the Court approved an equitable lien over municipal bonds transferred to a company to facilitate its business. When a supplier of the company suspended shipments because of delinquent debts, the individual who had transferred the bonds assured the supplier that "'any indebtedness that they may be owing you at any time, shall be paid before the return to me of these bonds . . . and that these bonds . . . are at the risk of the business of [the company], so far as any claim you may have against [it].'" *Id.*, at 663, 17 S. Ct. 453, 41 L. Ed. 865. The Court found that this undertaking created an equitable lien on the bonds, which the supplier could enforce against the individual after the bonds had been returned to him when the company became insolvent. *Id.*, at 666, 17 S. Ct. 453, 41 L. Ed. 865. As in *Barnes*, the Court resolved the case by applying general equitable principles, stating that "[t]o dedicate property to a particular purpose, to provide that a specified creditor and that creditor alone shall be authorized to seek payment of his debt from the property or its value, is unmistakably to create an equitable lien." 165 U.S. at 666, 17 S. Ct. 453, 41 L. Ed. 865.

C

Shifting gears, the Sereboffs contend that the lower courts erred in allowing enforcement of the "Acts of Third Parties" provision, without imposing various limitations that they say would apply to "truly equitable relief grounded in principles of subrogation." Reply Brief for Petitioners 5. According to the Sereboffs, they would in an equitable *subrogation* action be able to assert certain equitable defenses, such as the defense that subrogation may be pursued only after a victim had been made whole for his injuries. *Id.,* at 5-6. Such defenses should be available against Mid Atlantic's action, the Sereboffs claim, despite the plan provision that "[Mid Atlantic's] share of the recovery will not be reduced because [the beneficiary] has not received the full damages claimed, unless [Mid Atlantic] agrees in writing to a reduction." App. to Pet. for Cert. 38a.

But Mid Atlantic's claim is not considered equitable because it is a subrogation claim. As explained, Mid Atlantic's action to enforce the "Acts of Third Parties" provision qualifies as an equitable remedy because it is indistinguishable from an action to enforce an equitable lien established by agreement, of the sort epitomized by our decision in *Barnes*. See 4 Palmer, Law of Restitution § 23.18*(d)*, at 470 (A subrogation lien "is not an express lien based on agreement, but instead is an equitable lien impressed on moneys on the ground that they ought to go to the insurer"). Mid Atlantic need not characterize its claim as a freestanding action for equitable subrogation. Accordingly, the parcel of equitable defenses the Sereboffs claim accompany any such action are beside the point. [2]

> [2] The Sereboffs argue that, even if the relief Mid Atlantic sought was "equitable" under § 502(a)(3), it was not "appropriate" under that provision in that it contravened principles like the make-whole doctrine. Neither the District Court nor the Court of Appeals considered the argument that Mid Atlantic's claim was not "appropriate" apart from the contention that it was not "equitable," and from our examination of the record it does not appear that the Sereboffs raised this distinct assertion below. We decline to consider it for the first time here. See *National Collegiate Athletic Assn* v. *Smith*, 525 U.S. 459, 470, 119 S. Ct. 924, 142 L. Ed. 2d 929 (1999).

* * *

Under the teaching of *Barnes* and similar cases, Mid Atlantic's action in the District Court properly sought "equitable relief" under § 502(a)(3); the judgment of the Fourth Circuit is affirmed in relevant part.

It is so ordered.

LORENZO L. JONES, Petitioner
v.
BARBARA BOCK, WARDEN, et al.

TIMOTHY WILLIAMS, Petitioner
v.
WILLIAM S. OVERTON, et al.

JOHN H. WALTON, Petitioner
v.
BARBARA BOUCHARD, et al.

05-7058 & 05-7142
SUPREME COURT
OF THE UNITED STATES

549 U.S. 199

October 30, 2006, Argued
January 22, 2007, Decided

ON WRIT OF CERTIORARI TO THE UNITED STATES COURT OF APPEALS FOR THE SIXTH CIRCUIT.

Chief Justice Roberts delivered the opinion of the Court.

In an effort to address the large number of prisoner complaints filed in federal court, Congress enacted the Prison Litigation Reform Act of 1995 (PLRA), 110 Stat. 1321-71, as amended, 42 U.S.C. § 1997e *et seq.* Among other reforms, the PLRA mandates early judicial screening of prisoner complaints and requires prisoners to exhaust prison grievance procedures before filing suit. 28 U.S.C. § 1915A; 42 U.S.C. § 1997e(a). The Sixth Circuit, along with some other lower courts, adopted several procedural rules designed to implement this exhaustion requirement and facilitate early judicial screening. These rules require a prisoner to allege and demonstrate exhaustion in his complaint, permit suit only against defendants who were identified by the prisoner in his grievance, and require courts to dismiss the entire action if the prisoner fails to satisfy the exhaustion requirement as to any single claim in his complaint. Other lower courts declined to adopt such rules. We granted certiorari to resolve the conflict and now conclude that these rules are not required by the PLRA, and that crafting and imposing them exceeds the proper limits on the judicial role.

I

Prisoner litigation continues to "account for an outsized share of filings" in federal district courts. *Woodford* v. *Ngo*, 548 U.S. 81, 94, n. 4, 126 S. Ct. 2378, 165 L. Ed. 2d 368, 381 (2006). In 2005, nearly 10 percent of all civil cases filed in federal courts nationwide were prisoner complaints challenging prison conditions or claiming civil rights violations.[1] Most of these cases have no merit; many are frivolous. Our legal system, however, remains committed to guaranteeing that prisoner claims of illegal conduct by their custodians are fairly handled according to law. The challenge lies in ensuring that the flood of nonmeritorious claims does not submerge and effectively preclude consideration of the allegations with merit. See *Neitzke* v. *Williams*, 490 U.S. 319, 327, 109 S. Ct. 1827, 104 L. Ed. 2d 338 (1989).

> 1 See Administrative Office of the United States Courts, Judicial Facts and Figures, Tables 4.4, 4.6, http://www.uscourts.gov/judicialfactsfigures/contents.html (as visited Jan. 17, 2007, and available in Clerk of Court's case file). That number *excludes* habeas corpus petitions and motions to vacate a sentence. If these filings are included, prisoner complaints constituted 24 percent of all civil filings in 2005.

Congress addressed that challenge in the PLRA. What this country needs, Congress decided, is fewer and better prisoner suits. See *Porter* v. *Nussle*, 534 U.S. 516, 524, 122 S. Ct. 983, 152 L. Ed. 2d 12 (2002) (PLRA intended to "reduce the quantity and improve the quality of prisoner suits"). To that end, Congress enacted a variety of reforms designed to filter out the bad claims and facilitate consideration of the good. Key among these was the requirement that inmates complaining about prison conditions exhaust prison grievance remedies before initiating a lawsuit.

The exhaustion provision of the PLRA states:

> "No action shall be brought with respect to prison conditions under [42 U.S.C. § 1983], or any other Federal law, by a prisoner confined in any jail, prison, or other correctional facility until such administrative remedies as are available are exhausted." 42 U.S.C. § 1997e(a).

Requiring exhaustion allows prison officials an opportunity to resolve disputes concerning the exercise of their responsibilities before being haled into court. This has the potential to reduce the number of inmate suits, and also to improve the quality of suits that are filed by producing a useful administrative record. *Woodford, supra*, at   , 126 S. Ct. 2378, 165 L. Ed. 2d, at 380-81 . In an attempt to implement the exhaustion requirement, some lower courts have imposed procedural rules that have become the subject of varying levels of disagreement among the federal courts of appeals.

The first question presented centers on a conflict over whether exhaustion under the PLRA is a pleading requirement the prisoner must satisfy in his complaint or an affirmative defense the defendant must plead and prove.[2] The Sixth Circuit, adopting the former view, requires prisoners to attach proof of exhaustion--typically copies of the grievances--to their complaints to avoid dismissal. If no written record of the grievance is available, the inmate must plead with specificity how and when he exhausted the grievance procedures. *Knuckles El* v. *Toombs*, 215 F.3d 640, 642 (2000).

> 2 Compare *Steele* v. *Federal Bureau of Prisons*, 355 F.3d 1204, 1210 (CA10 2003) (pleading requirement); *Brown* v. *Toombs*, 139 F.3d 1102, 1104 (CA6 1998) *(per curiam)* (same); *Rivera* v. *Allin*, 144 F.3d 719, 731 (CA11 1998) (same), with *Anderson* v. *XYZ Correctional Health Servs., Inc.*, 407 F.3d 674, 681 (CA4 2005) (affirmative defense); *Wyatt* v. *Terhune*, 315 F.3d 1108, 1119 (CA9 2003) (same); *Casanova* v. *Dubois*, 304 F.3d 75, 77, n. 3 (CA1 2002) (same); *Ray* v. *Kertes*, 285 F.3d 287, 295 (CA3 2002) (same); *Foulk* v. *Charrier*, 262 F.3d 687, 697 (CA8 2001) (same); *Massey* v. *Helman*, 196 F.3d 727, 735 (CA7 1999) (same); *Jenkins* v. *Haubert*, 179 F.3d 19, 28-29 (CA2 1999) (same). See also *Johnson* v. *Johnson*, 385 F.3d 503, 516, n. 7 (CA5 2004) (noting the conflict but not deciding the question); *Jackson* v. *District of Columbia*, 349 U.S. App. D.C. 185, 254 F.3d 262, 267 (CADC 2001) (treating exhaustion as an affirmative defense).

The next issue concerns how courts determine whether a prisoner has properly exhausted administrative remedies--specifically, the level of detail required in a grievance to put the prison and individual officials on notice of the claim. The Sixth Circuit requires that a prisoner have identified, in the first step of the grievance process, each individual later named in the lawsuit to properly exhaust administrative remedies. *Burton* v. *Jones*, 321 F.3d 569, 575 (2003). Other Circuits have taken varying approaches to this question, see, *e.g., Butler v. Adams*, 397 F.3d 1181, 1183 (CA9 2005) (proper exhaustion requires use of the administrative process provided by the State; if that process does not require identification of specific persons, neither does the PLRA); *Johnson* v. *Johnson*, 385 F.3d 503, 522 (CA5 2004) ("[T]he grievance must provide administrators with a fair opportunity under the circumstances to address the problem that will later form the basis of the suit"); *Riccardo* v. *Rausch*, 375 F.3d 521, 524 (CA7 2004) (exhaustion satisfied if grievance "served its function of alerting the state and inviting corrective action"), none going as far as the Sixth Circuit in requiring in every case that the defendants have been named from the beginning of the grievance process.

Finally, the Circuits are divided over what the PLRA requires when both exhausted and unexhausted claims are included in a complaint.[3] Some Circuits, including the Sixth Circuit, apply a "total exhaustion" rule, under which no part of the suit may proceed if any single claim in the action is not properly exhausted. See, *e.g., Jones Bey* v. *Johnson*, 407 F.3d 801, 805 (CA6 2005). Among Circuits requiring total exhaustion there is further disagreement over what to do if the requirement is not met. Most courts allow the prisoner to amend his complaint to include only exhausted claims, *e.g., Kozohorsky* v. *Harmon*, 332 F.3d 1141, 1144 (CA8 2003), but the Sixth Circuit denies leave to amend, dismisses the action, and requires that it be filed anew with only unexhausted claims, *Baxter* v. *Rose*, 305 F.3d 486, 488 (2002); *Jones Bey, supra*, at 807. See also *McGore* v. *Wrigglesworth*, 114 F.3d 601, 612 (1997). Other Circuits reject total exhaustion altogether, instead dismissing only unexhausted claims and considering the rest on the merits. See, *e.g., Ortiz* v. *McBride*, 380 F.3d 649, 663 (CA2 2004).

> [3] Compare *Jones Bey* v. *Johnson*, 407 F.3d 801, 805 (CA6 2005) (requiring dismissal of the entire action if one unexhausted claim is present); *Ross* v. *County of Bernalillo*, 365 F.3d 1181, 1189 (CA10 2004) (same); *Vazquez* v. *Ragonese*, 142 Fed. Appx. 606, 607 (CA3 2005) *(per curiam)* (same); *Kozohorsky* v. *Harmon*, 332 F.3d 1141, 1144 (CA8 2003) (same), with *Lira* v. *Herrera*, 427 F.3d 1164, 1175 (CA9 2005) (allowing dismissal of only unexhausted claims); *Ortiz* v. *McBride*, 380 F.3d 649, 663 (CA2 2004) (same); *Lewis* v. *Washington*, 300 F.3d 829, 835 (CA7 2002) (same). See also *Johnson, supra,* at 523, n. 5 (suggesting that total exhaustion is an open question in the Fifth Circuit).

A

Petitioners are inmates in the custody of the Michigan Department of Corrections (MDOC). At the time petitioners filed their grievances, MDOC Policy Directive 03.02.130 (Nov. 1, 2000) set forth the applicable grievance procedures. 1 App. 138-157.[4] The policy directive describes what issues are grievable and contains instructions for filing and processing grievances.

> [4] MDOC has since revised its policy. See Policy Directive 03.02.130 (effective Dec. 19, 2003), App. to Brief for Respondents 1b. The new policy is not at issue in these cases.

Inmates must first attempt to resolve a problem orally within two business days of becoming aware of the grievable issue. *Id.,* at 147. If oral resolution is unsuccessful, the inmate may proceed to Step I of the grievance process, and submit a completed grievance form within five business days of the attempted oral resolution. *Id.,* at 147, 149-150. The Step I grievance form provided by MDOC (a one-page form on which the inmate fills out identifying information and is given space to describe the complaint) advises inmates to be "brief and concise in describing your grievance issue." 2 *id.,* at 1. The inmate submits the grievance to a designated grievance coordinator, who assigns it to a respondent--generally the supervisor of the person being grieved. 1 *id.,* at 150.

If the inmate is dissatisfied with the Step I response, he may appeal to Step II by obtaining an appeal form within five business days of the response, and submitting the appeal within five business days of obtaining the form. *Id.,* at 152. The respondent at Step II is designated by the policy, *id.,* at 152-153 (*e.g.,* the regional health administrator for medical care grievances). If still dissatisfied after Step II, the inmate may further appeal to Step III using the same appeal form; the MDOC director is designated as respondent for all Step III appeals. *Id.,* at 154.

Lorenzo Jones

Petitioner Lorenzo Jones is incarcerated at MDOC's Saginaw Correctional Facility. In November 2000, while in MDOC's custody, Jones was involved in a vehicle accident and suffered significant injuries to his neck and back. Several months later Jones was given a work assignment he allegedly could not perform in light of his injuries. According to Jones, respondent Paul Morrison--in charge of work assignments at the prison--made the inappropriate assignment, even though he knew of Jones's injuries. When Jones reported to the assignment, he informed the staff member in charge-- respondent Michael Opanasenko--that he could not perform the work; Opanasenko allegedly told him to do the work or "'suffer the consequences.'" *Id.,* at 20. Jones performed the required tasks and allegedly aggravated his injuries. After unsuccessfully seeking redress through MDOC's grievance process, Jones filed a complaint in the Eastern District of Michigan under 42 U.S.C. § 1983 for deliberate indifference to medical needs, retaliation, and harassment. Jones named as defendants, in addition to Morrison and Opanasenko, respondents Barbara Bock (the warden), Valerie Chaplin (a deputy warden), Janet Konkle (a registered nurse), and Ahmad Aldabaugh (a physician).

A Magistrate Judge recommended dismissal for failure to state a claim with respect to Bock, Chaplin, Konkle, and Aldabaugh, and the District Court agreed. 1 App. 41. With respect to Morrison and Opanasenko, however, the Magistrate Judge recommended that the suit proceed, finding that Jones had exhausted his administrative remedies as to those two. *Id.,* at 18-29. The District Court Judge disagreed. In his complaint, Jones provided the dates on which his claims were filed at various steps of the MDOC grievance procedures. *Id.,* at 41. He did not, however, attach copies of the grievance forms or describe the proceedings with specificity. Respondents attached copies of all of Jones's grievances to their own motion to dismiss, but the District Judge ruled that Jones's failure to meet his burden to plead exhaustion in his complaint could not be cured by respondents. *Id.,* at 42. The Sixth Circuit agreed, holding both that Jones failed to comply with the specific pleading requirements applied to PLRA suits, 135 Fed. Appx. 837, 839 (2005) *(per curiam)* (citing *Knuckles El,* 215 F.3d at 642), and that, even if Jones had shown that he exhausted the claims against Morrison and Opanasenko, dismissal was still required under the total exhaustion rule, 135 Fed. Appx., at 839 (citing *Jones Bey,* 407 F.3d, 806).

Timothy Williams

Petitioner Timothy Williams is incarcerated at MDOC's Adrian Correctional Facility. He suffers from noninvoluting cavernous hemangiomas in his right arm, a medical condition that causes pain, immobility, and disfigurement of the limb, and for which he has undergone several surgeries. An MDOC physician recommended further surgery to provide pain relief, but MDOC's Correctional Medical Services denied the recommendation (and subsequent appeals by the doctor) on the ground that the danger of surgery outweighed the benefits, which it viewed as cosmetic. The MDOC Medical Services Advisory Committee upheld this decision. After Correctional Medical Services indicated that it would take the request under advisement, Williams filed a grievance objecting to the quality of his medical care and seeking authorization for the surgery. He later filed another grievance complaining that he was denied a single-occupancy handicapped cell, allegedly necessary to accommodate his medical condition. After both grievances were denied at all stages, Williams filed a complaint in the Eastern District of Michigan under § 1983, naming as respondents William Overton (former director of MDOC), David Jamrog (the warden), Mary Jo Pass and Paul Klee (assistant deputy wardens), Chad Markwell (corrections officer), Bonnie Peterson (health unit manager), and Dr. George Pramstaller (chief medical officer for MDOC).

The District Judge found that Williams had failed to exhaust his administrative remedies with regard to his medical care claim because he had not identified any of the respondents named in his lawsuit during the grievance process.5 Although Williams's claim concerning the handicapped cell had been properly exhausted, the District Judge--applying the total exhaustion rule--dismissed the entire suit. The Sixth Circuit affirmed. 136 Fed. Appx. 859, 861-863 (2005) (citing *Burton*, 321 F.3d, at 574, *Curry* v. *Scott*, 249 F.3d 493, 504-505 (CA6 2001), and *Jones Bey*, supra, at 805).

> 5 Dr. Pramstaller was mentioned at Step III of the grievance process, but was apparently never served with the complaint initiating the lawsuit. The Magistrate Judge stated that even if the claims against Pramstaller had been properly exhausted they nonetheless were subject to dismissal under the total exhaustion rule. 1 App. 86, 101. It also appears that under the Sixth Circuit's rule requiring a defendant to be named at Step I of the grievance process, the claims against Pramstaller, who was not mentioned until Step III, would not have been exhausted. See *supra*, at _, 166 L. Ed. 2d, at 807; n 7, *infra*. Because Pramstaller was never served, he is not a respondent in this Court.

John Walton

Petitioner John Walton is incarcerated at MDOC's Alger Maximum Correctional Facility. After assaulting a guard, he was sanctioned with an indefinite "upper slot" restriction.6 Several months later, upon learning that other prisoners had been given upper slot restrictions of only three months for the same infraction, he filed a grievance claiming that this disparity was the result of racial discrimination (Walton is black, the two other prisoners he identified in his grievances are white). After the grievance was denied, Walton filed a complaint in the Western District of Michigan under § 1983, claiming race discrimination. He named as respondents Barbara Bouchard (former warden), Ken Gearin, David Bergh, and Ron Bobo (assistant deputy wardens), Catherine Bauman (resident unit manager), and Denise Gerth (assistant resident unit supervisor).

> 6 An upper slot restriction limits the inmate to receiving food and paperwork via the lower slot of the cell door. Brief for Respondents 5-6. Presumably, this is less desirable than access through the upper slot; the record does not reveal how effective this particular sanction is in discouraging assaults on staff.

The District Judge dismissed the lawsuit because Walton had not named any respondent other than Bobo in his grievance. His claims against the other respondents were thus not properly exhausted, and the court dismissed the entire action under the total exhaustion rule. The Sixth Circuit affirmed, reiterating its requirement that a prisoner must "file a grievance against the person he ultimately seeks to sue," *Curry, supra,* at 505, and that this requirement can only be satisfied by naming each defendant at Step I of the MDOC grievance process. Because Walton had exhausted prison remedies only as to respondent Bobo, the Sixth Circuit affirmed the District Court's dismissal of the entire action. 136 Fed. Appx. 846, 848-849 (2005).

B

Jones sought review in a petition for certiorari, arguing that the Sixth Circuit's heightened pleading requirement and total exhaustion rule contravene the clear language of the Federal Rules of Civil Procedure and the PLRA. Williams and Walton filed a joint petition under this Court's Rule 12.4, contending that the rule requiring every defendant to be named during the grievance process is not required by the PLRA, and also challenging the total exhaustion rule. We granted both petitions for certiorari, 547 U.S. 1002, 126 S. Ct. 1463, 164 L. Ed. 2d 246 (2006), and consolidated the cases for our review.

II

There is no question that exhaustion is mandatory under the PLRA and that unexhausted claims cannot be brought in court. *Porter,* 534 U.S., at 524, 122 S. Ct. 983, 152 L. Ed. 2d 12 . What is less clear is whether it falls to the prisoner to plead and demonstrate exhaustion in the complaint, or to the defendant to raise lack of exhaustion as an affirmative defense. The minority rule, adopted by the Sixth Circuit, places the burden of pleading exhaustion in a case covered by the PLRA on the prisoner; most courts view failure to exhaust as an affirmative defense. See n 2, *supra.*

We think petitioners, and the majority of courts to consider the question, have the better of the argument. Federal Rule of Civil Procedure 8(a) requires simply a "short and plain statement of the claim" in a complaint, while Rule 8(c) identifies a nonexhaustive list of affirmative defenses that must be pleaded in response. The PLRA itself is not a source of a prisoner's claim; claims covered by the PLRA are typically brought under 42 U.S.C. § 1983, which does not require exhaustion at all, see *Patsy* v. *Board of Regents of Fla.,* 457 U.S. 496, 516, 102 S. Ct. 2557, 73 L. Ed. 2d 172 (1982). Petitioners assert that courts typically regard exhaustion as an affirmative defense in other contexts, see Brief for Petitioners 34-36, and nn 12-13 (citing cases), and respondents do not seriously dispute the general proposition. We have referred to exhaustion in these terms, see, *e.g.*, *Wright* v. *Universal Maritime Service Corp.*, 525 U.S. 70, 75, 119 S. Ct. 391, 142 L. Ed. 2d 361 (1998) (referring to "failure to exhaust" as an "affirmative defens[e]"), including in the similar statutory scheme governing habeas corpus, Day v. McDonough, 547 U.S. 198, 208, 126 S. Ct. 1675, 164 L. Ed. 2d 376, 386 (2006) (referring to exhaustion as a "defense"). The PLRA dealt extensively with the subject of exhaustion, see 42 U.S.C. §§ 1997e(a), (c)(2), but is silent on the issue whether exhaustion must be pleaded by the plaintiff or is an affirmative defense. This is strong evidence that the usual practice should be followed, and the usual practice under the Federal Rules is to regard exhaustion as an affirmative defense.

In a series of recent cases, we have explained that courts should generally not depart from the usual practice under the Federal Rules on the basis of perceived policy concerns. Thus, in *Leatherman* v. *Tarrant County Narcotics Intelligence and Coordination Unit*, 507 U.S. 163, 113 S. Ct. 1160, 122 L. Ed. 2d 517 (1993), we unanimously reversed the Court of Appeals for imposing a heightened pleading standard in § 1983 suits against municipalities. We explained that "[p]erhaps if [the] Rules . . . were rewritten today, claims against municipalities under § 1983 might be subjected to the added specificity requirement . . . . But that is a result which must be obtained by the process of amending the Federal Rules, and not by judicial interpretation." *Id.,* at 168, 113 S. Ct. 1160, 122 L. Ed. 2d 517.

In *Swierkiewicz* v. *Sorema N. A.*, 534 U.S. 506, 122 S. Ct. 992, 152 L. Ed. 2d 1 (2002), we unanimously reversed the Court of Appeals for requiring employment discrimination plaintiffs to specifically allege the elements of a prima facie case of discrimination. We explained that "the Federal Rules do not contain a heightened pleading standard for employment discrimination suits," and a "requirement of greater specificity for particular claims" must be obtained by amending the Federal Rules. *Id.,* at 515, 122 S. Ct. 992, 152 L. Ed. 2d 1 (citing *Leatherman*). And just last Term, in *Hill* v. *McDonough*, 547 U.S. 573, 126 S. Ct. 2096, 165 L. Ed. 2d 44 (2006), we unanimously rejected a proposal that § 1983 suits challenging a method of execution must identify an acceptable alternative: "Specific pleading requirements are mandated by the Federal Rules of Civil Procedure, and not, as a general rule, through case-by-case determinations of the federal courts." Id., at 582, 126 S. Ct. 2096, 165 L. Ed. 2d 44 (citing *Swierkiewicz*).

The Sixth Circuit and other courts requiring prisoners to plead and demonstrate exhaustion in their complaints contend that if the "new regime" mandated by the PLRA for prisoner complaints is to function effectively, prisoner complaints must be treated outside of this typical framework. See *Baxter*, 305 F.3d, at 489. These courts explain that the PLRA not only imposed a new mandatory exhaustion requirement, but also departed in a fundamental way from the usual procedural ground rules by requiring judicial screening to filter out nonmeritorious claims: Courts are to screen inmate complaints "before docketing, if feasible or, . . . as soon as practicable after docketing," and dismiss the complaint if it is "frivolous, malicious, . . . fails to state a claim upon which relief may be granted[,] or . . . seeks monetary relief from a defendant who is immune from such relief." 28 U.S.C. § 1915A(a), (b). All this may take place before any responsive pleading is filed--unlike in the typical civil case, defendants do not have to respond to a complaint covered by the PLRA until required to do so by the court, and waiving the right to reply does not constitute an admission of the allegations in the complaint. See 42 U.S.C. § 1997e(g)(1), (2). According to respondents, these departures from the normal litigation framework of complaint and response mandate a different pleading requirement for prisoner complaints, if the screening is to serve its intended purpose. See, *e.g., Baxter, supra*, at 489 ("This court's heightened pleading standards for complaints covered by the PLRA are designed to facilitate the Act's screening requirements . . ."); *Knuckles El*, 215 F.3d, at 642. See also Brief for Respondents 17.

We think that the PLRA's screening requirement does not--explicitly or implicitly--justify deviating from the usual procedural practice beyond the departures specified by the PLRA itself. Before the PLRA, the *in forma pauperis* provision of § 1915, applicable to most prisoner litigation, permitted *sua sponte* dismissal only if an action was frivolous or malicious. 28 U.S.C. § 1915(d) (1994 ed.); see also *Neitzke*, 490 U.S., at 320, 109 S. Ct. 1827, 104 L. Ed. 2d 338 (concluding that a complaint that fails to state a claim was not frivolous under § 1915(d) and thus could not be dismissed *sua sponte*). In the PLRA, Congress added failure to state a claim and seeking monetary relief from a defendant immune from such relief as grounds for *sua sponte* dismissal of *in forma pauperis* cases, § 1915(e)(2)(B) (2000 ed.), and provided for judicial screening and *sua sponte* dismissal of prisoner suits on the same four grounds, § 1915A(b); 42 U.S.C. § 1997e(c)(1). Although exhaustion was a "centerpiece" of the PLRA, *Woodford*, 548 U.S., at 84, 126 S. Ct. 2378, 165 L. Ed. 2d 368, failure to exhaust was notably not added in terms to this enumeration. There is thus no reason to suppose that the normal pleading rules have to be altered to facilitate judicial screening of complaints specifically for failure to exhaust.

Some courts have found that exhaustion is subsumed under the PLRA's enumerated ground authorizing early dismissal for "fail[ure] to state a claim upon which relief may be granted." 28 U.S.C. §§ 1915A(b)(1), 1915(e)(2)(B); 42 U.S.C. § 1997e(c)(1). See *Baxter, supra*, at 489; *Steele* v. *Federal Bureau of Prisons*, 355 F.3d 1204, 1210 (CA10 2003); *Rivera* v. *Allin*, 144 F.3d 719, 731 (CA11 1998). The point is a bit of a red herring. A complaint is subject to dismissal for failure to state a claim if the allegations, taken as true, show the

37

plaintiff is not entitled to relief. If the allegations, for example, show that relief is barred by the applicable statute of limitations, the complaint is subject to dismissal for failure to state a claim; that does not make the statute of limitations any less an affirmative defense, see Fed. Rule Civ. Proc. 8(c). Whether a particular ground for opposing a claim may be the basis for dismissal for failure to state a claim depends on whether the allegations in the complaint suffice to establish that ground, not on the nature of the ground in the abstract. See *Leveto* v. *Lapina*, 258 F.3d 156, 161 (CA3 2001) ("[A] complaint may be subject to dismissal under Rule 12(b)(6) when an affirmative defense . . . appears on its face" (internal quotation marks omitted)). See also *Lopez-Gonzalez* v. *Comerio*, 404 F.3d 548, 551 (CA1 2005) (dismissing a complaint barred by the statute of limitations under Rule 12(b)(6)); *Pani* v. *Empire Blue Cross Blue Shield*, 152 F.3d 67, 74-75 (CA2 1998) (dismissing a complaint barred by official immunity under Rule 12(b)(6)). See also 5B C. Wright & A. Miller, Federal Practice and Procedure § 1357, pp 708-710, 721-729 (3d ed. 2004). Determining that Congress meant to include failure to exhaust under the rubric of "failure to state a claim" in the screening provisions of the PLRA would thus not support treating exhaustion as a pleading requirement rather than an affirmative defense.

The argument that screening would be more effective if exhaustion had to be shown in the complaint proves too much; the same could be said with respect to any affirmative defense. The rejoinder that the PLRA focused on exhaustion rather than other defenses simply highlights the failure of Congress to include exhaustion in terms among the enumerated grounds justifying dismissal upon early screening. As noted, that is not to say that failure to exhaust cannot be a basis for dismissal for failure to state a claim. It is to say that there is no basis for concluding that Congress implicitly meant to transform exhaustion from an affirmative defense to a pleading requirement by the curiously indirect route of specifying that courts should screen PLRA complaints and dismiss those that fail to state a claim.

Respondents point to 42 U.S.C. § 1997e(g) as confirming that the usual pleading rules should not apply to PLRA suits, but we think that provision supports petitioners. It specifies that defendants can waive their right to reply to a prisoner complaint without the usual consequence of being deemed to have admitted the allegations in the complaint. See § 1997e(g)(1) (allowing defendants to waive their response without admitting the allegations "[n]otwithstanding any other law or rule of procedure"). This shows that when Congress meant to depart from the usual procedural requirements, it did so expressly.

We conclude that failure to exhaust is an affirmative defense under the PLRA, and that inmates are not required to specially plead or demonstrate exhaustion in their complaints. We understand the reasons behind the decisions of some lower courts to impose a pleading requirement on plaintiffs in this context, but that effort cannot fairly be viewed as an interpretation of the PLRA. "Whatever temptations the statesmanship of policy-making might wisely suggest," the judge's job is to construe the statute--not to make it better. Frankfurter, Some Reflections on the Reading of Statutes, 47 Colum. L. Rev. 527, 533 (1947). The judge "must not read in by way of creation," but instead abide by the "duty of restraint, th[e] humility of function as merely the translator of another's command." *Id.,* at 533-534. See *United States* v. *Goldenberg,* 168 U.S. 95, 103, 18 S. Ct. 3, 42 L. Ed. 394 (1897) ("No mere omission . . . which it may seem wise to have specifically provided for, justif[ies] any judicial addition to the language of the statute"). Given that the PLRA does not itself require plaintiffs to plead exhaustion, such a result "must be obtained by the process of amending the Federal Rules, and not by judicial interpretation." *Leatherman,* 507 U.S., at 168, 113 S. Ct. 1160, 122 L. Ed. 2d 517.

III

The Sixth Circuit threw out the Williams and Walton suits because those prisoners had not identified in their initial grievances each defendant they later sued. 136 Fed. Appx., at 862-863; *id.,* at 848-849. See *Burton,* 321 F.3d, at 575.[7] Here again the lower court's procedural rule lacks a textual basis in the PLRA. The PLRA requires exhaustion of "such administrative remedies as are available," 42 U.S.C. § 1997e(a), but nothing in the statute imposes a "name all defendants" requirement along the lines of the Sixth Circuit's judicially created rule. Respondents argue that without such a rule the exhaustion requirement would become a "'useless appendage,'" Brief for Respondents 44 (quoting *Woodford,* 548 U.S., at 93, 126 S. Ct. 2378, 165 L. Ed. 2d 368, 380), but the assertion is hyperbole, and the citation of *Woodford* misplaced.

> 7 This "name all defendants" rule apparently applies even when a prisoner does not learn the identity of the responsible party until a later step of the grievance process. Upon learning the identity of the responsible party, the prisoner is required to bring an entirely new grievance to properly exhaust. 136 Fed. Appx. 846, 849 (CA6 2005) ("At that point [after he learned, in response to a Step I grievance, that Gearin was responsible for the upper slot restriction], Walton was armed with all of the information that he needed to file a Step I grievance against . . . Gearin--and a federal complaint against Gearin once the claim had been exhausted--but he simply chose not to follow

this route"). At oral argument, Michigan admitted that it did not agree with at least this application of the rule. Tr. of Oral Arg. 44-45.

Woodford held that "proper exhaustion" was required under the PLRA, and that this requirement was not satisfied when grievances were dismissed because prisoners had missed deadlines set by the grievance policy. *Id.,* at 93, 126 S. Ct. 2378, 165 L. Ed. 2d 368, 381-82. At the time each of the grievances at issue here was filed, in contrast, the MDOC policy did not contain any provision specifying who must be named in a grievance. MDOC's policy required only that prisoners "be as specific as possible" in their grievances, 1 App. 148, while at the same time the required forms advised them to "[b]e brief and concise," 2 *id.,* at 1. The MDOC grievance form does not require a prisoner to identify a particular responsible party, and the respondent is not necessarily the allegedly culpable prison official, but rather an administrative official designated in the policy to respond to particular types of grievances at different levels. *Supra,* at 207, 166 L. Ed. 2d, at 808. The grievance policy specifically provides that the grievant at Step I "shall have the opportunity to explain the grievance more completely at [an] interview, enabling the Step I respondent to gather any additional information needed to respond to the grievance." 1 App. 151. Nothing in the MDOC policy itself supports the conclusion that the grievance process was improperly invoked simply because an individual later named as a defendant was not named at the first step of the grievance process.

Nor does the PLRA impose such a requirement. In *Woodford,* we held that to properly exhaust administrative remedies prisoners must "complete the administrative review process in accordance with the applicable procedural rules," 548 U.S., at 88, 126 S. Ct. 2378, 165 L. Ed. 2d 368, 377 --rules that are defined not by the PLRA, but by the prison grievance process itself. Compliance with prison grievance procedures, therefore, is all that is required by the PLRA to "properly exhaust." The level of detail necessary in a grievance to comply with the grievance procedures will vary from system to system and claim to claim, but it is the prison's requirements, and not the PLRA, that define the boundaries of proper exhaustion. As MDOC's procedures make no mention of naming particular officials, the Sixth Circuit's rule imposing such a prerequisite to proper exhaustion is unwarranted.

We have identified the benefits of exhaustion to include allowing a prison to address complaints about the program it administers before being subjected to suit, reducing litigation to the extent complaints are satisfactorily resolved, and improving litigation that does occur by leading to the preparation of a useful record. See *id.,* at 88-91, 126 S. Ct. 2378, 165 L. Ed. 2d, at 377; *Porter,* 534 U.S., at 524-525, 122 S. Ct. 983, 152 L. Ed. 2d 12. The Sixth Circuit rule may promote early notice to those who might later be sued, but that has not been thought to be one of the leading purposes of the exhaustion requirement. See *Johnson*, 385 F.3d, at 522 ("We are mindful that the primary purpose of a grievance is to alert prison officials to a problem, not to provide personal notice to a particular official that he may be sued; the grievance is not a summons and complaint that initiates adversarial litigation"); see also Brief for American Civil Liberties Union et al. as *Amici Curiae* 8-9, and n 6 (collecting grievance procedures and noting that the majority do not require prisoners to identify specific individuals).

We do not determine whether the grievances filed by petitioners satisfied the requirement of "proper exhaustion," *Woodford, supra*, at , 126 S. Ct. 2378, 165 L. Ed. 2d, at 380-81, but simply conclude that exhaustion is not *per se* inadequate simply because an individual later sued was not named in the grievances. We leave it to the court below in the first instance to determine the sufficiency of the exhaustion in these cases.

IV

The final issue concerns how courts should address complaints in which the prisoner has failed to exhaust some, but not all, of the claims asserted in the complaint.⁸ All agree that no unexhausted claim may be considered. The issue is whether the court should proceed with the exhausted claims, or instead--as the Sixth Circuit has held--dismiss the entire action if any one claim is not properly exhausted. See *Jones Bey*, 407 F.3d, at 807.⁹

> 8 Although we reverse the Sixth Circuit's rulings on the substantive exhaustion requirements as to all three petitioners, the question whether a total exhaustion rule is contemplated by the PLRA is not moot. In Jones's case, the Sixth Circuit ruled in the alternative that total exhaustion required dismissal. 135 Fed. Appx. 837, 839 (2005) (per curiam) ("[E]ven if Jones had shown he had exhausted some of his claims, the district court properly dismissed the complaint because Jones did not show that he had exhausted all of his claims").
>
> 9 After we granted certiorari, the Sixth Circuit suggested that the adoption of a total exhaustion rule in that Circuit in *Jones Bey* ran contrary to previous panel decisions and was therefore not controlling. *Spencer* v. *Bouchard*, 449 F.3d 721, 726 (2006). See also Rule 206(c) (CA6 2006). As total exhaustion was applied in the cases under review, and the Sixth Circuit is not the only court to apply this rule, we do not concern ourselves with this possible intracircuit split.

Here the Sixth Circuit can point to language in the PLRA in support of its rule. Section 1997e(a) provides that "[n]o action shall be brought" unless administrative procedures are exhausted. Respondents argue that if Congress intended courts to dismiss only unexhausted claims while retaining the balance of the lawsuit, the word "claim" rather than "action" would have been used in this provision.

This statutory phrasing--"no action shall be brought"--is boilerplate language. There are many instances in the Federal Code where similar language is used, but such language has not been thought to lead to the dismissal of an entire action if a single claim fails to meet the pertinent standards. Statutes of limitations, for example, are often introduced by a variant of the phrase "no action shall be brought," see, *e.g., Beach* v. *Ocwen Fed. Bank,* 523 U.S. 410, 416, 118 S. Ct. 1408, 140 L. Ed. 2d 566 (1998); 18 U.S.C. § 1030(g) (2000 ed., Supp. IV), but we have never heard of an entire complaint being thrown out simply because one of several discrete claims was barred by the statute of limitations, and it is hard to imagine what purpose such a rule would serve. The same is true with respect to other uses of the "no action shall be brought" phrasing. See, *e.g., Hawksbill Sea Turtle* v. *Federal Emergency Management Agency,* 126 F.3d 461, 471, 37 V.I. 526 (CA3 1997) (dismissing only claims that fail to comply with the citizen suit notification requirement of 16 U.S.C. § 1540(g)(2), which states that "[n]o action may be commenced" until an agency has declined to act after being given written notice).

More generally, statutory references to an "action" have not typically been read to mean that every claim included in the action must meet the pertinent requirement before the "action" may proceed. See, *e.g., Exxon Mobil Corp.* v. *Allapattah Services, Inc.,* 545 U.S. 546, 560-563, 125 S. Ct. 2611, 162 L. Ed. 2d 502 (2005) (District Court had jurisdiction over a "civil action" under 28 U.S.C. § 1367(a), even if it might not have jurisdiction over each separate claim pressed in the action); *Chicago* v. *International College of Surgeons,* 522 U.S. 156, 166, 118 S. Ct. 523, 139 L. Ed. 2d 525 (1997) (District Court had jurisdiction over removed "civil action" even if every claim did not satisfy jurisdictional prerequisites).

As a general matter, if a complaint contains both good and bad claims, the court proceeds with the good and leaves the bad. "[O]nly the bad claims are dismissed; the complaint as a whole is not. If Congress meant to depart from this norm, we would expect some indication of that, and we find none." *Robinson* v. *Page,* 170 F.3d 747, 748-749 (CA7 1999) (considering § 1997e(e)).

Respondents note an exception to this general rule, the total exhaustion rule in habeas corpus. In *Rose* v. *Lundy,* 455 U.S. 509, 522, 102 S. Ct. 1198, 71 L. Ed. 2d 379 (1982), we held that "mixed" habeas petitions--containing both exhausted and unexhausted claims--cannot be adjudicated. This total exhaustion rule applied in habeas was initially derived from considerations of "comity and federalism," not any statutory command. *Rhines* v. *Weber*, 544 U.S. 269, 273, 125 S. Ct. 1528, 161 L. Ed. 2d 440 (2005); *id.,* at 274, 125 S. Ct. 1528, 161 L. Ed. 2d 440 (noting that Congress "preserved *Lundy*'s total exhaustion requirement" in 28 U.S.C. § 2254(b)(1)(A)). Separate claims in a single habeas petition generally seek the same relief from custody, and success on one is often as good as success on another. In such a case it makes sense to require exhaustion of all claims in state court before allowing the federal action to proceed. A typical PLRA suit with multiple claims, on the other hand, may combine a wide variety of discrete complaints, about interactions with guards, prison conditions, generally applicable rules, and so on, seeking different relief on each claim. There is no reason failure to exhaust on one necessarily affects any other. In any event, even if the habeas total exhaustion rule is pertinent, it does not in fact depart from the usual practice--as we recently held, a court presented with a mixed habeas petition "should allow the petitioner to delete the unexhausted claims and to proceed with the exhausted claims . . . ." *Rhines, supra,* at 278, 125 S. Ct. 1528, 161 L. Ed. 2d 440. This is the opposite of the rule the Sixth Circuit adopted, and precisely the rule that respondents argue against.

Respondents' reading of 42 U.S.C. § 1997e(a) to contain a total exhaustion rule is bolstered by the fact that other sections of the PLRA distinguish between actions and claims. Section 1997e(c)(1), for example, provides that a court shall dismiss an *action* for one of four enumerated deficiencies, while § 1997e(c)(2) allows a court to dismiss a *claim* for one of these reasons without first determining whether the claim is exhausted. Similarly, 28 U.S.C. § 1915A(b) directs district courts to dismiss "the complaint, or any portion of the complaint," before docketing under certain circumstances. This demonstrates that Congress knew how to differentiate between the entire action and particular claims when it wanted to, and suggests that its use of "action" rather than "claim" in 42 U.S.C. § 1997e(a) should be given effect.

But the interpretation respondents advocate creates its own inconsistencies. Section 1997e(e) contains similar language, "[n]o . . . action may be brought . . . for mental or emotional injury suffered while in custody without a prior showing of physical injury," yet respondents cite no case interpreting this provision to require dismissal of the entire lawsuit if only one claim does not comply, and again we see little reason for such an approach. Accord, *Cassidy* v. *Indiana Dep't of Corrections*, 199 F.3d 374, 376-377 (CA7 2000) (dismissing only the portions of the complaint barred by § 1997e(e)); see also *Williams* v. *Ollis*, 230 F.3d 1361 [2000 U.S. App. LEXIS 23671] (CA6 2000) (unpublished table decision) (same). Interpreting the phrase "no action shall be brought" to require dismissal of the entire case under § 1997e(a) but not § 1997e(e) would contravene our normal rules of statutory construction. *National Credit Union*

Admin. v. *First Nat. Bank & Trust Co.*, 522 U.S. 479, 501-502, 118 S. Ct. 927, 140 L. Ed. 2d 1 (1998).

In pressing the total exhaustion argument, respondents also marshal the policy and purpose underlying the PLRA--this time in a supporting rather than lead role. The invigorated exhaustion requirement is a "centerpiece" of the statute, *Woodford*, 548 U.S., at 84, 126 S. Ct. 2378, 165 L. Ed. 2d, at 374, and if the exhaustion requirement of § 1997e(a) is not effectuated by a total exhaustion rule, they argue, inmates will have little incentive to ensure that they have exhausted all available administrative remedies before proceeding to court. The PLRA mandated early judicial screening to reduce the burden of prisoner litigation on the courts; a total exhaustion rule allows courts promptly to dismiss an action upon identifying an unexhausted claim. The alternative approach turns judges into editors of prisoner complaints, rather than creating an incentive for prisoners to exhaust properly. See *Ross* v. *County of Bernalillo*, 365 F.3d 1181, 1190 (CA10 2004).

We are not persuaded by these policy arguments. In fact, the effect of a total exhaustion rule could be that inmates will file various claims in separate suits, to avoid the possibility of an unexhausted claim tainting the others. That would certainly not comport with the purpose of the PLRA to reduce the quantity of inmate suits. Additionally, district judges who delve into a prisoner complaint only to realize it contains an unexhausted claim, requiring dismissal of the entire complaint under the total exhaustion rule, will often have to begin the process all over again when the prisoner refiles. In light of typically short prison grievance time limits, prisoners' refiled complaints will often be identical to what the district court would have considered had it simply dismissed unexhausted claims as it encountered them and proceeded with the exhausted ones. Perhaps filing fees and concerns about the applicability of the "three strikes" rule, 28 U.S.C. § 1915(g), would mitigate these effects, but the debate about consequences is close enough that there is no clear reason to depart from the more typical claim-by-claim approach.

* * *

We are not insensitive to the challenges faced by the lower federal courts in managing their dockets and attempting to separate, when it comes to prisoner suits, not so much wheat from chaff as needles from haystacks. We once again reiterate, however--as we did unanimously in *Leatherman, Swierkiewicz,* and *Hill* --that adopting different and more onerous pleading rules to deal with particular categories of cases should be done through established rulemaking procedures, and not on a case-by-case basis by the courts.

The judgments of the United States Court of Appeals for the Sixth Circuit are reversed, and the cases are remanded for further proceedings consistent with this opinion.

It is so ordered.

Roberts Unanimous

JOHN F. HINCK, et ux., Petitioners
v.
UNITED STATES

No. 06-376
SUPREME COURT
OF THE UNITED STATES

550 U.S. 501

April 23, 2007, Argued
May 21, 2007, Decided

ON WRIT OF CERTIORARI TO THE UNITED STATES COURT OF APPEALS FOR THE FEDERAL CIRCUIT

Chief Justice Roberts delivered the opinion of the Court.

Bad things happen if you fail to pay federal income taxes when due. One of them is that interest accrues on the unpaid amount. Sometimes it takes a while for the Internal Revenue Service (IRS) to determine that taxes should have been paid that were not. Section 6404(e)(1) of the Internal Revenue Code permits the Secretary of the Treasury to abate interest--to forgive it, partially or in whole--if the assessment of interest on a deficiency is attributable to unreasonable error or delay on the part of the IRS. Section 6404(h) allows for judicial review of the Secretary's decision not to grant such relief. The question presented in this case is whether this review may be obtained only in the Tax Court, or may also be secured in the district courts and the Court of Federal Claims. We hold that the Tax Court provides the exclusive forum for judicial review of a refusal to abate interest under § 6404(e)(1), and affirm.

I

The Internal Revenue Code provides that if any amount of assessed federal income tax is not paid "on or before the last date prescribed for payment," interest "shall be paid for the period from such last date to the date paid." 26 U.S.C. § 6601(a). Section 6404 of the Code authorizes the Secretary of the Treasury to abate any tax or related liability in certain circumstances. As part of the Tax Reform Act of 1986, Congress amended § 6404 to add subsection (e)(1), which, as enacted, provided in pertinent part:

"In the case of any assessment of interest on . . . any deficiency attributable in whole or in part to any error or delay by an officer or employee of the Internal Revenue Service (acting in his official capacity) in performing a ministerial act . . . the Secretary may abate the assessment of all or any part of such interest for any period." 26 U.S.C. § 6404(e)(1) (1994 ed.).

In the years following passage of § 6404(e)(1), the federal courts uniformly held that the Secretary's decision not to grant an abatement was not subject to judicial review. See, *e.g., Argabright* v. *United States*, 35 F.3d 472, 476 (CA9 1994); *Selman* v. *United States*, 941 F.2d 1060, 1064 (CA10 1991); *Horton Homes, Inc.* v. *United States*, 936 F.2d 548, 554 (CA11 1991); see also *Bax* v. *Commissioner*, 13 F.3d 54, 58 (CA2 1993). These decisions recognized that § 6404(e)(1) gave the Secretary complete discretion to determine whether to abate interest, "neither indicat[ing] that such authority should be used universally nor provid[ing] any basis for distinguishing between the instances in which abatement should and should not be granted." *Selman, supra*, at 1063. Any decision by the Secretary was accordingly "committed to agency discretion by law" under the Administrative Procedure Act, 5 U.S.C. § 701(a)(2), and thereby insulated from judicial review. See, *e.g., Webster* v. *Doe*, 486 U.S. 592, 599, 108 S. Ct. 2047, 100 L. Ed. 2d 632 (1988); *Heckler* v. *Chaney*, 470 U.S. 821, 830, 105 S. Ct. 1649, 84 L. Ed. 2d 714 (1985).

In 1996, as part of the Taxpayer Bill of Rights 2, Congress again amended § 6404, adding what is now subsection (h). As relevant, that provision states:

"Review of denial of request for abatement of interest.

"(1) In general

The Tax Court shall have jurisdiction over any action brought by a taxpayer who meets the requirements referred to in section 7430(c)(4)(A)(ii) to determine whether the Secretary's failure to abate interest under this section was an abuse of discretion, and may order an abatement, if such action is brought within 180 days after the date of the mailing of the Secretary's final determination not to abate such interest." 26 U.S.C. § 6404(h)(1) (2000 ed., Supp. IV).

Section 7430(c)(4)(A)(ii) in turn incorporates 28 U.S.C. § 2412(d)(2)(B), which refers to individuals with a net worth not exceeding $2 million and businesses with a net worth not exceeding $7 million. Congress made subsection (h) effective for all requests for abatement submitted to the IRS after July 30, 1996, regardless of the tax year involved. § 302(b), 110 Stat. 1458.[1]

1 The Taxpayer Bill of Rights 2 also modified 26 U.S.C. § 6404(e)(1)(A) to add the word "unreasonable" before the words "error or delay" and to change "ministerial act" to "ministerial or managerial act." § 301(a), 110 Stat. 1457. These changes, however, only apply to interest accruing on deficiencies for tax years beginning after July 30, 1996, see § 301(c), *ibid.,* and thus are not implicated in this case.

II

In 1986, petitioner John Hinck was a limited partner in an entity called Agri-Cal Venture Associates (ACVA). Along with his wife, petitioner Pamela Hinck, Hinck filed a joint return for 1986 reporting his share of losses from the partnership. The IRS later examined the tax returns for ACVA and proposed adjustments to deductions that the partnership had claimed for 1984, 1985, and 1986. In 1990, the IRS issued a final notice regarding the partnership's returns, disallowing tens of millions of dollars of deductions. While the partnership sought administrative review of this decision, the Hincks, in May 1996, made an advance remittance of $93,890 to the IRS toward any personal deficiency that might result from a final adjustment of ACVA's returns. In March 1999, the Hincks reached a settlement with the IRS concerning the ACVA partnership adjustments, to the extent they affected the Hincks' return. Shortly thereafter, as a result of the adjustments, the IRS imposed additional liability against the Hincks: $16,409 in tax and $21,669.22 in interest. The IRS applied the Hincks' advance remittance to this amount and refunded them the balance of $55,811.78.

The Hincks filed a claim with the IRS contending that, because of IRS errors and delays, the interest assessed against them for the period from March 21, 1989, to April 1, 1993, should be abated under § 6404(e)(1). The IRS denied the request. The Hincks then filed suit in the United States Court of Federal Claims seeking review of the refusal to abate. That court granted the Government's motion to dismiss, 64 Fed. Cl. 71, 81 (2005), and the United States Court of Appeals for the Federal Circuit affirmed, 446 F.3d 1307, 1313-1314 (2006), holding that § 6404(h) vests exclusive jurisdiction to review interest abatement claims under § 6404(e)(1) in the Tax Court. Because this decision conflicted with the Fifth Circuit's decision in *Beall* v. *United States,* 336 F.3d 419, 430 (2003) (holding that § 6404(h) grants concurrent rather than exclusive jurisdiction to the Tax Court), we granted certiorari, 549 U.S. 1162, 127 S. Ct. 1055, 166 L. Ed. 2d 797 (2007).

III

Our analysis is governed by the well-established principle that, in most contexts, "'a precisely drawn, detailed statute pre-empts more general remedies.'" *EC Term of Years Trust v. United States, ante,* at 434, 127 S. Ct. 1763, 167 L. Ed. 2d 729 (2007) (quoting *Brown* v. *GSA,* 425 U.S. 820, 834, 96 S. Ct. 1961, 48 L. Ed. 2d 402 (1976)); see also *Block* v. *North Dakota ex rel. Board of Univ. and School Lands,* 461 U.S. 273, 284-286, 103 S. Ct. 1811, 75 L. Ed. 2d 840 (1983). We are also guided by our past recognition that when Congress enacts a specific remedy when no remedy was previously recognized, or when previous remedies were "problematic," the remedy provided is generally regarded as exclusive. *Id.,* at 285, 103 S. Ct. 1811, 75 L. Ed. 2d 840; *Brown, supra,* at 826-829, 96 S. Ct. 1961, 48 L. Ed. 2d 402.

Section 6404(h) fits the bill on both counts. It is a "precisely drawn, detailed statute" that, in a single sentence, provides a forum for adjudication, a limited class of potential plaintiffs, a statute of limitations, a standard of review, and authorization for judicial relief. And Congress enacted this provision against a backdrop of decisions uniformly rejecting the possibility of any review for taxpayers wishing to challenge the Secretary's § 6404(e)(1) determination. Therefore, despite Congress's failure explicitly to define the Tax Court's jurisdiction as exclusive, we think it quite plain that the terms of § 6404(h) --a "precisely drawn, detailed statute" filling a perceived hole in the law--control all requests for review of § 6404(e)(1) determinations. Those terms include the forum for adjudication.

The Hincks' primary argument against exclusive Tax Court jurisdiction is that by providing a standard of review--abuse of discretion--in § 6404(h), Congress eliminated the primary barrier to judicial review that courts had previously recognized; accordingly, they maintain, taxpayers may seek review of § 6404(e)(1) determinations under statutes granting jurisdiction to the district courts and the Court of Federal Claims to review tax refund actions. See 28 U.S.C. §§ 1346(a)(1), 1491(a)(1); 26 U.S.C. § 7422(a). Or, as the Fifth Circuit reasoned: "[T]he federal district courts have always possessed *jurisdiction* over challenges brought to section 6404(e)(1) denials[;] they simply determined that the taxpayers had no *substantive right* whatever to a favorable exercise of the Secretary's discretion . . . . [I]n enacting section 6404(h), Congress indicated that such is no longer the case, and thereby removed any impediment to district court review." *Beall, supra,* at 428 (emphasis in original).

It is true that by providing an abuse-of-discretion standard, Congress removed one of the obstacles courts had held foreclosed judicial review of § 6404(e)(1) determinations. See, *e.g., Argabright,* 35 F.3d at 476 (noting an absence of "'judicially manageable standards'" (quoting *Heckler,* 470 U.S., at 830, 105 S. Ct. 1649, 84 L. Ed. 2d 714)). But in enacting § 6404(h), Congress did not simply supply this single missing ingredient; rather, it set out a carefully circumscribed, time-limited, plaintiff-specific provision, which also precisely defined the appropriate forum. We cannot accept the Hincks' invitation to isolate one feature of this "precisely drawn, detailed statute"--the portion specifying a standard of review--and use it to permit taxpayers to circumvent the other limiting features Congress placed in the *same* statute--restrictions such as a shorter statute of limitations than general refund suits, compare § 6404(h) (180-day limitations period) with § 6532(a)(1) (2-year limitations period), or a net-worth ceiling for plaintiffs eligible to bring suit. Taxpayers could "effortlessly evade" these specific limitations by bringing interest abatement claims as tax refund actions in the district courts or the Court of Federal Claims, disaggregating a statute Congress plainly envisioned as a package deal. *EC Term of Years Trust, ante,* at _, 127 S. Ct. 1763, 167 L. Ed. 2d 729; see also *Block, supra,* at 284-285, 103 S. Ct. 1811, 75 L. Ed. 2d 840; *Brown, supra,* at 832-833, 96 S. Ct. 1961, 48 L. Ed. 2d 402.

The Hincks' other contentions are equally unavailing. First, they claim that reading § 6404(h) to vest exclusive jurisdiction in the Tax Court impliedly repeals the pre-existing jurisdiction of the district courts and Court of Federal Claims, despite our admonition that "repeals by implication are not favored." *Morton* v. *Mancari,* 417 U.S. 535, 549, 94 S. Ct. 2474, 41 L. Ed. 2d 290 (1974) (internal quotation marks omitted). But the implied-repeal doctrine is not applicable here, for when Congress passed § 6404(h), § 6404(e)(1) had been interpreted not to provide *any* right of review for taxpayers. There is thus no indication of any "language on the statute books that [Congress] wishe[d] to change," *United States* v. *Fausto,* 484 U.S. 439, 453, 108 S. Ct. 668, 98 L. Ed. 2d 830 (1988), implicitly or explicitly. Congress simply prescribed a limited form of review where none had previously been found to exist.

Second, the Hincks assert that vesting jurisdiction over § 6404(e)(1) abatement decisions exclusively in the Tax Court runs contrary to the "entire structure of tax controversy jurisdiction," Brief for Petitioners 30, under which the Tax Court generally hears prepayment challenges to tax liability, see § 6213(a), while postpayment actions are brought in the district courts or Court of Federal Claims. In a related vein, the Hincks point out that the Government's position would force taxpayers seeking postpayment review of their tax liabilities to separate their § 6404(e)(1) abatement claims from their refund claims and bring each in a different court. Even assuming, *arguendo,* that we were inclined to depart from the face of the statute, these arguments are undercut on two fronts. To begin with, by expressly granting to the Tax Court *some* jurisdiction over § 6404(e)(1) decisions, Congress has already broken with the general scheme the Hincks identify. No one doubts that an action seeking review of a § 6404(e)(1) determination may be maintained in the Tax Court even if the interest has already been paid, see, *e.g., Dadian* v. *Comm'r,*87 T.C.M. (CCH) 1344, T.C. Memo 2004-121, P2004-121 RIA Memo TC, p. 790-2004 (2004); *Miller* v. *Comm'r,* T.C. Memo 2000-196, 79 T.C.M. (CCH) 2213, T.C.M.

(RIA) P53930, p. 1120-2000 (2000), aff'd, 310 F.3d 640 (CA9 2002), and the Hincks point to no case where the Tax Court has refused to exercise jurisdiction under such circumstances.

In addition, an interest abatement claim under § 6404(e)(1) involves no questions of substantive tax law, but rather is premised on issues of bureaucratic administration (whether, for example, there was "error or delay" in the performance of a "ministerial" act, § 6404(e)(1)(A)). Judicial review of decisions not to abate requires an evaluation of the internal processes of the IRS, not the underlying tax liability of the taxpayer. We find nothing tellingly awkward about channeling such discrete and specialized questions of administrative operations to one particular court, even if in some respects it "may not appear to be efficient" as a policy matter to separate refund and interest abatement claims. 446 F.3d at 1316.[2]

> 2 We note that the Hincks sought only interest abatement in the Court of Federal Claims, thus failing to implicate the "claim-splitting" and efficiency concerns they condemn. See Brief for Petitioners 49.

Last, the Hincks contend that Congress would not have intended to vest jurisdiction exclusively in the Tax Court because it would lead to the "unreasonable" result that taxpayers with net worths greater than $2 million (for individuals) or $7 million (for businesses) would be foreclosed from seeking judicial review of § 6404(e)(1) refusals to abate. Brief for Petitioners 46; see also *Beall*, 336 F.3d at 430. But we agree with the Federal Circuit that this outcome "was contemplated by Congress." 446 F.3d at 1316. The net-worth limitation in § 6404(h) reflects Congress's judgment that wealthier taxpayers are more likely to be able to pay a deficiency before contesting it, thereby avoiding accrual of interest during their administrative and legal challenges. In contrast, taxpayers with comparatively fewer resources are more likely to contest their assessed deficiency before first paying it, thus exposing themselves to interest charges if their challenge is ultimately unsuccessful. There is nothing "unreasonable" about Congress's decision to grant the possibility of judicial relief only to those taxpayers most likely to be in need of it.[3]

> 3 The Hincks also argue that the net-worth limitations on § 6404(h) review violate the due process rights of those taxpayers who exceed them. The court below did not pass upon this constitutional challenge, nor do we, for as the Hincks concede, the record contains no findings concerning their own net worth, Brief for Petitioners 44, and they offer no reasons to deviate from our general rule that a party "must assert his own legal rights and interests, and cannot rest his claim to relief on

the legal rights or interests of third parties," *Kowalski* v. *Tesmer*, 543 U.S. 125, 129, 125 S. Ct. 564, 160 L. Ed. 2d 519 (2004) (quoting *Warth* v. *Seldin*, 422 U.S. 490, 499, 95 S. Ct. 2197, 45 L. Ed. 2d 343 (1975); internal quotation marks omitted).

The judgment of the United States Court of Appeals for the Federal Circuit is affirmed.

It is so ordered.

Roberts Unanimous

CSX TRANSPORTATION, INC., Petitioner
v.
GEORGIA STATE BOARD OF EQUALIZATION et al.

06-1287
SUPREME COURT
OF THE UNITED STATES

552 U.S. 9

November 5, 2007, Argued
December 4, 2007, Decided

ON WRIT OF CERTIORARI TO THE UNITED STATES COURT OF APPEALS FOR THE ELEVENTH CIRCUIT

Chief Justice Roberts delivered the opinion of the Court.

The Railroad Revitalization and Regulatory Reform Act of 1976 prohibits States from discriminating against railroads by taxing railroad property more heavily than other commercial property in the State. Two decades ago, we held that this statute permits an aggrieved railroad to challenge a State's valuation of its property for tax purposes. *Burlington Northern R. Co.* v. *Oklahoma Tax Comm'n,* 481 U.S. 454, 462, 107 S. Ct. 1855, 95 L. Ed. 2d 404 (1987). Because the railroad in that case challenged only the State's *application* of its valuation methods, we expressly reserved the question whether a railroad may challenge the State's methods themselves. We answer that question today, and hold that railroads may challenge state methods for determining the value of railroad property, as well as how those methods are applied. The statute provides for nothing less.

I

Congress enacted the Railroad Revitalization and Regulatory Reform Act in 1976. 90 Stat. 31.[1] Called the "4-R Act" for brevity, the law aimed to halt the economic decline of the rail industry by, among other means, barring "discriminatory state taxation of railroad property." *Burlington Northern, supra,* at 457, 107 S. Ct. 1855, 95 L. Ed. 2d 404; see also *Department of Revenue of Ore.* v. *ACF Industries, Inc.,* 510 U.S. 332, 336, 114 S. Ct. 843, 127 L. Ed. 2d 165 (1994). The 4-R Act prohibits four separate forms of discriminatory state taxation of railroads.[2] Only the first is at issue here: States, the Act provides, may not "[a]ssess rail transportation property at a value that has a higher ratio to the [property's] true market value . . . than the ratio" between the assessed and true market values of other commercial and industrial property in the same taxing jurisdiction. 49 U.S.C. § 11501(b)(1). If the railroad ratio exceeds the ratio for other property by at least five percent, the district court may enjoin the tax. § 11501(c).[3]

> 1 The portion of the Act that concerns us here, § 306, was originally codified at 49 U.S.C. § 26c (1976 ed.). In 1978, Congress recodified it at 49 U.S.C. § 11503 (1976 ed., Supp. II). Congress recodified it again in 1995, without substantive change, this time as § 11501. For convenience, all references to the statute are to the text of § 11501.
>
> 2 Section 11501 reads, in relevant part: "(b) The following acts unreasonably burden and discriminate against interstate commerce, and a State, subdivision of a State, or authority acting for a State or subdivision of a State may not do any of them: "(1) Assess rail transportation property at a value that has a higher ratio to the true market value of the rail transportation property than the ratio that the assessed value of other commercial and industrial property in the same assessment jurisdiction has to the true market value of the other commercial and industrial property. "(2) Levy or collect a tax on an assessment that may not be made under paragraph (1) of this subsection. "(3) Levy or collect an ad valorem property tax on rail transportation property at a tax rate that exceeds the tax rate applicable to commercial and industrial property in the same assessment jurisdiction. "(4) Impose another tax that discriminates against a rail carrier providing transportation subject to the jurisdiction of the Board under this part."
>
> 3 Section 11501(c) provides: "Notwithstanding section 1341 of title 28 and without regard to the amount in controversy or citizenship of the parties, a district court of the United States has jurisdiction, concurrent with other jurisdiction of courts of the United States and the States, to prevent a violation of subsection (b) of this section. Relief may be granted under this subsection only if the ratio of assessed value to true market value of rail transportation property exceeds by at least 5 percent the ratio of assessed value to true market value of other commercial and industrial property in the same assessment jurisdiction. The burden of proof in determining assessed value and true market value is governed by State law. If the ratio of the assessed value of other commercial and industrial property in the assessment jurisdiction to the true market value of all other commercial and industrial property cannot be determined to the satisfaction of the district court through

the random-sampling method known as a sales assessment ratio study (to be carried out under statistical principles applicable to such a study), the court shall find, as a violation of this section-- "(1) an assessment of the rail transportation property at a value that has a higher ratio to the true market value of the rail transportation property than the assessed value of all other property subject to a property tax levy in the assessment jurisdiction has to the true market value of all other commercial and industrial property; and "(2) the collection of an ad valorem property tax on the rail transportation property at a tax rate that exceeds the tax ratio rate applicable to taxable property in the taxing district."

Petitioner CSX Transportation, Inc., is a freight rail carrier with multiple routes across the State of Georgia. As a consequence, it is subject to Georgia's ad valorem tax on real property. Under Georgia law, most commercial and industrial property is valued locally by county boards. Public utilities such as railroads, however, are initially valued by the State, which then certifies the proposed valuations to the county boards for adoption or alteration. In 2001, Georgia's State Board of Equalization, a respondent here, put CSX's ad valorem tax liability at $4.6 million. A year later, the State's appraiser used a different combination of methodologies to determine the market value of CSX's in-state property.[4] The result was a significantly higher tax levy. The State estimated the railroad's 2002 market value at approximately $7.8 billion, 472 F.3d 1281, 1285 (CA11 2006), a 47 percent increase over the previous year. That brought the assessed value of CSX's Georgia property to $514.9 million, for a final property tax bill of $6.5 million. Brief for Petitioner 15.

---

[4] Georgia assesses public utilities using the "unit rule." Under this rule, "an appraiser first determines the value of all assets of an entity, regardless of location," then multiplies "by the percentage of the entity located within [the State] to determine what portion of the value of the company should be allocated to the state." 472 F.3d 1281, 1283 (CA11 2006). The parties agree the unit rule is the appropriate rule for valuing CSX's property. There are, however, numerous methods available to value property under the unit rule, and many of these methods themselves have multiple variations. See *id.*, at 1284.

CSX filed suit in the United States District Court for the Northern District of Georgia, contending that the State's 2002 tax assessment violated the 4-R Act. The railroad alleged that Georgia had grossly overestimated the market value of its in-state property while accurately valuing other commercial and industrial property in the State. The result, according to CSX, was that its rail property was taxed at a ratio of assessed-to-market value considerably more than five percent greater than the same ratio for the other property in the State.

To make its case, CSX submitted the testimony of its own expert appraiser, who relied on a combination of valuation methods different from those used by the appraiser for Georgia. The CSX appraiser calculated the 2002 market value of the railroad's property to be $6 billion, not the $7.8 billion figure used by the State. 472 F.3d at 1285-1286. CSX maintained that the state appraiser's valuation methodologies were flawed, and urged the District Court to accept the market value estimated by its expert as more accurate.

The District Court refused to do so. Following a bench trial, the court ruled Georgia had not discriminated against CSX in violation of the 4-R Act because the State had used widely accepted valuation methods to arrive at its estimate of true market value. 448 F. Supp. 2d 1330, 1341 (ND Ga. 2005). In the judgment of the District Court, the Act "does not generally allow a railroad to challenge the state's chosen methodology," as long as the State's methods are rational and not motivated by discriminatory intent. *Ibid.*

A divided panel of the Court of Appeals for the Eleventh Circuit affirmed. 472 F.3d 1281. The majority reasoned that the "text of the Act does not clearly state that railroads may challenge valuation methodologies," and that such a clear statement was required in light of the intrusion on state taxing prerogatives. *Id.*, at 1289. Judge Fay dissented. *Id.*, at 1292. Recognizing the division on this question among the Circuits, compare *Consolidated Rail Corp.* v. *Hyde Park*, 47 F.3d 473, 481-482 (CA2 1995) (a railroad may challenge a State's valuation methodology), and *Burlington Northern R. Co.* v. *Department of Revenue of Wash.*, 23 F.3d 239, 240-241 (CA9 1994) (same), with *Chesapeake Western R. Co.* v. *Forst*, 938 F.2d 528, 531 (CA4 1991) (a railroad may not challenge a State's valuation methodology), and 472 F.3d at 1289 (case below), we granted certiorari, 550 U.S. 968, 127 S. Ct. 2879, 167 L. Ed. 2d 1151 (2007), and now reverse.

II

"[T]he language of § 1150[1] plainly declares the congressional purpose." *Burlington Northern*, 481 U.S., at 461,107 S. Ct. 1855, 95 L. Ed. 2d 404. States may not tax railroad property at a ratio of assessed-to-true-market value higher than the ratio for other commercial and industrial property in the same jurisdiction. In order to apply the Act, district courts must calculate the true market value of in-state railroad property. A court cannot undertake the comparison of ratios the statute requires without that figure at hand. We said as much in *Burlington Northern:* "It is clear from [the Act's] language that in order to compare the actual assessment ratios, it is necessary to determine what the 'true market values' are." *Ibid.*

We do not see how a court can go about determining true market value if it may not look behind the State's choice of valuation methods. Georgia insists there is a clear and important distinction between valuation methodologies and their application. As the State would have it, the statute allows courts to question only the latter. We find no distinction between method and application in the language of the Act, and see no passage limiting district court factfinding in the manner the State proposes. The total lack of textual support for Georgia's position is not surprising. The dichotomy the State presses would eviscerate the statute by forcing courts to defer to the valuation estimate of the State, when discriminatory taxation by States was the very evil the Act aimed to ban.

Georgia's position is untenable given the way market value is calculated. Valuation is not a matter of mathematics, as if the district court could prevent discriminatory taxation simply by doublechecking the State's assessment equations. Rather, the calculation of true market value is an applied science, even a craft. Most appraisers estimate market value by employing not one methodology but a combination. These various methods generate a range of possible market values which the appraiser uses to derive what he considers to be an accurate estimate of market value, based on careful scrutiny of all the data available. Appraisal Institute, The Appraisal of Real Estate 49-50 (12th ed. 2001).

Georgia's appraiser in the instant case, for example, used three different valuation techniques--the discounted cashflow approach, a market multiple approach, and a stock and debt approach. He derived five values from these three methods, ranging from $8.126 billion to $12.346 billion. After selecting a number at the low end of the range and then subtracting another $400 million to account for intangible property not subject to ad valorem taxation, he settled on $7.8 billion as his final estimate of the true market value. 472 F.3d at 1284-1285.

Appraisers typically employ a combination of methods because no one approach is entirely accurate, at least in the absence of an established market for the type of property at issue. The individual methods yield sometimes more, sometimes less reliable results depending on the peculiar features of the property evaluated. As the variation in the state appraiser's market-value range reveals, different methods can produce substantially different estimates. W. Kinnard, Income Property Valuation: Principles and Techniques of Appraising Income-Producing Real Estate 52 (1971).

Given the extent to which the chosen methods can affect the determination of value, preventing courts from scrutinizing state valuation methodologies would render § 11501 a largely empty command. It would force district courts to accept as "true" the market value estimated by the State, one of the parties to the litigation. States, in turn, would be free to employ appraisal techniques that routinely overestimate the market worth of railroad assets. By then levying taxes based on those overestimates, States could implement the very discriminatory taxation Congress sought to eradicate. On Georgia's reading of the statute, courts would be powerless to stop them, and the Act would ultimately guarantee railroads nothing more than mathematically accurate discriminatory taxation. We do not find this interpretation compelling. Instead, we agree with Judge Fay in dissent below: "Since the objective of any methodology is a determination of *true market value*, a railroad should be allowed to challenge the method[s] used [by the State] in an attempt to prove that the result . . . was not the *true market value* of its property." 472 F.3d at 1294.

The State agrees that it may not be possible to fix true market value with any precision. But it draws a different conclusion from this premise. Because any number of estimates are plausible, Georgia argues, the court is as likely to get an accurate result by verifying the application of the State's methods--so long as they are broadly reasonable--as it is by employing another method altogether. The State warns that allowing railroads to introduce their own valuation estimates based on different methodologies will inevitably lead to a futile clash of experts, which courts will have no reasonable way to settle. At least one of the Courts of Appeals shares this concern. See *Chesapeake Western*, 938 F.2d at 532 ("There is no absolute way to test the assertions of competing valuations . . ." (internal quotation marks and brackets omitted)).

Congress was not similarly troubled. It directed courts to find true market value, however elusive. It made that value the objective benchmark for courts' evaluation of state taxes on railroad property. True market value may well not be a single, precise number, but Congress obviously believed it was susceptible to judicial inquiry and that some approximations were better than others.

Georgia's grim prophecies notwithstanding, the inquiry the statute mandates is not unfamiliar to courts. Valuation of property, though admittedly complex, is at bottom just "an issue of fact about possible market prices," *Suitum* v. *Tahoe Regional Planning Agency*, 520 U.S. 725, 741, 117 S. Ct. 1659, 137 L. Ed. 2d 980 (1997), an issue district courts are used to addressing. Railroad property is not frequently sold, but "determinations of market value are routinely made in judicial proceedings without the benefit of a market transaction." *Id.*, at 742, 117 S. Ct. 1659, 137 L. Ed. 2d 980. The District

Court in this case made clear that it knew how to find true market value: "In a more typical case, the court would look at both [the railroad expert's] appraisal and [the State's] appraisal to determine the true market value of [the railroad]." 448 F. Supp. 2d, at 1338, n. 8. It refused to do so not because true market value is inherently elusive, but because it believed the Act did not allow it to question the State's methods.

In light of the statute's directive making true market value a factual question to be determined by the district court, what Georgia is really asking for is a limitation on the types of evidence courts may consider as part of their factual inquiry. If Congress had wanted to impose such a limit by reserving to States the prerogative of selecting which valuation methods may be used, it surely could have done so. Out of deference to the States, for example, § 11501(c) provides that "[t]he burden of proof in determining . . . true market value [shall be] governed by State law." Congress could easily have included similar language insulating the State's chosen methodologies from judicial scrutiny. It did not. Like Oklahoma's argument in *Burlington Northern*, Georgia's position in this case ultimately "depends upon the addition of words to a statutory provision which is complete as it stands." 481 U. S., at 463, 107 S. Ct. 1855, 95 L. Ed. 2d 404. We decline to find distinctions in the statute where they do not exist, especially where, as here, those distinctions would thwart the law's operation.

III

Considering the clarity of the statute, we are tempted to leave the discussion at that. "When we find the terms of a statute unambiguous, judicial inquiry is complete . . . ." *Rubin* v. *United States*, 449 U.S. 424, 430, 101 S. Ct. 698, 66 L. Ed. 2d 633 (1981). Georgia, however, lodges two objections to our interpretation, each of which merits a reply. First, the State argues that any interpretation of the Act allowing courts to question state valuation methods ignores the background principles of federalism against which the statute was enacted. The majority below expressed a similar concern. "The selection of a valuation methodology," it ruled, "is part of th[e] fundamental power of a state [to tax]," 472 F.3d at 1288, and should not be limited absent a clear statement from Congress. We have long held that the means States adopt to collect their taxes "should be interfered with as little as possible." *Dows* v. *Chicago*, 78 U.S. 108, 11 Wall. 108, 110, 20 L. Ed. 65 (1871). But we are persuaded that allowing railroads to challenge a State's valuation methodologies has been clearly authorized by the terms of the 4-R Act.

As an initial matter, we question Georgia's contention that its selection of valuation methodologies is an important state policy choice intimately connected to its tax power. Georgia does not prescribe any particular methodology as a matter of state law. Its appraisers use different methodologies in different combinations, as they see fit. See 472 F.3d at 1284-1285 (explaining that the state appraiser employed multiple methods and selected a value according to his best judgment). This suit, in fact, is the result of an individual appraiser's decision to employ a different combination of assessment techniques than that used by his immediate predecessors. The methods he selected were his choice, not the dictate of any state statute or regulation. *Ibid.*

But even if important questions of state policy are, as the Eleventh Circuit believed, "intertwined with the selection of a valuation methodology," *id.*, at 1288, judicial scrutiny of those methodologies is authorized by the 4-R Act's clear command to find true market value. As we explained above, the power to calculate true market value necessarily includes the power to look behind a State's valuation methods. That the statute should vest this authority in the Nation's courts is hardly surprising, given Congress's conclusion that the States were assessing railroad property unfairly.

Our decision in *Department of Revenue of Ore.* v. *ACF Industries, Inc.*, 510 U.S. 332, 114 S. Ct. 843, 127 L. Ed. 2d 165 (1994), is not to the contrary. That case concerned a different provision of the 4-R Act--namely, the command in § 11501(b)(4) preventing a State from "[i]mpos[ing] another tax that discriminates against a rail carrier providing transportation" in the taxing jurisdiction. This bar on facially discriminatory taxes, we held, did not prevent a State from exempting certain nonrailroad property from otherwise generally applicable ad valorem taxes. *Id.*, 510 U.S., at 343, 114 S. Ct. 843, 127 L. Ed. 2d 165. At the time the 4-R Act was adopted, a majority of States exempted one or more classes of business property from ad valorem taxation, "including business inventories, raw materials used in textile manufacturing, . . . and mechanics tools," to name just a few. *Id.*, at 344, 114 S. Ct. 843, 127 L. Ed. 2d 165. The States had provided such property tax exemptions for years. In the face of this widespread and historical practice, we declined to read the 4-R Act to prohibit a type of tax exemption the text did not expressly mention. *Ibid.*

By contrast, we pointedly noted that the Act "prohibit[s] discriminatory tax rates and assessment ratios in no uncertain terms . . . and set[s] forth precise standards for judicial scrutiny of challenged rate and assessment practices." *Id.*, at 343, 114 S. Ct. 843, 127 L. Ed. 2d 165. Georgia's claim that court review of state valuation methodologies is not authorized by a clear statement in the Act ignores the statute's explicit prohibition of discriminatory assessment ratios. A district court cannot accurately calculate or compare those ratios without determining true market value. Congress clearly permitted courts to question state valuation methodologies when it banned discriminatory assessment ratios and made true market value a question to be litigated in federal court.

Georgia also protests that our interpretation will destroy the States' discretion to choose their own valuation methodologies. We disagree. A State may use whatever method or methods it likes, so long as the result is not discriminatory. The Act does not prohibit the use of any valuation methodology. It prohibits discrimination. Far from requiring States to follow a particular method, we hold only that nothing in the statute prevents a railroad from attempting to show that the methods chosen by the State result in a discriminatory determination of true market value.

The judgment of the Court of Appeals for the Eleventh Circuit is reversed.

It is so ordered.

MICHAEL J. KNIGHT, trustee of the
WILLIAM L. RUDKIN
TESTAMENTARY TRUST,
Petitioner
v.
COMMISSIONER OF
INTERNAL REVENUE

06-1286
SUPREME COURT
OF THE UNITED STATES

552 U.S. 181

November 27, 2007, Argued
January 16, 2008, Decided

ON WRIT OF CERTIORARI TO THE UNITED STATES COURT OF APPEALS FOR THE SECOND CIRCUIT

Chief Justice Roberts delivered the opinion of the Court.

Under the Internal Revenue Code, individuals may subtract from their adjusted gross income certain itemized deductions, but only to the extent the deductions exceed 2% of adjusted gross income. A trust may also claim those deductions, also subject to the 2% floor, except that costs incurred in the administration of the trust, which would not have been incurred if the trust property were not held by a trust, may be deducted without regard to the floor. In the case of individuals, investment advisory fees are subject to the 2% floor; the question presented is whether such fees are also subject to the floor when incurred by a trust. We hold that they generally are and therefore affirm the judgment below, albeit for different reasons than those given by the Court of Appeals.

I

The Internal Revenue Code imposes a tax on the "taxable income" of both individuals and trusts. 26 U.S.C. § 1(a). The Code instructs that the calculation of taxable income begins with a determination of "gross income," capaciously defined as "all income from whatever source derived." § 61(a). "Adjusted gross income" is then calculated by subtracting from gross income certain "above-the-line" deductions, such as trade and business expenses and losses from the sale or exchange of property. § 62(a). Finally, taxable income is calculated by subtracting from adjusted gross income "itemized deductions"--also known as "below-the-line" deductions--defined as all allowable deductions other than the "above-the-line" deductions identified in § 62(a) and the deduction for personal exemptions allowed under § 151 (2000 ed. and Supp. V). § 63(d) (2000 ed.).

Before the passage of the Tax Reform Act of 1986, 100 Stat. 2085, below-the-line deductions were deductible in full. This system resulted in significant complexity and potential for abuse, requiring "extensive [taxpayer] recordkeeping with regard to what commonly are small expenditures," as well as "significant administrative and enforcement problems for the Internal Revenue Service." H. R. Rep. No. 99-426, p 109 (1985).

In response, Congress enacted what is known as the "2% floor" by adding § 67 to the Code. Section 67(a) provides that "the miscellaneous itemized deductions for any taxable year shall be allowed only to the extent that the aggregate of such deductions exceeds 2 percent of adjusted gross income." The term "miscellaneous itemized deductions" is defined to include all itemized deductions other than certain ones specified in § 67(b). Investment advisory fees are deductible pursuant to 26 U.S.C. § 212. Because § 212 is not listed in § 67(b) as one of the categories of expenses that may be deducted in full, such fees are "miscellaneous itemized deductions" subject to the 2% floor. 26 CFR § 1.67-1T(a)(1)(ii) (2007).

Section 67(e) makes the 2% floor generally applicable not only to individuals but also to estates and trusts,[1] with one exception relevant here. Under this exception, "the adjusted gross income of an estate or trust shall be computed in the same manner as in the case of an individual, except that . . . the deductions for costs which are paid or incurred in connection with the administration of the estate or trust and which would not have been incurred if the property were not held in such trust or estate . . . shall be treated as allowable" and not subject to the 2% floor. § 67(e)(1).

---

[1] Because this case is only about trusts, we generally refer to trusts throughout, but the analysis applies equally to estates.

Petitioner Michael J. Knight is the trustee of the William L. Rudkin Testamentary Trust, established in the State of Connecticut in 1967. In 2000, the Trustee hired Warfield Associates, Inc., to provide advice with respect to investing the Trust's assets. At the beginning of the tax year, the Trust held approximately $2.9 million in marketable securities, and it paid Warfield

$22,241 in investment advisory fees for the year. On its fiduciary income tax return for 2000, the Trust reported total income of $624,816, and it deducted in full the investment advisory fees paid to Warfield. After conducting an audit, respondent Commissioner of Internal Revenue found that these investment advisory fees were miscellaneous itemized deductions subject to the 2% floor. The Commissioner therefore allowed the Trust to deduct the investment advisory fees, which were the only claimed deductions subject to the floor, only to the extent that they exceeded 2% of the Trust's adjusted gross income. The discrepancy resulted in a tax deficiency of $4,448.

The Trust filed a petition in the United States Tax Court seeking review of the assessed deficiency. It argued that the Trustee's fiduciary duty to act as a "prudent investor" under the Connecticut Uniform Prudent Investor Act, Conn. Gen. Stat. §§ 45a-541a to 45a-541*l* (2007),[2] required the Trustee to obtain investment advisory services, and therefore to pay investment advisory fees. The Trust argued that such fees are accordingly unique to trusts and therefore fully deductible under 26 U.S.C. § 67(e)(1). The Tax Court rejected this argument, holding that § 67(e)(1) allows full deductibility only for expenses that are not commonly incurred outside the trust setting. Because investment advisory fees are commonly incurred by individuals, the Tax Court held that they are subject to the 2% floor when incurred by a trust. *Rudkin Testamentary Trust* v. *Commissioner*, 124 T. C. 304, 309-311 (2005).

> 2 Forty-four States and the District of Columbia have adopted versions of the Uniform Prudent Investor Act. See 7B U. L. A. 1-2 (2006) (listing States that have enacted the Uniform Prudent Investor Act). Five of the remaining six States have adopted their own versions of the prudent investor standard. See Del. Code Ann., Tit. 12, § 3302 (1995 ed. and 2006 Supp.); Ga. Code Ann. § 53-12-287 (1997); La. Rev. Stat. Ann. § 9:2127 (West 2005); Md. Est. & Trusts Code Ann. § 15-114 (Lexis 2001); S. D. Codified Laws § 55-5-6 (2004). Kentucky, the only remaining State, applies the prudent investor standard only in certain circumstances. See Ky. Rev. Stat. Ann. § 286.3-277 (Lexis 2007 Cum. Supp.); §§ 386.454(1), 386.502 (Supp. 2007).

The Trust appealed to the United States Court of Appeals for the Second Circuit. The Court of Appeals concluded that, in determining whether costs such as investment advisory fees are fully deductible or subject to the 2% floor, § 67(e) "directs the inquiry toward the counterfactual condition of assets held individually instead of in trust," and requires "an objective determination of whether the particular cost is one that is peculiar to trusts and one that individuals are incapable of incurring." 467 F.3d 149, 155, 156 (2006). The court held that because investment advisory fees were "costs of a type that *could* be incurred if the property were held individually rather than in trust," deduction of such fees by the Trust was subject to the 2% floor. *Id.,* at 155-156.

The Courts of Appeals are divided on the question presented. The Sixth Circuit has held that investment advisory fees are fully deductible. *O'Neill* v. *Commissioner,* 994 F.2d 302, 304 (1993). In contrast, both the Fourth and Federal Circuits have held that such fees are subject to the 2% floor, because they are "commonly" or "customarily" incurred outside of trusts. See *Scott* v. *United States,* 328 F.3d 132, 140 (CA4 2003); *Mellon Bank, N. A.* v. *United States,* 265 F.3d 1275, 1281 (CA Fed. 2001). The Court of Appeals below came to the same conclusion, but as noted announced a more exacting test, allowing "full deduction only for those costs that *could not* have been incurred by an individual property owner." 467 F.3d at 156 (emphasis added). We granted the Trustee's petition for certiorari to resolve the conflict, 551 U.S. 1144, 127 S. Ct. 3005, 168 L. Ed. 2d 725 (2007), and now affirm.

II

"We start, as always, with the language of the statute." *Williams* v. *Taylor,* 529 U.S. 420, 431, 120 S. Ct. 1479, 146 L. Ed. 2d 435 (2000). Section 67(e) sets forth a general rule: "[T]he adjusted gross income of [a] . . . trust shall be computed in the same manner as in the case of an individual." That is, trusts can ordinarily deduct costs subject to the same 2% floor that applies to individuals' deductions. Section 67(e) provides for an exception to the 2% floor when two conditions are met. First, the relevant cost must be "paid or incurred in connection with the administration of the . . . trust." § 67(e)(1). Second, the cost must be one "which would not have been incurred if the property were not held in such trust." *Ibid.*

In applying the statute, the Court of Appeals below asked whether the cost at issue *could* have been incurred by an individual.[3] This approach flies in the face of the statutory language. The provision at issue asks whether the costs "would not have been incurred if the property were not held" in trust, *ibid.,* not, as the Court of Appeals would have it, whether the costs "could not have been incurred" in such a case, 467 F.3d at 156. The fact that an individual could not do something is one reason he would not, but not the only possible reason. If Congress had intended the Court of Appeals' reading, it easily could have replaced "would" in the statute with "could," and presumably would have. The fact that it did not adopt this readily available and apparent alternative strongly supports rejecting the Court of Appeals' reading.[4]

3 The Solicitor General embraces this position in this Court, arguing that the Court of Appeals' approach represents the best reading of the statute and establishes an easily administrable rule. See Brief for Respondent 17-20, 22. Indeed, after the Court of Appeals' decision, the Commissioner adopted that court's reading of the statute in a proposed regulation. See Section 67 Limitations on Estates or Trusts, 72 Fed. Reg. 41245 (2007) (notice of proposed rulemaking) (a trust-related cost is exempted from the 2% floor only if "an individual *could not* have incurred that cost in connection with property not held in an estate or trust" (emphasis added)). The Government did not advance this argument before the Court of Appeals. See Brief for Appellee in No. 05-5151-AG (CA2), pp 3-4, 22-24. In fact, the notice of proposed rulemaking appears to be the first time the Government has ever taken this position, and we are the first Court to which the argument has been made in a brief. See Brief for United States in *Mellon Bank, N.A. v. United States*, No. 01-5015 (CA Fed.), p 27 ("[I]f a trust-related administrative expense is also customarily or habitually incurred outside of trusts, then it is subject to the two-percent floor"); Brief for United States in *Scott v. United States*, No. 02-1464 (CA4), p 27 (same).

4 In pressing the Court of Appeals' approach, the Solicitor General argues that "to say that a team would not have won the game if it were not for the quarterback's outstanding play is to say that the team could not have won without the quarterback." Brief for Respondent 19. But the Solicitor General simply posits the truth of a proposition--that the team would not have won the game if it were not for the quarterback's outstanding play--and then states its equivalent. The statute, in contrast, does not posit any proposition. Rather, it asks a question: whether a particular cost *would* have been incurred if the property were held by an individual instead of a trust.

Moreover, if the Court of Appeals' reading were correct, it is not clear why Congress would have included in the statute the first clause of § 67(e)(1). If the only costs that are fully deductible are those that *could* not be incurred outside the trust context--that is, that could *only* be incurred by trusts--then there would be no reason to place the further condition on full deductibility that the costs be "paid or incurred in connection with the administration of the . . . trust," § 67(e)(1). We can think of no expense that could be incurred exclusively by a trust but would nevertheless *not* be "paid or incurred in connection with" its administration.

The Trustee argues that the exception in § 67(e)(1) "establishes a straightforward causation test." Brief for Petitioner 22. The proper inquiry, the Trustee contends, is "whether a particular expense of a particular trust or estate was caused by the fact that the property was held in the trust or estate." *Ibid.* Investment advisory fees incurred by a trust, the argument goes, meet this test because these costs are caused by the trustee's obligation "to obtain advice on investing trust assets in compliance with the Trustees' particular fiduciary duties." *Ibid.* We reject this reading as well.

On the Trustee's view, the statute operates only to distinguish costs that are incurred by virtue of a trustee's fiduciary duties from those that are not. But all (or nearly all) of a trust's expenses are incurred because the trustee has a duty to incur them; otherwise, there would be no reason for the trust to incur the expense in the first place. See G. Bogert & G. Bogert, Law of Trusts and Trustees § 801, p 134 (2d rev. ed. 1981) ("[T]he payment for expenses must be reasonably necessary to facilitate administration of the trust"). As an example of a type of trust-related expense that would be subject to the 2% floor, the Trustee offers "expenses for routine maintenance of real property" held by a trust. Brief for Petitioner 23. But such costs would appear to be fully deductible under the Trustee's own reading because a trustee is obligated to incur maintenance expenses in light of the fiduciary duty to maintain trust property. See 1 Restatement (Second) of Trusts § 176, p 381 (1957) ("The trustee is under a duty to the beneficiary to use reasonable care and skill to preserve the trust property").

Indeed, the Trustee's formulation of its argument is circular: "Trust investment advice fees are caused by the fact the property is held in trust." Brief for Petitioner 19. But "trust investment advice fees" are only aptly described as such because the property is held in trust; the statute asks whether such costs would be incurred by an individual if the property were not. Even when there is a clearly analogous category of costs that would be incurred by individuals, the Trustee's reading would exempt most or all trust costs as fully deductible merely because they derive from a trustee's fiduciary duty. Adding the modifier "trust" to costs that otherwise would be incurred by an individual surely cannot be enough to escape the 2% floor.

What is more, if the Trustee's position were correct, then only the first clause of § 67(e)(1)--providing that the cost be "incurred in connection with the administration of the . . . trust"--would be necessary. The statute's second, limiting condition--that the cost also be one "which would not have been incurred if the property were not held in such trust"--would do no work; we see no difference in saying, on the one hand, that costs are "caused by" the fact that the property is held in trust and, on the other, that costs are incurred "in connection with the administration" of the trust. Thus, accepting the

Trustee's approach "would render part of the statute entirely superfluous, something we are loath to do." *Cooper Industries, Inc.* v. *Aviall Services, Inc.*, 543 U.S. 157, 166, 125 S. Ct. 577, 160 L. Ed. 2d 548 (2004).

The Trustee's reading is further undermined by our inclination, "[i]n construing provisions . . . in which a general statement of policy is qualified by an exception, [to] read the exception narrowly in order to preserve the primary operation of the provision." *Commissioner* v. *Clark*, 489 U.S. 726, 739, 109 S. Ct. 1455, 103 L. Ed. 2d 753 (1989). As we have said, § 67(e) sets forth a general rule for purposes of the 2% floor established in § 67(a): "For purposes of this section, the adjusted gross income of an estate or trust shall be computed in the same manner as in the case of an individual." Under the Trustee's reading, § 67(e)(1)'s exception would swallow the general rule; most (if not all) expenses incurred by a trust would be fully deductible. "Given that Congress has enacted a general rule . . ., we should not eviscerate that legislative judgment through an expansive reading of a somewhat ambiguous exception." *Ibid.*

More to the point, the statute by its terms does not "establis[h] a straightforward causation test," Brief for Petitioner 22, but rather invites a hypothetical inquiry into the treatment of the property were it held outside a trust. The statute does not ask whether a cost was incurred *because* the property is held by a trust; it asks whether a particular cost "would not have been incurred if the property were not held in such trust," § 67(e)(1). "Far from examining the nature of the cost at issue from the perspective of whether it was caused by the trustee's duties, the statute instead looks to the counterfactual question of whether *individuals* would have incurred such costs in the *absence* of a trust." Brief for Respondent 9.

This brings us to the test adopted by the Fourth and Federal Circuits: Costs incurred by trusts that escape the 2% floor are those that would not "commonly" or "customarily" be incurred by individuals. See *Scott*, 328 F.3d at 140 ("Put simply, trust-related administrative expenses are subject to the 2% floor if they constitute expenses commonly incurred by individual taxpayers"); *Mellon Bank*, 265 F.3d at 1281 (§ 67(e) "treats as fully deductible only those trust-related administrative expenses that are unique to the administration of a trust and not customarily incurred outside of trusts"). The Solicitor General also accepts this view as an alternative reading of the statute. See Brief for Respondent 20-21. We agree with this approach.

The question whether a trust-related expense is fully deductible turns on a prediction about what would happen if a fact were changed--specifically, if the property were held by an individual rather than by a trust. In the context of making such a prediction, when there is uncertainty about the answer, the word "would" is best read as "express[ing] concepts such as custom, habit, natural disposition, or probability." *Scott, supra*, at 139. See Webster's Third New International Dictionary 2637-2638 (1993); American Heritage Dictionary 2042, 2059 (3d ed. 1996). The Trustee objects that the statutory text "does not ask whether expenses are 'customarily' incurred outside of trusts," Reply Brief for Petitioner 15, but that is the direct import of the language in context. The text requires determining what would happen if a fact were changed; such an exercise necessarily entails a prediction; and predictions are based on what would customarily or commonly occur. Thus, in asking whether a particular type of cost "would *not* have been incurred" if the property were held by an individual, § 67(e)(1) excepts from the 2% floor only those costs that it would be *un*common (or unusual, or unlikely) for such a hypothetical individual to incur.

III

Having decided on the proper reading of § 67(e)(1), we come to the application of the statute to the particular question in this case: whether investment advisory fees incurred by a trust escape the 2% floor.

It is not uncommon or unusual for individuals to hire an investment adviser. Certainly the Trustee, who has the burden of establishing its entitlement to the deduction, has not demonstrated that it is. See *INDOPCO, Inc.* v. *Commissioner*, 503 U.S. 79, 84, 112 S. Ct. 1039, 117 L. Ed. 2d 226 (1992) (noting the "'familiar rule' that 'an income tax deduction is a matter of legislative grace and that the burden of clearly showing the right to the claimed deduction is on the taxpayer'" (quoting *Interstate Transit Lines* v. *Commissioner*, 319 U.S. 590, 593, 63 S. Ct. 1279, 87 L. Ed. 1607, 1943-1 C.B. 1016 (1943))); Tax Court Rule 142(a)(1) (stating that the "burden of proof shall be upon the petitioner," with certain exceptions not relevant here). The Trustee's argument is that individuals cannot incur trust investment advisory fees, not that individuals do not commonly incur investment advisory fees.

Indeed, the essential point of the Trustee's argument is that he engaged an investment adviser because of his fiduciary duties under Connecticut's Uniform Prudent Investor Act, Conn. Gen. Stat. § 45a-541a(a) (2007). The Act eponymously requires trustees to follow the "prudent investor rule." See n 2, *supra*. To satisfy this standard, a trustee must "invest and manage trust assets *as a prudent investor would*, by considering the purposes, terms, distribution requirements and other circumstances of the trust." § 45a-541b(a) (emphasis added). The prudent investor standard plainly does not refer to a prudent *trustee*; it would not be very helpful to explain that a trustee should act as a prudent trustee would. Rather, the standard looks to what a prudent investor with the same investment objectives handling his own affairs would do--*i.e.*, a prudent individual investor. See Restatement (Third) of Trusts (Prudent Investor Rule) Reporter's Notes on § 227, p 58 (1990) ("The prudent investor rule of this Section has its origins in the dictum of Harvard College v. Amory, 9 Pick. (26 Mass.) 446, 461 (1830), stating that trustees must 'observe how men of prudence, discretion, and intelligence manage their own affairs, not in regard to speculation, but in regard to the permanent disposition of their funds, considering the probable income, as well as the probable safety of the capital to be invested'"). See also, *e.g.*, *In re Musser's Estate*, 341 Pa. 1, 9-10, 17 A.2d 411, 415 (1941) (noting the "general rule" that "a trustee must exercise such prudence and diligence in conducting the affairs of the trust as men of average diligence and discretion would employ in their own affairs"). And we have no reason to doubt the Trustee's claim that a hypothetical prudent investor in his position would have solicited investment advice, just as he did. Having accepted all this, it is quite difficult to say that investment advisory fees "would not have been incurred"--that is, that it would be unusual or uncommon for such fees to have been incurred--if the property were held by an individual investor with the same objectives as the Trust in handling his own affairs.

We appreciate that the inquiry into what is common may not be as easy in other cases, particularly given the absence of regulatory guidance. But once you depart in the name of ease of administration from the language chosen by Congress, there is more than one way to skin the cat: The Trustee raises administrability concerns in support of his causation test, Reply Brief for Petitioner 6, but so does the Government in explaining why it prefers the Court of Appeals' approach to the one it has successfully advanced before the Tax Court and two Federal Circuits. Congress's decision to phrase the pertinent inquiry in terms of a prediction about a hypothetical situation inevitably entails some uncertainty, but that is no excuse for judicial amendment of the statute. The Code elsewhere poses similar questions--such as whether expenses are "ordinary," see §§ 162(a), 212; see also *Deputy, Administratrix* v. *Du Pont*, 308 U.S. 488, 495, 60 S. Ct. 363, 84 L. Ed. 416, 1940-1 C.B. 118 (1940) (noting that "[o]rdinary has the connotation of normal, usual, or customary")--and the inquiry is in any event what § 67(e)(1) requires.

As the Solicitor General concedes, some trust-related investment advisory fees may be fully deductible "if an investment advisor were to impose a special, additional charge applicable only to its fiduciary accounts." Brief for Respondent 25. There is nothing in the record, however, to suggest that Warfield charged the Trustee anything extra, or treated the Trust any differently than it would have treated an individual with similar objectives, because of the Trustee's fiduciary obligations. See App. 24-27. It is conceivable, moreover, that a trust may have an unusual investment objective, or may require a specialized balancing of the interests of various parties, such that a reasonable comparison with individual investors would be improper. In such a case, the incremental cost of expert advice beyond what would normally be required for the ordinary taxpayer would not be subject to the 2% floor. Here, however, the Trust has not asserted that its investment objective or its requisite balancing of competing interests was distinctive. Accordingly, we conclude that the investment advisory fees incurred by the Trust are subject to the 2% floor.

The judgment of the Court of Appeals is affirmed.

It is so ordered.

UNITED STATES, Petitioner
v.
CLINTWOOD ELKHORN MINING COMPANY et al.

07-308
SUPREME COURT
OF THE UNITED STATES

553 U.S. 1

March 24, 2008, Argued
April 15, 2008, Decided

ON WRIT OF CERTIORARI TO THE UNITED STATES COURT OF APPEALS FOR THE FEDERAL CIRCUIT

Chief Justice Roberts delivered the opinion of the Court.

The Internal Revenue Code provides that taxpayers seeking a refund of taxes unlawfully assessed must comply with tax refund procedures set forth in the Code. Under those procedures, a taxpayer must file an administrative claim with the Internal Revenue Service before filing suit against the Government. Such a claim must be filed within three years of the filing of a return or two years of payment of the tax, whichever is later. The Tucker Act, in contrast, is more forgiving, allowing claims to be brought against the United States within six years of the challenged conduct. The question in this case is whether a taxpayer suing for a refund of taxes collected in violation of the Export Clause of the Constitution may proceed under the Tucker Act, when his suit does not meet the time limits for refund actions in the Internal Revenue Code. The answer is no.

I

A taxpayer seeking a refund of taxes erroneously or unlawfully assessed or collected may bring an action against the Government either in United States district court or in the United States Court of Federal Claims. 28 U.S.C. § 1346(a)(1); *EC Term of Years Trust* v. *United States,* 550 U.S. 429, 431, and n 2, 127 S. Ct. 1763, 167 L. Ed. 2d 729 (2007). The Internal Revenue Code specifies that before doing so, the taxpayer must comply with the tax refund scheme established in the Code. *United States* v. *Dalm,* 494 U.S. 596, 609-610,

110 S. Ct. 1361, 108 L. Ed. 2d 548 (1990). That scheme provides that a claim for a refund must be filed with the Internal Revenue Service (IRS) before suit can be brought, and establishes strict timeframes for filing such a claim. In particular, 26 U.S.C. § 7422(a) specifies:

> "No suit or proceeding shall be maintained in any court for the recovery of any internal revenue tax alleged to have been erroneously or illegally assessed or collected, or of any penalty claimed to have been collected without authority, or of any sum alleged to have been excessive or in any manner wrongfully collected, until a claim for refund or credit has been duly filed with the [IRS]."

The Code further establishes a time limit for filing such a refund claim with the IRS: To receive a "refund of an overpayment of any tax imposed by this title in respect of which tax the taxpayer is required to file a return," a refund claim must be filed no later than "3 years from the time the return was filed or 2 years from the time the tax was paid, whichever of such periods expires the later." § 6511(a). And § 6511(b)(1) mandates that "[n]o credit or refund shall be allowed or made" if a claim is not filed within the time limits set forth in § 6511(a). "Read together, the import of these sections is clear: unless a claim for refund of a tax has been filed within the time limits imposed by § 6511(a), a suit for refund . . . may not be maintained in any court." *Dalm, supra,* at 602, 110 S. Ct. 1361, 108 L. Ed. 2d 548.

In 1978, Congress levied a tax "on coal from mines located in the United States sold by the producer," 26 U.S.C. § 4121(a)(1), and specifically applied this tax to coal exports, see § 4221(a) (1994 ed.) (excepting from the general ban on taxing exports those taxes imposed under, *inter alia,* § 4121). In 1998, a group of companies challenged the tax in the District Court for the Eastern District of Virginia, contending that it violated the Export Clause of the Constitution. That Clause provides that "No Tax or Duty shall be laid on Articles exported from any State." Art. I, § 9, cl. 5. The District Court agreed and held the tax unconstitutional. *Ranger Fuel Corp.* v. *United States,* 33 F. Supp. 2d 466, 469 (1998). The Government did not appeal, and the IRS acquiesced in the District Court's holding. See IRS Notice 2000-28, 2000-1 Cum. Bull. 1116, 1116-1117 (IRS Notice).

The respondents here, three coal companies, had all paid taxes on coal exports under § 4121(a) "[s]ince as early as 1978." App. to Pet. for Cert. 36a. After § 4121(a) was held unconstitutional as applied to coal exports, the companies filed timely administrative claims in accordance with the refund scheme outlined above, seeking a refund of coal taxes they had paid in 1997, 1998, and 1999. The IRS refunded those taxes, with interest.

The companies also filed suit in the Court of Federal Claims seeking a refund of $ 1,065,936 in taxes paid between 1994 and 1996. They did not file any claim for those taxes with the IRS; any such claim would of course have been denied, given the limits set forth in § 6511. See IRS Notice, at 1117 ("Claims [for a refund of taxes paid under § 4121] must be filed within the period prescribed by § 6511"). Notwithstanding the failure of the companies to file timely administrative refund claims, the Court of Federal Claims allowed the companies to pursue their suit directly under the Export Clause. Jurisdiction rested on the Tucker Act, 28 U.S.C. § 1491(a)(1), and the companies limited their claim to taxes paid within that statute's 6-year limitations period, § 2501 (2000 ed. and Supp. V).

In allowing the companies to proceed outside the confines of the Internal Revenue Code refund procedures, the court relied on the decision of the Court of Appeals for the Federal Circuit in *Cyprus Amax Coal Co.* v. *United States,* 205 F.3d 1369 (2000). *Andalex Resources, Inc.* v. *United States,* 54 Fed. Cl. 563, 564 (2002). The Court of Federal Claims did not, however, allow the companies to recover interest on the taxes paid under 28 U.S.C. § 2411. That provision requires the Government to pay interest "for any overpayment in respect of any internal-revenue tax," but the court held that the statute applied only to refund claims brought under the Code, not to claims brought directly under the Export Clause. 54 Fed. Cl., at 566.

The Court of Appeals affirmed in part and reversed in part. It first refused to revisit its holding in *Cyprus Amax*, and therefore upheld the ruling that the companies could pursue their claim under the Export Clause, despite having failed to file timely administrative refund claims. 473 F.3d 1373, 1374-1375 (CA Fed. 2007). The Court of Appeals reversed the Court of Federal Claims interest holding, however, finding that the Government was required to pay the companies interest on the 1994-1996 amounts under § 2411. *Id.,* at 1376.

We granted certiorari, 552 U.S. 1061, 128 S. Ct. 710, 169 L. Ed. 2d 552 (2007), and now reverse.

II

A

The outcome here is clear given the language of the pertinent statutory provisions. Title 26 U.S.C. § 7422(a) states that "*[n]o suit* . . . shall be maintained in *any court* for the recovery of *any internal revenue tax* alleged to have been erroneously or illegally assessed or collected, or of *any penalty* claimed to have been collected without authority, or of *any sum* alleged to have been excessive or *in any manner* wrongfully collected, until a claim for refund . . . has been duly filed with" the IRS. (Emphasis added.) Here the companies did not file a refund claim with the IRS for the 1994-1996 taxes, and therefore may bring "[n]o suit" in "any court" to recover "any internal revenue tax" or "any sum" alleged to have been wrongfully collected "in any manner." Five "any's" in one sentence and it begins to seem that Congress meant the statute to have expansive reach.

Moreover, the time limits for filing administrative refund claims in § 6511 -- set forth in an "unusually emphatic form," *United States* v. *Brockamp,* 519 U.S. 347, 350, 117 S. Ct. 849, 136 L. Ed. 2d 818 (1997)--apply to "*any* tax imposed by this title," 26 U.S.C. § 6511(a) (emphasis added). The statute further provides that "[n]o credit or refund shall be allowed or made after the expiration of the period of limitation prescribed in subsection (a) . . . unless a claim for credit or refund is filed by the taxpayer within such period." § 6511(b)(1). Again, this language on its face plainly covers the companies' claim for a "refund" of "tax[es] imposed by" Title 26, specifically 26 U.S.C. § 4121. The companies argue that these statutory provisions are ambiguous, Brief for Respondents 43-45, but we cannot imagine what language could more clearly state that taxpayers seeking refunds of unlawfully assessed taxes must comply with the Code's refund scheme before bringing suit, including the requirement to file a timely administrative claim.

Indeed, we all but decided the question presented over six decades ago in *United States* v. *A. S. Kreider Co.,* 313 U.S. 443, 61 S. Ct. 1007, 85 L. Ed. 1447 (1941). Section 1113(a) of the Revenue Act of 1926, like the refund claim provision in § 7422(a) of the current Code, prescribed that "[n]o suit or proceeding shall be maintained in any court for the recovery of any internal-revenue tax alleged to have been erroneously or illegally assessed or collected, or of any penalty claimed to have been collected without authority, or of any sum alleged to have been excessive or in any manner wrongfully collected until a claim for refund or credit has been duly filed with the Commissioner of Internal Revenue," and established a time limit for bringing suit once the claim-filing requirement had been met. 44 Stat. 116. Like the companies here, A. S. Kreider had failed to file a tax refund action within that limitations period. See 313 U.S., at 446, 61 S. Ct. 1007, 85 L. Ed. 1447. And, like the companies here, A. S. Kreider argued that it was instead subject only to the longer 6-year statute of limitations under the Tucker Act. *Id.,* at 447, 61 S. Ct. 1007, 85 L. Ed. 1447.

We rejected the claim, holding that the Tucker Act limitations period "was intended merely to place an outside limit on the period within which all suits might be initiated" under that Act, and that "Congress left it open to provide less liberally for particular actions which, because of special considerations, required different treatment." *Ibid.* We held that the limitations period in § 1113(a) was "precisely that type of provision," finding that Congress created a shorter statute of limitations for tax claims because "suits against the United States for the recovery of taxes impeded effective administration of the revenue laws." *Ibid.* If such suits were allowed to be brought subject only to the 6-year limitations period in the Tucker Act, we explained, § 1113(a) would have "no meaning whatever." *Id.,* at 448, 61 S. Ct. 1007, 85 L. Ed. 1447. So too here. The refund scheme in the current Code would have "no meaning whatever" if taxpayers failing to comply with it were nonetheless allowed to bring suit subject only to the Tucker Act's longer time bar.

B

The companies gamely argue for a different result here because the coal tax at issue was assessed in violation of the Export Clause of the Constitution. They spend much of their brief arguing that the Export Clause itself creates a cause of action against the Government, which can be brought directly under the Tucker Act. See Brief for Respondents 8-25. We need not decide this question here, because it does not matter. If the companies' claims are subject to the Code provisions, those claims are barred whatever the source of the cause of action. We therefore turn to the companies' assertion that their claims are somehow exempt from the broad sweep of the Code provisions.

The companies do not argue for such an exemption simply because their claims are based on a constitutional violation. As they acknowledge, *id.,* at 34, a "constitutional claim can become time-barred just as any other claim can," *Block* v. *North Dakota ex rel. Board of Univ. and School Lands,* 461 U.S. 273, 292, 103 S. Ct. 1811, 75 L. Ed. 2d 840 (1983). Further, Congress has the authority to require administrative exhaustion before allowing a suit against the Government, even for a constitutional violation. See, *e.g., Ruckelshaus* v. *Monsanto Co.,* 467 U.S. 986, 1018, 104 S. Ct. 2862, 81 L. Ed. 2d 815 (1984); *Christian* v. *New York State Dep't of Labor, Div. of Employment,* 414 U.S. 614, 622, 94 S. Ct. 747, 39 L. Ed. 2d 38 (1974); *Aircraft & Diesel Equipment Corp.* v. *Hirsch,* 331 U.S. 752, 766-767, 67 S. Ct. 1493, 91 L. Ed. 1796 (1947).

These principles are fully applicable to claims of unconstitutional taxation, a point highlighted by what we have said in other cases about the Anti-Injunction Act. That statute commands that (absent certain exceptions) "no suit for the purpose of restraining the assessment or collection of any tax shall be maintained in any court." 26 U.S.C. § 7421(a). The "decisions of this Court make it unmistakably clear that the constitutional nature of a taxpayer's claim . . . is of no consequence" to whether the prohibition against tax injunctions applies. *Alexander* v. *"Americans United" Inc.,* 416 U.S. 752, 759, 94 S. Ct. 2053, 40 L. Ed. 2d 518 (1974). This is so even though the Anti-

Injunction Act's prohibitions impose upon the wronged taxpayer requirements at least as onerous as those mandated by the refund scheme--the taxpayer must succumb to an unconstitutional tax, and seek recourse only after it has been unlawfully exacted. We see no reason why compliance with straightforward administrative requirements and reasonable time limits to seek a refund once a tax has been paid should lead to a different result.

The companies assert that Export Clause claims in particular must be treated differently from constitutional claims in general. This is so, they argue, because the Clause is not simply a limitation on the taxing authority but a prohibition that "carves one particular economic activity completely out of Congress's power." Brief for Respondents 11. That distinction is without substance and totally manipulable: If the pertinent authority is regarded as the power to tax exports, the Clause is indeed a complete prohibition on congressional power. But if the pertinent authority is instead viewed as the "Power To lay and collect Taxes," U.S. Const., Art. I, § 8, cl. 1, then the Clause is properly regarded as a limitation on that power. We do not question the importance of the Export Clause to the success of the enterprise in Philadelphia in 1787, see Brief for Respondents 11-13, but we see no basis for treating taxes collected in violation of its terms differently from taxes challenged on other grounds.

Indeed, the companies more or less give up the game when they acknowledge that their claims are subject to the Tucker Act's statute of limitations. See *id.*, at 34. The question is thus not whether the companies' refund claim under the Export Clause can be limited, but rather which limitation applies. The companies are therefore left to argue that, despite the explicit and expansive statutory language described above, the refund scheme in Title 26 does not apply to their case as a matter of statutory interpretation. We find this ambitious argument unavailing.

The companies seek to support it by characterizing the refund scheme set out in the Code as "pro-government and revenue-protective," and therefore "constitutionally dubious" as applied to Export Clause cases. *Id.*, at 28-29. Given this potential constitutional infirmity, the companies argue, Congress could not have intended the refund scheme to apply to taxes assessed in violation of the Export Clause. See *Ashwander* v. *TVA*, 297 U.S. 288, 341, 56 S. Ct. 466, 80 L. Ed. 688 (1936) (Brandeis, J., concurring). We disagree. To begin with, any argument that Congress did not mean to require those in the companies' position to comply with the tax refund scheme runs into a powerful impediment, for "[t]he 'strong presumption' that the plain language of the statute expresses congressional intent is rebutted only in 'rare and exceptional circumstances.'" *Ardestani* v. *INS*, 502 U.S. 129, 135, 112 S. Ct. 515, 116 L. Ed. 2d 496 (1991) (quoting *Rubin* v. *United States*, 449 U.S. 424,

430, 101 S. Ct. 698, 66 L. Ed. 2d 633 (1981)). As we have already explained, the language of the relevant statutes emphatically covers the facts of this case.

In any event, we see no constitutional problem at all. Congress has indeed established a detailed refund scheme that subjects complaining taxpayers to various requirements before they can bring suit. This scheme is designed "to advise the appropriate officials of the demands or claims intended to be asserted, so as to insure an orderly administration of the revenue," *United States* v. *Felt & Tarrant Mfg. Co.,* 283 U.S. 269, 272, 51 S. Ct. 376, 75 L. Ed. 1025, 72 Ct. Cl. 734, 1931-1 C.B. 431 (1931), to provide that refund claims are made promptly, and to allow the IRS to avoid unnecessary litigation by correcting conceded errors. Even when the constitutionality of a tax is challenged, taxing authorities do in fact have an "exceedingly strong interest in financial stability," *McKesson Corp.* v. *Division of Alcoholic Beverages and Tobacco, Fla. Dept. of Business Regulation,* 496 U.S. 18, 37, 110 S. Ct. 2238, 110 L. Ed. 2d 17 (1990), an interest they may pursue through provisions of the sort at issue here.

We do not see why invocation of the Export Clause would deprive Congress of the power to protect this "exceedingly strong interest." Congress may not impose a tax in violation of the Export Clause (or any other constitutional provision, for that matter). But it is certainly within Congress's authority to ensure that allegations of taxes unlawfully assessed--whether the asserted illegality is based upon the Export Clause or any other provision of law--are processed in an orderly and timely manner, and that costly litigation is avoided when possible. The companies' claim that the Code procedures are themselves excessively burdensome is belied by the companies' own invocation of those procedures for taxes paid within the Code's limitations period, which resulted in full refunds with interest.

C

As a fallback argument, the companies maintain that even if the refund scheme applies to Export Clause cases generally, it does not "apply to taxes that are, on their face, unconstitutional." Brief for Respondents 39. They rely for this proposition on *Enochs* v. *Williams Packing & Nav. Co.,* 370 U.S. 1, 82 S. Ct. 1125, 8 L. Ed. 2d 292 (1962), a case dealing with the Anti-Injunction Act, 26 U.S.C. § 7421(a). Despite that Act's broad and mandatory language, we explained that "if it is clear that under no circumstances could the Government ultimately prevail, . . . the attempted collection may be enjoined if equity jurisdiction otherwise exists. In such a situation the exaction is merely in 'the guise of a tax.'" 370 U.S., at 7, 82 S. Ct. 1125, 8 L. Ed. 2d 292 (quoting *Miller* v. *Standard Nut Margarine Co. of Fla.,* 284 U.S. 498, 509, 52 S. Ct. 260, 76 L. Ed. 422, 1932 C.B. 370, 1932-1 C.B. 370 (1932)). See also *Bob Jones*

Univ. v. *Simon,* 416 U.S. 725, 745-746, 94 S. Ct. 2038, 40 L. Ed. 2d 496 (1974) (reaffirming the "under no circumstances" rule of *Williams Packing*).

On the force of *Williams Packing*, the companies argue that the refund scheme should similarly be read as inapplicable to situations in which there are "no circumstances" under which the tax imposed could be held valid under the Export Clause. The trouble with this is that § 7422, the primary statute governing the refund process, is written much more broadly than § 7421(a), the statute at issue in *Williams Packing*. Section 7422(a) states that "[n]o suit . . . shall be maintained in any court for the recovery of any *internal revenue tax* alleged to have been erroneously or illegally assessed or collected . . . until a claim for refund or credit has been duly filed with the" IRS. (Emphasis added.) This language generally tracks that of the Anti-Injunction Act, which also applies to suits "restraining the assessment or collection of any *tax*." § 7421(a) (emphasis added). But § 7422(a) goes on to apply its prohibition against suit absent a proper refund claim to "*any sum* alleged to have been excessive or in any manner wrongfully collected." (Emphasis added.) Even if we agreed that a facially unconstitutional tax for purposes of the tax refund scheme is "merely in 'the guise of a tax,'" *Williams Packing, supra,* at 7, 82 S. Ct. 1125, 8 L. Ed. 2d 292 (quoting *Standard Nut Margarine, supra,* at 509, 52 S. Ct. 260, 76 L. Ed. 422), and therefore not a "tax alleged to have been erroneously or illegally assessed or collected," § 7422(a), it would nevertheless clearly fall into the broader category of "any sum . . . in any manner wrongfully collected," *ibid.*

Moreover, even if we were to accept the companies' argument that the "under no circumstances" limitation on the Anti-Injunction Act applies to the refund scheme, they still would not prevail. We made clear in *Williams Packing* that "the question of whether the Government has a chance of ultimately prevailing is to be determined on the basis of the information available to it at the time of suit. Only if it is then apparent that, under the most liberal view of the law and the facts, the United States cannot establish its claim, may the suit for an injunction be maintained." 370 U.S., at 7, 82 S. Ct. 1125, 8 L. Ed. 2d 292. A tax injunction suit, of course, is brought at the time the Government attempts to assess a tax on the taxpayer. Thus, if we applied the *Williams Packing* "under no circumstances" rule to the refund scheme, we would judge the Government's chances of success as of the time the tax was assessed.

In this case, the companies seek refunds for taxes paid between 1994 and 1996. At that time, the scope of the Export Clause was sufficiently debatable that we granted certiorari in 1995, see *United States* v. *International Business Machines Corp.,* 516 U.S. 1021, 116 S. Ct. 594, 133 L. Ed. 2d 514, and again in 1997, see *United States* v. *United States Shoe Corp.,* 522 U.S. 944, 118 S. Ct. 361,

139 L. Ed. 2d 281, to clear it up. What is more, the District Court that struck down the application of § 4121(a) to coal exports partially relied on these cases in arriving at its decision, *Ranger Fuel Corp.,* 33 F. Supp. 2d, at 469, and the IRS cited, *inter alia, International Business Machines, supra,* in its acquiescence notice, see IRS Notice, at 1116. Indeed, we would think that if the unconstitutionality of the coal export tax were so obvious that the Government had no chance of prevailing, someone paying the tax--such as these companies--would have successfully challenged it earlier than 20 years after its enactment.

We therefore hold that the plain language of 26 U.S.C. §§ 7422(a) and 6511 requires a taxpayer seeking a refund for a tax assessed in violation of the Export Clause, just as for any other unlawfully assessed tax, to file a timely administrative refund claim before bringing suit against the Government. Because we find that the Court of Appeals erred in allowing the companies to bring suit seeking a refund for the 1994-1996 taxes, we do not reach the question whether the Court of Appeals also erred in awarding the companies interest on those amounts under 28 U.S.C. § 2411. The judgment of the Court of Appeals is reversed.

It is so ordered.

ERICA P. JOHN FUND, INC., fka ARCHDIOCESE OF MILWAUKEE SUPPORTING FUND, INC., Petitioner
v.
HALLIBURTON CO. et al.

No. 09-1403

SUPREME COURT OF THE UNITED STATES

563 U.S. 804

April 25, 2011, Argued
June 6, 2011, Decided

ON WRIT OF CERTIORARI TO THE UNITED STATES COURT OF APPEALS FOR THE FIFTH CIRCUIT

Chief Justice Roberts delivered the opinion of the Court.

To prevail on the merits in a private securities fraud action, investors must demonstrate that the defendant's deceptive conduct caused their claimed economic loss. This requirement is commonly referred to as "loss causation." The question presented in this case is whether securities fraud plaintiffs must also prove loss causation in order to obtain class certification. We hold that they need not.

I

Petitioner Erica P. John Fund, Inc. (EPJ Fund), is the lead plaintiff in a putative securities fraud class action filed against Halliburton Co. and one of its executives (collectively Halliburton). The suit was brought on behalf of all investors who purchased Halliburton common stock between June 3, 1999, and December 7, 2001.

EPJ Fund alleges that Halliburton made various misrepresentations designed to inflate its stock price, in violation of § 10(b) of the Securities Exchange Act of 1934 and Securities and Exchange Commission Rule 10b-5. See 48 Stat. 891, 15 U.S.C. § 78j(b); 17 CFR § 240.10b-5 (2010). The complaint asserts that Halliburton deliberately made false statements about (1) the scope of its potential liability in asbestos litigation, (2) its expected revenue from certain construction contracts, and (3) the benefits of its merger with another company. EPJ Fund contends that Halliburton later made a number of corrective disclosures that caused its stock price to drop and, consequently, investors to lose money.

After defeating a motion to dismiss, EPJ Fund sought to have its proposed class certified pursuant to Federal Rule of Civil Procedure 23. The parties agreed, and the District Court held, that EPJ Fund satisfied the general requirements for class actions set out in Rule 23(a): The class was sufficiently numerous, there were common questions of law or fact, the claims of the representative parties were typical, and the representative parties would fairly and adequately protect the interests of the class. See App. to Pet. for Cert. 3a.

The District Court also found that the action could proceed as a class action under Rule 23(b)(3), but for one problem: Circuit precedent required securities fraud plaintiffs to prove "loss causation" in order to obtain class certification. *Id.*, at 4a, and n. 2 (citing *Oscar Private Equity Invs.* v. *Allegiance Telecom, Inc.*, 487 F.3d 261, 269 (CA5 2007)). As the District Court explained, loss causation is the " 'causal connection between the material misrepresentation and the [economic] loss' " suffered by investors. App. to Pet. for Cert. 5a, and n. 3 (quoting *Dura Pharms., Inc.* v. *Broudo*, 544 U.S. 336, 342, 125 S. Ct. 1627, 161 L. Ed. 2d 577 (2005)). After reviewing the alleged misrepresentations and corrective disclosures, the District Court concluded that it could not certify the class in this case because EPJ Fund had "failed to establish loss causation with respect to any" of its claims. App. to Pet. for Cert. 54a. The court made clear, however, that absent "this stringent loss causation requirement," it would have granted EPJ Fund's certification request. *Ibid.*

The Court of Appeals affirmed the denial of class certification. See 597 F.3d 330 (CA5 2010). It confirmed that, "[i]n order to obtain class certification on its claims, [EPJ Fund] was required to prove loss causation, i.e., that the corrected truth of the former falsehoods actually caused the stock price to fall and resulted in the losses." *Id.*, at 334. Like the District Court, the Court of Appeals concluded that EPJ Fund had failed to meet the "requirements for proving loss causation at the class certification stage." *Id.*, at 344.

We granted EPJ Fund's petition for certiorari, 562 U.S. 1127, 131 S. Ct. 856, 178 L. Ed. 2d 622 (2011), to resolve a conflict among the Circuits as to whether securities fraud plaintiffs must prove loss causation in order to obtain class certification. Compare 597 F.3d, at 334 (case below), with *In re Salomon Analyst Metromedia Litigation*, 544 F.3d 474, 483 (CA2 2008) (not requiring investors to prove loss causation at class certification stage); *Schleicher* v. *Wendt*, 618 F.3d 679, 687 (CA7 2010) (same); *In re DVI, Inc. Secs. Litig.*, 639 F.3d 623, 636-637 (CA3, 2011) (same; decided after certiorari was granted).

II

EPJ Fund contends that the Court of Appeals erred by requiring proof of loss causation for class certification. We agree.

A

As noted, the sole dispute here is whether EPJ Fund satisfied the prerequisites of Rule 23(b)(3). In order to certify a class under that Rule, a court must find "that the questions of law or fact common to class members predominate over any questions affecting only individual members, and that a class action is superior to other available methods for fairly and efficiently adjudicating the controversy." Fed. Rule Civ. Proc. 23(b)(3). Considering whether "questions of law or fact common to class members predominate" begins, of course, with the elements of the underlying cause of action. The elements of a private securities fraud claim based on violations of § 10(b) and Rule 10b-5 are: " '(1) a material misrepresentation or omission by the defendant; (2) scienter; (3) a connection between the misrepresentation or omission and the purchase or sale of a security; (4) reliance upon the misrepresentation or omission; (5) economic loss; and (6) loss causation.' *Matrixx Initiatives, Inc.* v. *Siracusano*, ante, at 37-38 (quoting *Stoneridge Investment Partners, LLC* v. *Scientific-Atlanta, Inc.*, 552 U.S. 148, 157, 128 S. Ct. 761, 169 L. Ed. 2d 627 (2008)).

Whether common questions of law or fact predominate in a securities fraud action often turns on the element of reliance. The courts below determined that EPJ Fund had to prove the separate element of loss causation in order to establish that reliance was capable of resolution on a common, classwide basis.

"Reliance by the plaintiff upon the defendant's deceptive acts is an essential element of the § 10(b) private cause of action." *Id.*, at 159, 128 S. Ct. 761, 169 L. Ed. 2d 627. This is because proof of reliance ensures that there is a proper "connection between a defendant's misrepresentation and a plaintiff's injury." *Basic Inc.* v. *Levinson*, 485 U.S. 224, 243, 108 S. Ct. 978, 99 L. Ed. 2d 194 (1988). The traditional (and most direct) way a plaintiff can demonstrate reliance is by showing that he was aware of a company's statement and engaged in a relevant transaction--*e.g.*, purchasing common stock--based on that specific misrepresentation. In that situation, the plaintiff plainly would have relied on the company's deceptive conduct. A plaintiff unaware of the relevant statement, on the other hand, could not establish reliance on that basis.

We recognized in *Basic*, however, that limiting proof of reliance in such a way "would place an unnecessarily unrealistic evidentiary burden on the Rule 10b-5 plaintiff who has traded on an impersonal market." *Id.*, at 245, 108 S. Ct. 978, 99 L. Ed. 2d 194. We also observed that " [r]equiring proof of individualized reliance from each member of the proposed plaintiff class effectively would" prevent such plaintiffs "from proceeding with a class action, since individual issues" would "overwhelm[ ] the common ones." *Id.*, at 242, 108 S. Ct. 978, 99 L. Ed. 2d 194.

The Court in *Basic* sought to alleviate those related concerns by permitting plaintiffs to invoke a rebuttable presumption of reliance based on what is known as the "fraud-on-the-market" theory. According to that theory, "the market price of shares traded on well-developed markets reflects all publicly available information, and, hence, any material misrepresentations." *Id.*, at 246, 108 S. Ct. 978, 99 L. Ed. 2d 194. Because the market "transmits information to the investor in the processed form of a market price," we can assume, the Court explained, that an investor relies on public misstatements whenever he "buys or sells stock at the price set by the market." *Id.*, at 244, 247, 108 S. Ct. 978, 99 L. Ed. 2d 194 (internal quotation marks omitted); see also *Stoneridge*, *supra*, at 159, 128 S. Ct. 761, 169 L. Ed. 2d 627; *Dura Pharmaceuticals*, 544 U.S., at 341-342, 125 S. Ct. 1627, 161 L. Ed. 2d 577. The Court also made clear that the presumption was just that, and could be rebutted by appropriate evidence. See *Basic*, *supra*, at 248, 108 S. Ct. 978, 99 L. Ed. 2d 194.

B

It is undisputed that securities fraud plaintiffs must prove certain things in order to invoke *Basic*'s rebuttable presumption of reliance. It is common ground, for example, that plaintiffs must demonstrate that the alleged misrepresentations were publicly known (else how would the market take them into account?), that the stock traded in an efficient market, and that the relevant transaction took place "between the time the misrepresentations were made and the time the truth was revealed." *Basic*, 485 U.S., at 248, n. 27, 108 S. Ct. 978, 99 L. Ed. 2d 194; *id.*, at 241-247, 108 S. Ct. 978, 99 L. Ed. 2d 194; see also *Stoneridge*, *supra*, at 159, 128 S. Ct. 761, 169 L. Ed. 2d 627.

According to the Court of Appeals, EPJ Fund also had to establish loss causation at the certification stage to "trigger the fraud-on-the-market presumption." 597 F.3d, at 335 (internal quotation marks omitted); see *ibid.* (EPJ Fund must "establish a causal link between the alleged falsehoods and its losses in order to invoke the fraud-on-the-market presumption"). The court determined that, in order to invoke a rebuttable presumption of reliance, EPJ Fund needed to prove that the decline in Halliburton's stock was "because of the correction to a prior misleading statement" and "that the subsequent loss could not otherwise be explained by some additional factors revealed then to the market." *Id.*, at 336 (emphasis deleted). This is the loss causation requirement as we have described it. See *Dura Pharmaceuticals*, *supra*, at 342, 125 S. Ct. 1627, 161 L. Ed. 2d 577; see also 15 U.S.C. § 78u-4(b)(4).

The Court of Appeals' requirement is not justified by *Basic* or its logic. To begin, we have never before mentioned loss causation as a precondition for invoking *Basic*'s rebuttable presumption of reliance. The term "loss causation" does not even appear in our *Basic* opinion. And for good reason: Loss causation addresses a matter different from whether an investor relied on a misrepresentation, presumptively or otherwise, when buying or selling a stock.

We have referred to the element of reliance in a private Rule 10b-5 action as "transaction causation," not loss causation. *Dura Pharmaceuticals, supra,* at 341-342, 125 S. Ct. 1627, 161 L. Ed. 2d 577 (citing *Basic, supra,* at 248-249, 108 S. Ct. 978, 99 L. Ed. 2d 194). Consistent with that description, when considering whether a plaintiff has relied on a misrepresentation, we have typically focused on facts surrounding the investor's decision to engage in the transaction. See *Dura Pharmaceuticals, supra,* at 342, 125 S. Ct. 1627, 161 L. Ed. 2d 577. Under *Basic*'s fraud-on-the-market doctrine, an investor presumptively relies on a defendant's misrepresentation if that "information is reflected in [the] market price" of the stock at the time of the relevant transaction. See *Basic, supra,* at 247, 108 S. Ct. 978, 99 L. Ed. 2d 194.

Loss causation, by contrast, requires a plaintiff to show that a misrepresentation that affected the integrity of the market price *also* caused a subsequent economic loss. As we made clear in *Dura Pharmaceuticals*, the fact that a stock's "price on the date of purchase was inflated because of [a] misrepresentation" does not necessarily mean that the misstatement is the cause of a later decline in value. 544 U.S., at 342, 125 S. Ct. 1627, 161 L. Ed. 2d 577 (emphasis deleted; internal quotation marks omitted). We observed that the drop could instead be the result of other intervening causes, such as "changed economic circumstances, changed investor expectations, new industry-specific or firm-specific facts, conditions, or other events." *Id.,* at 342-343, 125 S. Ct. 1627, 161 L. Ed. 2d 577. If one of those factors were responsible for the loss or part of it, a plaintiff would not be able to prove loss causation to that extent. This is true even if the investor purchased the stock at a distorted price, and thereby presumptively relied on the misrepresentation reflected in that price.

According to the Court of Appeals, however, an inability to prove loss causation would prevent a plaintiff from invoking the rebuttable presumption of reliance. Such a rule contravenes *Basic*'s fundamental premise--that an investor presumptively relies on a misrepresentation so long as it was reflected in the market price at the time of his transaction. The fact that a subsequent loss may have been caused by factors other than the revelation of a misrepresentation has nothing to do with whether an investor relied on the misrepresentation in the first place, either directly or presumptively through the fraud-on-the-market theory. Loss causation has no logical connection to the facts necessary to establish the efficient market predicate to the fraud-on-the-market theory.

The Court of Appeals erred by requiring EPJ Fund to show loss causation as a condition of obtaining class certification.

C

Halliburton concedes that securities fraud plaintiffs should not be required to prove loss causation in order to invoke *Basic*'s presumption of reliance or otherwise achieve class certification. See Tr. of Oral Arg. 26-29. Halliburton nonetheless defends the judgment below on the ground that the Court of Appeals did not actually require plaintiffs to prove "loss causation" as we have used that term. See *id.*, at 27 ("it's not loss causation as this Court knows it in *Dura*"). According to Halliburton, "loss causation" was merely "shorthand" for a different analysis. Brief for Respondents 18. The lower court's actual inquiry, Halliburton insists, was whether EPJ Fund had demonstrated "price impact"--that is, whether the alleged misrepresentations affected the market price in the first place. See, *e.g.*, *id.*, at 16-19, 24-27, 50-51; see also Tr. of Oral Arg. 27 (stating that the Court of Appeals' "test is simply price impact" and that EPJ Fund's "only burden under the Fifth Circuit case law was to show price impact").*

> * Halliburton further concedes that, even if its conception of what the Court of Appeals meant by "loss causation" is correct, the Court of Appeals erred by placing the initial burden on EPJ Fund. See Tr. of Oral Arg. 29 ("We agree . . . that the Fifth Circuit put the initial burden of production on the plaintiff, and that's contrary to *Basic*"). According to Halliburton, a plaintiff must prove price impact only after *Basic*'s presumption has been successfully rebutted by the defendant. Tr. of Oral Arg. 28, 38-40. We express no views on the merits of such a framework.

"Price impact" simply refers to the effect of a misrepresentation on a stock price. Halliburton's theory is that if a misrepresentation does not affect market price, an investor cannot be said to have relied on the misrepresentation merely because he purchased stock at that price. If the price is unaffected by the fraud, the price does not reflect the fraud.

We do not accept Halliburton's wishful interpretation of the Court of Appeals' opinion. As we have explained, loss causation is a familiar and distinct concept in securities law; it is not price impact. While the opinion below may include some language consistent with a "price impact" approach, see, *e.g.*, 597 F.3d, at 336, we simply cannot ignore the Court of Appeals' repeated and explicit references to "loss causation," see *id.*, at 334 (three times), 334, n. 2, 335, 335, n. 10 (twice), 335, n. 11, 336, 336, n. 19, 336, n. 20, 337, 338, 341 (twice), 341, n. 46, 342, n. 47, 343, 344 (three times).

Whatever Halliburton thinks the Court of Appeals meant to say, what it said was loss causation: "[EPJ Fund] was required to prove loss causation, i.e., that the corrected truth of the former falsehoods actually caused the stock price to fall and resulted in the losses." *Id.*, at 334; see *id.*, at 335 ("we require plaintiffs to establish loss causation in order to trigger the fraud-on-the-market presumption" (internal quotation marks omitted)). We take the Court of Appeals at its word. Based on those words, the decision below cannot stand.

* * *

Because we conclude the Court of Appeals erred by requiring EPJ Fund to prove loss causation at the certification stage, we need not, and do not, address any other question about *Basic*, its presumption, or how and when it may be rebutted. To the extent Halliburton has preserved any further arguments against class certification, they may be addressed in the first instance by the Court of Appeals on remand.

The judgment of the Court of Appeals is vacated, and the case is remanded for further proceedings consistent with this opinion.

It is so ordered.

JERRY W. GUNN, et al., Petitioners
v.
VERNON F. MINTON

11-1118
SUPREME COURT
OF THE UNITED STATES

568 U.S. 251

January 16, 2013, Argued
February 20, 2013, Decided

ON WRIT OF CERTIORARI TO THE SUPREME COURT OF TEXAS

Chief Justice Roberts delivered the opinion of the Court.

Federal courts have exclusive jurisdiction over cases "arising under any Act of Congress relating to patents." 28 U.S.C. §1338(a). The question presented is whether a state law claim alleging legal malpractice in the handling of a patent case must be brought in federal court.

I

In the early 1990s, respondent Vernon Minton developed a computer program and telecommunications network designed to facilitate securities trading. In March 1995, he leased the system--known as the Texas Computer Exchange Network, or TEXCEN--to R. M. Stark & Co., a securities brokerage. A little over a year later, he applied for a patent for an interactive securities trading system that was based substantially on TEXCEN. The U.S. Patent and Trademark Office issued the patent in January 2000.

Patent in hand, Minton filed a patent infringement suit in Federal District Court against the National Association of Securities Dealers, Inc. (NASD) and the NASDAQ Stock Market, Inc. He was represented by Jerry Gunn and the other petitioners. NASD and NASDAQ moved for summary judgment on the ground that Minton's patent was invalid under the "on sale" bar, 35 U.S.C. §102(b). That provision specifies that an inventor is not entitled to a patent if "the invention was . . . on sale in [the United States], more than one year prior to the date of the application," and Minton had leased TEXCEN to Stark more than one year prior to filing his patent application. Rejecting Minton's argument that there were differences between TEXCEN and the patented system that precluded application of the on-sale bar, the District Court granted the summary judgment motion and declared Minton's patent invalid. *Minton* v. *National Assn. of Securities Dealers, Inc.*, 226 F. Supp. 2d 845, 873, 883-884 (ED Tex. 2002).

Minton then filed a motion for reconsideration in the District Court, arguing for the first time that the lease agreement with Stark was part of ongoing testing of TEXCEN and therefore fell within the "experimental use" exception to the on-sale bar. See generally *Pfaff* v. *Wells Electronics, Inc.*, 525 U.S. 55, 64, 119 S. Ct. 304, 142 L. Ed. 2d 261 (1998) (describing the exception). The District Court denied the motion. *Minton* v. *NASD*, No. 9:00-cv-00019, 2002 U.S. Dist. LEXIS 26587 (ED Tex., July 15, 2002).

Minton appealed to the U.S. Court of Appeals for the Federal Circuit. That court affirmed, concluding that the District Court had appropriately held Minton's experimental-use argument waived. See *Minton v. NASD*, 336 F.3d 1373, 1379-1380 (CA Fed. 2003).

Minton, convinced that his attorneys' failure to raise the experimental-use argument earlier had cost him the lawsuit and led to invalidation of his patent, brought this malpractice action in Texas state court. His former lawyers defended on the ground that the lease to Stark was not, in fact, for an experimental use, and that therefore Minton's patent infringement claims would have failed even if the experimental-use argument had been timely raised. The trial court agreed, holding that Minton had put forward "less than a scintilla of proof" that the lease had been for an experimental purpose. App. 213. It accordingly granted summary judgment to Gunn and the other lawyer defendants.

On appeal, Minton raised a new argument: Because his legal malpractice claim was based on an alleged error in a patent case, it "aris[es] under" federal patent law for purposes of 28 U.S.C. §1338(a). And because, under §1338(a), "[n]o State court shall have jurisdiction over any claim for relief arising under any Act of Congress relating to patents," the Texas court--where Minton had originally brought his malpractice claim--lacked subject matter jurisdiction to decide the case. Accordingly, Minton argued, the trial court's order should be vacated and the case dismissed, leaving Minton free to start over in the Federal District Court.

A divided panel of the Court of Appeals of Texas rejected Minton's argument. Applying the test we articulated in *Grable & Sons Metal Products, Inc.* v. *Darue Engineering & Mfg.*, 545 U.S. 308, 314, 125 S. Ct. 2363, 162 L. Ed. 2d 257 (2005), it held that the federal interests implicated by Minton's state law claim were not sufficiently substantial to trigger §1338 "arising under" jurisdiction. It also held that finding exclusive federal jurisdiction over state legal malpractice actions would, contrary to *Grable*'s commands, disturb the balance of federal

89

and state judicial responsibilities. Proceeding to the merits of Minton's malpractice claim, the Court of Appeals affirmed the trial court's determination that Minton had failed to establish experimental use and that arguments on that ground therefore would not have saved his infringement suit.

The Supreme Court of Texas reversed, relying heavily on a pair of cases from the U.S. Court of Appeals for the Federal Circuit. 355 S.W.3d 634, 641-642 (2011) (discussing *Air Measurement Technologies, Inc.* v. *Akin Gump Strauss Hauer & Feld, L. L. P.*, 504 F.3d 1262 (2007); *Immunocept, LLC* v. *Fulbright & Jaworski, LLP*, 504 F.3d 1281 (2007)). The Court concluded that Minton's claim involved "a substantial federal issue" within the meaning of *Grable* "because the success of Minton's malpractice claim is reliant upon the viability of the experimental use exception as a defense to the on-sale bar." 355 S.W.3d, at 644. Adjudication of Minton's claim in federal court was consistent with the appropriate balance between federal and state judicial responsibilities, it held, because "the federal government and patent litigants have an interest in the uniform application of patent law by courts well-versed in that subject matter." *Id.*, at 646 (citing *Immunocept, supra*, at 1285-1286; *Air Measurement Technologies, supra*, at 1272).

Justice Guzman, joined by Justices Medina and Willett, dissented. The dissenting justices would have held that the federal issue was neither substantial nor disputed, and that maintaining the proper balance of responsibility between state and federal courts precluded relegating state legal malpractice claims to federal court.

We granted certiorari. 568 U.S. _, 568 U.S. 936, 133 S. Ct. 420, 184 L. Ed. 2d 251 (2012).

II

"Federal courts are courts of limited jurisdiction," possessing "only that power authorized by Constitution and statute." *Kokkonen* v. *Guardian Life Ins. Co. of America*, 511 U.S. 375, 377, 114 S. Ct. 1673, 128 L. Ed. 2d 391 (1994). There is no dispute that the Constitution permits Congress to extend federal court jurisdiction to a case such as this one, see *Osborn* v. *Bank of United States*, 9 Wheat. 738, 823-824, 22 U.S. 738, 6 L. Ed. 204 (1824); the question is whether Congress has done so, see *Powell* v. *McCormack*, 395 U.S. 486, 515-516, 89 S. Ct. 1944, 23 L. Ed. 2d 491 (1969).

As relevant here, Congress has authorized the federal district courts to exercise original jurisdiction in "all civil actions arising under the Constitution, laws, or treaties of the United States," 28 U.S.C. §1331, and, more particularly, over "any civil action arising under any Act of Congress relating to patents," §1338(a). Adhering to the demands of "[l]inguistic consistency," we have interpreted the phrase "arising under" in both sections identically, applying our §1331 and §1338(a) precedents interchangeably. See *Christianson* v. *Colt Industries Operating Corp.*, 486 U.S. 800, 808-809, 108 S. Ct. 2166, 100 L. Ed. 2d 811 (1988). For cases falling within the patent-specific arising under jurisdiction of §1338(a), however, Congress has not only provided for federal jurisdiction but also eliminated state jurisdiction, decreeing that "[n]o State court shall have jurisdiction over any claim for relief arising under any Act of Congress relating to patents." §1338(a) (2006 ed., Supp. V). To determine whether jurisdiction was proper in the Texas courts, therefore, we must determine whether it would have been proper in a federal district court-- whether, that is, the case "aris[es] under any Act of Congress relating to patents."

For statutory purposes, a case can "aris[e] under" federal law in two ways. Most directly, a case arises under federal law when federal law creates the cause of action asserted. See *American Well Works Co.* v. *Layne & Bowler Co.*, 241 U.S. 257, 260, 36 S. Ct. 585, 60 L. Ed. 987 (1916) ("A suit arises under the law that creates the cause of action"). As a rule of inclusion, this "creation" test admits of only extremely rare exceptions, see, *e.g., Shoshone Mining Co.* v. *Rutter*, 177 U.S. 505, 20 S. Ct. 726, 44 L. Ed. 864 (1900), and accounts for the vast bulk of suits that arise under federal law, see *Franchise Tax Bd. of Cal.* v. *Construction Laborers Vacation Trust for Southern Cal.*, 463 U.S. 1, 9, 103 S. Ct. 2841, 77 L. Ed. 2d 420 (1983). Minton's original patent infringement suit against NASD and NASDAQ, for example, arose under federal law in this manner because it was authorized by 35 U.S.C. §§271, 281.

But even where a claim finds its origins in state rather than federal law--as Minton's legal malpractice claim indisputably does--we have identified a "special and small category" of cases in which arising under jurisdiction still lies. *Empire HealthChoice Assurance, Inc.* v. *McVeigh*, 547 U.S. 677, 699, 126 S. Ct. 2121, 165 L. Ed. 2d 131 (2006). In outlining the contours of this slim category, we do not paint on a blank canvas. Unfortunately, the canvas looks like one that Jackson Pollock got to first. See 13D C. Wright, A. Miller, E. Cooper, & R. Freer, Federal Practice and Procedure § 3562, pp. 175-176 (3d ed. 2008) (reviewing general confusion on question).

In an effort to bring some order to this unruly doctrine several Terms ago, we condensed our prior cases into the following inquiry: Does the "state-law claim necessarily raise a stated federal issue, actually disputed and substantial, which a federal forum may entertain without disturbing any congressionally approved balance of federal and state judicial responsibilities"? *Grable*, 545 U.S., at 314, 125 S. Ct. 2363, 162 L. Ed. 2d 257. That is, federal jurisdiction over a state law claim will lie if a federal issue is: (1) necessarily raised, (2) actually disputed, (3) substantial, and (4) capable of resolution in federal court without disrupting the federal-state balance approved by Congress. Where all four of these requirements are met, we held, jurisdiction is proper because there is a "serious federal interest in claiming the advantages thought to be inherent in a federal forum," which can be vindicated without disrupting Congress's intended division of labor between state and federal courts. *Id.,* at 313-314, 125 S. Ct. 2363, 162 L. Ed. 2d 257.

III

Applying *Grable*'s inquiry here, it is clear that Minton's legal malpractice claim does not arise under federal patent law. Indeed, for the reasons we discuss, we are comfortable concluding that state legal malpractice claims based on underlying patent matters will rarely, if ever, arise under federal patent law for purposes of §1338(a). Although such cases may necessarily raise disputed questions of patent law, those cases are by their nature unlikely to have the sort of significance for the federal system necessary to establish jurisdiction.

A

To begin, we acknowledge that resolution of a federal patent question is "necessary" to Minton's case. Under Texas law, a plaintiff alleging legal malpractice must establish four elements: (1) that the defendant attorney owed the plaintiff a duty; (2) that the attorney breached that duty; (3) that the breach was the proximate cause of the plaintiff's injury; and (4) that damages occurred. See *Alexander* v. *Turtur & Associates, Inc.*, 146 S.W.3d 113, 117 (Tex. 2004). In cases like this one, in which the attorney's alleged error came in failing to make a particular argument, the causation element requires a "case within a case" analysis of whether, had the argument been made, the outcome of the earlier litigation would have been different. 355 S.W.3d, at 639; see 4 R. Mallen & J. Smith, Legal Malpractice § 37:15, pp. 1509-1520 (2012). To prevail on his legal malpractice claim, therefore, Minton must show that he would have prevailed in his federal patent infringement case if only petitioners had timely made an experimental-use argument on his behalf. 355 S.W.3d, at 644. That will necessarily require application of patent law to the facts of Minton's case.

B

The federal issue is also "actually disputed" here--indeed, on the merits, it is the central point of dispute. Minton argues that the experimental-use exception properly applied to his lease to Stark, saving his patent from the on-sale bar; petitioners argue that it did not. This is just the sort of " 'dispute . . . respecting the . . . effect of [federal] law' " that *Grable* envisioned. 545 U.S., at 313, 125 S. Ct. 2363, 162 L. Ed. 2d 257 (quoting *Shulthis* v. *McDougal,* 225 U.S. 561, 569, 32 S. Ct. 704, 56 L. Ed. 1205 (1912)).

C

Minton's argument founders on *Grable*'s next requirement, however, for the federal issue in this case is not substantial in the relevant sense. In reaching the opposite conclusion, the Supreme Court of Texas focused on the importance of the issue to the plaintiff's case and to the parties before it. 355 S.W.3d, at 644 ("because the success of Minton's malpractice claim is reliant upon the viability of the experimental use exception as a defense to the on-sale bar, we hold that it is a substantial federal issue"); see also *Air Measurement Technologies*, 504 F.3d, at 1272 ("the issue is substantial, for it is a necessary element of the malpractice case"). As our past cases show, however, it is not enough that the federal issue be significant to the particular parties in the immediate suit; that will *always* be true when the state claim "necessarily raise[s]" a disputed federal issue, as *Grable* separately requires. The substantiality inquiry under *Grable* looks instead to the importance of the issue to the federal system as a whole.

In *Grable* itself, for example, the Internal Revenue Service had seized property from the plaintiff and sold it to satisfy the plaintiff's federal tax delinquency. 545 U.S., at 310-311, 125 S. Ct. 2363, 162 L. Ed. 2d 257. Five years later, the plaintiff filed a state law quiet title action against the third party that had purchased the property, alleging that the IRS had failed to comply with certain federally imposed notice requirements, so that the seizure and sale were invalid. *Ibid.* In holding that the case arose under federal law, we primarily focused not on the interests of the litigants themselves, but rather on the broader significance of the notice question for the Federal Government. We emphasized the Government's "strong interest" in being able to recover delinquent taxes through seizure and sale of property, which in turn "require[d] clear terms of notice to allow buyers . . . to satisfy themselves that the Service has touched the bases necessary for good title." *Id.,* at 315, 125 S. Ct. 2363, 162 L. Ed. 2d 257. The Government's "direct interest in the availability of a federal forum to vindicate its own administrative action" made the question "an important issue of federal law that sensibly belong[ed] in a federal court." *Ibid.*

A second illustration of the sort of substantiality we require comes from *Smith v. Kansas City Title & Trust Co.*, 255 U.S. 180, 41 S. Ct. 243, 65 L. Ed. 577 (1921), which *Grable* described as "[t]he classic example" of a state claim arising under federal law. 545 U.S., at 312, 125 S. Ct. 2363, 162 L. Ed. 2d 257. In *Smith*, the plaintiff argued that the defendant bank could not purchase certain bonds issued by the Federal Government because the Government had acted unconstitutionally in issuing them. 255 U.S., at 198, 41 S. Ct. 243, 65 L. Ed. 577. We held that the case arose under federal law, because the "decision depends upon the determination" of "the constitutional validity of an act of Congress which is directly drawn in question." *Id.,* at 201, 41 S. Ct.

243, 65 L. Ed. 577. Again, the relevant point was not the importance of the question to the parties alone but rather the importance more generally of a determination that the Government "securities were issued under an unconstitutional law, and hence of no validity." *Ibid.*; see also *Merrell Dow Pharmaceuticals Inc.* v. *Thompson*, 478 U.S. 804, 814, n. 12, 106 S. Ct. 3229, 92 L. Ed. 2d 650 (1986).

Here, the federal issue carries no such significance. Because of the backward-looking nature of a legal malpractice claim, the question is posed in a merely hypothetical sense: *If* Minton's lawyers had raised a timely experimental-use argument, would the result in the patent infringement proceeding have been different? No matter how the state courts resolve that hypothetical "case within a case," it will not change the real-world result of the prior federal patent litigation. Minton's patent will remain invalid.

Nor will allowing state courts to resolve these cases undermine "the development of a uniform body of [patent] law." *Bonito Boats, Inc.* v. *Thunder Craft Boats, Inc.*, 489 U.S. 141, 162, 109 S. Ct. 971, 103 L. Ed. 2d 118 (1989). Congress ensured such uniformity by vesting exclusive jurisdiction over actual patent cases in the federal district courts and exclusive appellate jurisdiction in the Federal Circuit. See 28 U.S.C. §§1338(a), 1295(a)(1). In resolving the nonhypothetical patent questions those cases present, the federal courts are of course not bound by state court case-within-a-case patent rulings. See *Tafflin* v. *Levitt*, 493 U.S. 455, 465, 110 S. Ct. 792, 107 L. Ed. 2d 887 (1990). In any event, the state court case-within-a-case inquiry asks what would have happened in the prior federal proceeding if a particular argument had been made. In answering that question, state courts can be expected to hew closely to the pertinent federal precedents. It is those precedents, after all, that would have applied had the argument been made. Cf. *ibid.* ("State courts adjudicating civil RICO claims will . . . be guided by federal court interpretations of the relevant federal criminal statutes, just as federal courts sitting in diversity are guided by state court interpretations of state law").

As for more novel questions of patent law that may arise for the first time in a state court "case within a case," they will at some point be decided by a federal court in the context of an actual patent case, with review in the Federal Circuit. If the question arises frequently, it will soon be resolved within the federal system, laying to rest any contrary state court precedent; if it does not arise frequently, it is unlikely to implicate substantial federal interests. The present case is "poles apart from *Grable*," in which a state court's resolution of the federal question "would be controlling in numerous other cases." *Empire HealthChoice Assurance, Inc.*, 547 U.S., at 700, 126 S. Ct. 2121, 165 L. Ed. 2d 131

Minton also suggests that state courts' answers to hypothetical patent questions can sometimes have real-world effect on other patents through issue preclusion. Brief for Respondent 33-36. Minton, for example, has filed what is known as a "continuation patent" application related to his original patent. See 35 U.S.C. §120; 4A D. Chisum, Patents §13.03 (2005) (describing continuation applications). He argues that, in evaluating this separate application, the patent examiner could be bound by the Texas trial court's interpretation of the scope of Minton's original patent. See Brief for Respondent 35-36. It is unclear whether this is true. The Patent and Trademark Office's Manual of Patent Examining Procedure provides that res judicata is a proper ground for rejecting a patent "only when the earlier decision was a decision of the Board of Appeals" or certain federal reviewing courts, giving no indication that state court decisions would have preclusive effect. See Dept. of Commerce, Patent and Trademark Office, Manual of Patent Examining Procedure § 706.03(w), p. 700-79 (rev. 8th ed. 2012); 35 U.S.C. §§134(a), 141, 145; Reply Brief 9-10. In fact, Minton has not identified any case finding such preclusive effect based on a state court decision. But even assuming that a state court's case-within-a-case adjudication may be preclusive under some circumstances, the result would be limited to the parties and patents that had been before the state court. Such "fact-bound and situation-specific" effects are not sufficient to establish federal arising under jurisdiction. *Empire HealthChoice Assurance, Inc., supra*, at 701, 126 S. Ct. 2121, 165 L. Ed. 2d 131.

Nor can we accept the suggestion that the federal courts' greater familiarity with patent law means that legal malpractice cases like this one belong in federal court. See *Air Measurement Technologies*, 504 F.3d, at 1272 ("The litigants will also benefit from federal judges who have experience in claim construction and infringement matters"); 355 S.W.3d, at 646 ("patent litigants have an interest in the uniform application of patent law by courts well-versed in that subject matter"). It is true that a similar interest was among those we considered in *Grable*. 545 U.S., at 314, 125 S. Ct. 2363, 162 L. Ed. 2d 257. But the possibility that a state court will incorrectly resolve a state claim is not, by itself, enough to trigger the federal courts' exclusive patent jurisdiction, even if the potential error finds its root in a misunderstanding of patent law.

There is no doubt that resolution of a patent issue in the context of a state legal malpractice action can be vitally important to the particular parties in that case. But something more, demonstrating that the question is significant to the federal system as a whole, is needed. That is missing here.

D

It follows from the foregoing that *Grable*'s fourth requirement is also not met. That requirement is concerned with the appropriate "balance of federal and state judicial responsibilities." *Ibid.* We have already explained the absence of a substantial federal issue within the meaning of *Grable*. The States, on the other hand, have "a special responsibility for maintaining standards among members of the licensed professions." *Ohralik* v. *Ohio State Bar Ass'n*, 436 U.S. 447, 460, 98 S. Ct. 1912, 56 L. Ed. 2d 444 (1978). Their "interest . . . in regulating lawyers is especially great since lawyers are essential to the primary governmental function of administering justice, and have historically been officers of the courts." *Goldfarb* v. *Virginia State Bar*, 421 U.S. 773, 792, 95 S. Ct. 2004, 44 L. Ed. 2d 572 (1975) (internal quotation marks omitted). We have no reason to suppose that Congress--in establishing exclusive federal jurisdiction over patent cases--meant to bar from state courts state legal malpractice claims simply because they require resolution of a hypothetical patent issue.

* * *

As we recognized a century ago, "[t]he Federal courts have exclusive jurisdiction of all cases arising under the patent laws, but not of all questions in which a patent may be the subject-matter of the controversy." *New Marshall Engine Co.* v. *Marshall Engine Co.*, 223 U.S. 473, 478, 32 S. Ct. 238, 56 L. Ed. 513, 1912 Dec. Comm'r Pat. 617 (1912). In this case, although the state courts must answer a question of patent law to resolve Minton's legal malpractice claim, their answer will have no broader effects. It will not stand as binding precedent for any future patent claim; it will not even affect the validity of Minton's patent. Accordingly, there is no "serious federal interest in claiming the advantages thought to be inherent in a federal forum," *Grable*, *supra*, at 313, 125 S. Ct. 2363, 162 L. Ed. 2d 257. Section 1338(a) does not deprive the state courts of subject matter jurisdiction.

The judgment of the Supreme Court of Texas is reversed, and the case is remanded for further proceedings not inconsistent with this opinion.

It is so ordered.

MARC J. GABELLI AND BRUCE ALPERT, Petitioners

v.

SECURITIES AND EXCHANGE COMMISSION

11-1274

SUPREME COURT
OF THE UNITED STATES

568 U.S. 442

January 8, 2013, Argued
February 27, 2013, Decided

ON WRIT OF CERTIORARI TO THE UNITED STATES COURT OF APPEALS FOR THE SECOND CIRCUIT

Chief Justice Roberts delivered the opinion of the Court.

The Investment Advisers Act makes it illegal for investment advisers to defraud their clients, and authorizes the Securities and Exchange Commission to seek civil penalties from advisers who do so. Under the general statute of limitations for civil penalty actions, the SEC has five years to seek such penalties. The question is whether the five-year clock begins to tick when the fraud is complete or when the fraud is discovered.

I

A

Under the Investment Advisers Act of 1940, it is unlawful for an investment adviser "to employ any device, scheme, or artifice to defraud any client or prospective client" or "to engage in any transaction, practice, or course of business which operates as a fraud or deceit upon any client or prospective client." 54 Stat. 852, as amended, 15 U.S.C. §§80b-6(1), (2). The SEC is authorized to bring enforcement actions against investment advisers who violate the Act, or individuals who aid and abet such violations. §80b-9(d).

As part of such enforcement actions, the SEC may seek civil penalties, §§80b-9(e), (f) (2006 ed. and Supp. V), in which case a five-year statute of limitations applies:

"Except as otherwise provided by Act of Congress, an action, suit or proceeding for the enforcement of any civil fine, penalty, or forfeiture, pecuniary or otherwise, shall not be entertained unless commenced within five years from the date when the claim first accrued if, within the same period, the offender or the property is found within the United States in order that proper service may be made thereon." 28 U.S.C. §2462.

This statute of limitations is not specific to the Investment Advisers Act, or even to securities law; it governs many penalty provisions throughout the U.S. Code. Its origins date back to at least 1839, and it took on its current form in 1948. See Act of Feb. 28, 1839, ch. 36, § 4, 5 Stat. 322.

B

Gabelli Funds, LLC, is an investment adviser to a mutual fund formerly known as Gabelli Global Growth Fund (GGGF). Petitioner Bruce Alpert is Gabelli Funds' chief operating officer, and petitioner Marc Gabelli used to be GGGF's portfolio manager.

In 2008, the SEC brought a civil enforcement action against Alpert and Gabelli. According to the complaint, from 1999 until 2002 Alpert and Gabelli allowed one GGGF investor--Headstart Advisers, Ltd.--to engage in "market timing" in the fund.

As this Court has explained, "[m]arket timing is a trading strategy that exploits time delay in mutual funds' daily valuation system." *Janus Capital Group, Inc.* v. *First Derivative Traders*, 564 U.S. 135, 139, n. 1, 131 S. Ct. 2296, 2300, 180 L. Ed. 2d 166 (2011). Mutual funds are typically valued once a day, at the close of the New York Stock Exchange. Because funds often hold securities traded on different exchanges around the world, their reported valuation may be based on stale information. If a mutual fund's reported valuation is artificially low compared to its real value, market timers will buy that day and sell the next to realize quick profits. Market timing is not illegal but can harm long-term investors in a fund. See *id.*, at 139, and n. 1, 131 S. Ct. 2296, 2300, 180 L. Ed. 2d 166

The SEC's complaint alleged that Alpert and Gabelli permitted Headstart to engage in market timing in exchange for Headstart's investment in a hedge fund run by Gabelli. According to the SEC, petitioners did not disclose Headstart's market timing or the *quid pro quo* agreement, and instead banned others from engaging in market timing and made statements indicating that the practice would not be tolerated. The complaint stated that during the relevant period, Headstart earned rates of return of up to 185%, while "the rate of return for long-term investors in GGGF was no more than negative 24.1 percent." App. 73.

The SEC alleged that Alpert and Gabelli aided and abetted violations of §§80b-6(1) and (2), and it sought civil penalties under §80b-9. Petitioners moved to dismiss, arguing in part that the claim for civil penalties was untimely. They invoked the five-year statute of limitations in §2462, pointing out that the complaint alleged market timing up until August 2002 but was not filed until April 2008. The District Court agreed and dismissed the SEC's civil penalty claim as time barred.[1]

> 1 The SEC also sought injunctive relief and disgorgement, claims the District Court found timely on the ground that they were not subject to §2462. Those issues are not before us.

The Second Circuit reversed. It acknowledged that §2462 required an action for civil penalties to be brought within five years "from the date when the claim first accrued," but accepted the SEC's argument that because the underlying violations sounded in fraud, the "discovery rule" applied to the statute of limitations. As explained by the Second Circuit, "[u]nder the discovery rule, the statute of limitations for a particular claim does not accrue until that claim is discovered, or could have been discovered with reasonable diligence, by the plaintiff." 653 F.3d 49, 59 (2011). The court concluded that while "this rule does not govern the accrual of most claims," it *does* govern the claims at issue here. *Ibid.* As the court explained, "for claims that sound in fraud a discovery rule is read into the relevant statute of limitation." *Id.,* at 60.[2]

> 2 The court distinguished the discovery rule, which governs when a claim accrues, from doctrines that toll the running of an applicable limitations period when the defendant takes steps beyond the challenged conduct itself to conceal that conduct from the plaintiff. 653 F.3d, at 59–60. The SEC abandoned any reliance on such doctrines below, and they are not before us. See Response and Reply Brief for SEC Appellant/Cross-Appellee in No. 10-3581 (CA2), p. 34 ("The Commission is not seeking application of the fraudulent concealment doctrine or other equitable tolling principles").

We granted certiorari. 567 U.S. 968, 133 S. Ct. 97, 183 L. Ed. 2d 737 (2012).

II

A

This case centers around the meaning of 28 U.S.C. §2462: "an action . . . for the enforcement of any civil fine, penalty, or forfeiture . . . shall not be entertained unless commenced within five years from the date when the claim first accrued." Petitioners argue that a claim based on fraud accrues--and the five-year clock begins to tick--when a defendant's allegedly fraudulent conduct occurs.

That is the most natural reading of the statute. "In common parlance a right accrues when it comes into existence . . . ." *United States* v. *Lindsay*, 346 U.S. 568, 569, 74 S. Ct. 287, 98 L. Ed. 300 (1954). Thus the "standard rule" is that a claim accrues "when the plaintiff has a complete and present cause of action." *Wallace* v. *Kato*, 549 U.S. 384, 388, 127 S. Ct. 1091, 166 L. Ed. 2d 973 (2007) (internal quotation marks omitted); see also, *e.g.,Bay Area Laundry and Dry Cleaning Pension Trust Fund* v. *Ferbar Corp. of Cal.*, 522 U.S. 192, 201, 118 S. Ct. 542, 139 L. Ed. 2d 553 (1997); *Clark* v. *Iowa City*, 87 U.S. 583, 20 Wall. 583, 589, 22 L. Ed. 427 (1875). That rule has governed since the 1830's when the predecessor to §2462 was enacted. See, *e.g., Bank of United States* v. *Daniel*, 37 U.S. 32, 12 Pet. 32, 56, 9 L. Ed. 989 (1838); *Evans* v. *Gee*, 36 U.S. 80, 11 Pet. 80, 84, 9 L. Ed. 639 (1837). And that definition appears in dictionaries from the 19th century up until today. See, *e.g.,* 1 A. Burrill, A Law Dictionary and Glossary 17 (1850) ("an action *accrues* when the plaintiff has a right to commence it"); Black's Law Dictionary 23 (9th ed. 2009) (defining "accrue" as "[t]o come into existence as an enforceable claim or right").

This reading sets a fixed date when exposure to the specified Government enforcement efforts ends, advancing "the basic policies of all limitations provisions: repose, elimination of stale claims, and certainty about a plaintiff's opportunity for recovery and a defendant's potential liabilities." *Rotella* v. *Wood*, 528 U.S. 549, 555, 120 S. Ct. 1075, 145 L. Ed. 2d 1047 (2000). Statutes of limitations are intended to "promote justice by preventing surprises through the revival of claims that have been allowed to slumber until evidence has been lost, memories have faded, and witnesses have disappeared." *Railroad Telegraphers* v. *Railway Express Agency, Inc.*, 321 U.S. 342, 348-349, 64 S. Ct. 582, 88 L. Ed. 788 (1944). They provide "security and stability to human affairs." *Wood* v. *Carpenter*, 101 U.S. 135, 139, 25 L. Ed. 807 (1879). We have deemed them "vital to the welfare of society," *ibid.,* and concluded that "even wrongdoers are entitled to assume that their sins may be forgotten," *Wilson* v. *Garcia*, 471 U.S. 261, 271, 105 S. Ct. 1938, 85 L. Ed. 2d 254 (1985).

B

Notwithstanding these considerations, the Government argues that the discovery rule should apply instead. Under this rule, accrual is delayed "until the plaintiff has 'discovered' " his cause of action. *Merck & Co.* v. *Reynolds,* 559 U.S. 633, 644, 130 S. Ct. 1784, 1798, 176 L. Ed. 2d 582 (2010). The doctrine arose in 18th-century fraud cases as an "exception" to the standard rule, based on the recognition that "something different was needed in the case of fraud, where a defendant's deceptive conduct may prevent a plaintiff from even *knowing* that he or she has been defrauded." *Ibid.* This Court has held that "where a plaintiff has been injured by fraud and 'remains in ignorance of it without any fault or want of diligence or care on his part, the bar of the statute does not begin to run until the fraud is discovered.' " *Holmberg* v. *Armbrecht,* 327 U.S. 392, 397, 66 S. Ct. 582, 90 L. Ed. 743 (1946) (quoting *Bailey* v. *Glover,* 88 U.S. 342, 21 Wall. 342, 348, 22 L. Ed. 636 (1875)). And we have explained that "fraud is deemed to be discovered when, in the exercise of reasonable diligence, it could have been discovered." *Merck & Co., supra,* at 645, 130 S. Ct. 1784, 1794, 176 L. Ed. 2d 582 (internal quotation marks and alterations omitted).

But we have never applied the discovery rule in this context, where the plaintiff is not a defrauded victim seeking recompense, but is instead the Government bringing an enforcement action for civil penalties. Despite the discovery rule's centuries-old roots, the Government cites no lower court case before 2008 employing a fraud-based discovery rule in a Government enforcement action for civil penalties. See Brief for Respondent 23 (citing *SEC* v. *Tambone,* 550 F.3d 106, 148-149 (CA1 2008); *SEC* v. *Koenig,* 557 F.3d 736, 739 (CA7 2009)). When pressed at oral argument, the Government conceded that it was aware of no such case. Tr. of Oral Arg. 25. The Government was also unable to point to any example from the first 160 years after enactment of this statute of limitations where it had even asserted that the fraud discovery rule applied in such a context. *Id.,* at 26-27 (citing only *United States* v. *Maillard,* 26 F. Cas. 1140, 1142, F. Cas. No. 15709 (No. 15,709) (SDNY 1871), a "fraudulent concealment" case, see n. 2, *supra*).

Instead the Government relies heavily on *Exploration Co.* v. *United States,* 247 U.S. 435, 38 S. Ct. 571, 62 L. Ed. 1200 (1918), in an attempt to show that the discovery rule should benefit the Government to the same extent as private parties. See, *e.g.,* Brief for Respondent 10-11, 16, 17, 33-34, 41-45. In that case, a company had fraudulently procured land from the United States, and the United States sued to undo the transaction. The company raised the statute of limitations as a defense, but this Court allowed the case to proceed, concluding that the rule "that statutes of limitations upon suits to set aside fraudulent transactions shall not begin to run until the discovery of the fraud" applied "in favor of the Government as well as a private individual." *Exploration Co., supra*, at 449, 38 S. Ct. 571, 62 L. Ed. 1200. But in *Exploration Co.*, the Government was itself a victim; it had been defrauded and was suing to recover its loss. The Government was not bringing an enforcement action for penalties. *Exploration Co.* cannot save the Government's case here.

There are good reasons why the fraud discovery rule has not been extended to Government enforcement actions for civil penalties. The discovery rule exists in part to preserve the claims of victims who do not know they are injured and who reasonably do not inquire as to any injury. Usually when a private party is injured, he is immediately aware of that injury and put on notice that his time to sue is running. But when the injury is self-concealing, private parties may be unaware that they have been harmed. Most of us do not live in a state of constant investigation; absent any reason to think we have been injured, we do not typically spend our days looking for evidence that we were lied to or defrauded. And the law does not require that we do so. Instead, courts have developed the discovery rule, providing that the statute of limitations in fraud cases should typically begin to run only when the injury is or reasonably could have been discovered.

The same conclusion does not follow for the Government in the context of enforcement actions for civil penalties. The SEC, for example, is not like an individual victim who relies on apparent injury to learn of a wrong. Rather, a central "mission" of the SEC is to "investigat[e] potential violations of the federal securities laws." SEC, Enforcement Manual 1 (2012). Unlike the private party who has no reason to suspect fraud, the SEC's very purpose is to root it out, and it has many legal tools at hand to aid in that pursuit. It can demand that securities brokers and dealers submit detailed trading information. *Id.,* at 44. It can require investment advisers to turn over their comprehensive books and records at any time. 15 U.S.C. §80b-4 (2006 ed. and Supp. V). And even without filing suit, it can subpoena any documents and witnesses it deems relevant or material to an investigation. See §§77s(c), 78u(b), 80a-41(b), 80b-9(b) (2006 ed.).

The SEC is also authorized to pay monetary awards to whistleblowers, who provide information relating to violations of the securities laws. §78u-6 (2006 ed., Supp. V). In addition, the SEC may offer "cooperation agreements" to violators to procure information about others in exchange for more lenient treatment. See Enforcement Manual, at 119-137. Charged with this mission and armed with these weapons, the SEC as enforcer is a far cry from the defrauded victim the discovery rule evolved to protect.

In a civil penalty action, the Government is not only a different kind of plaintiff, it seeks a different kind of relief. The discovery rule helps to ensure that the injured receive recompense. But this case involves penalties, which go beyond compensation, are intended to punish, and label defendants wrongdoers. See *Meeker* v. *Lehigh Valley R. Co.*, 236 U.S. 412, 423, 35 S. Ct. 328, 59 L. Ed. 644 (1915) (a penalty covered by the predecessor to §2462 is "something imposed in a punitive way for an infraction of a public law"); see also *Tull* v. *United States*, 481 U.S. 412, 422, 107 S. Ct. 1831, 95 L. Ed. 2d 365 (1987) (penalties are "intended to punish culpable individuals," not "to extract compensation or restore the status quo").

Chief Justice Marshall used particularly forceful language in emphasizing the importance of time limits on penalty actions, stating that it "would be utterly repugnant to the genius of our laws" if actions for penalties could "be brought at any distance of time." *Adams* v. *Woods*, 6 U.S. 336, 2 Cranch 336, 342, 2 L. Ed. 297 (1805). Yet grafting the discovery rule onto §2462 would raise similar concerns. It would leave defendants exposed to Government enforcement action not only for five years after their misdeeds, but for an additional uncertain period into the future. Repose would hinge on speculation about what the Government knew, when it knew it, and when it should have known it. See *Rotella*, 528 U.S., at 554, 120 S. Ct. 1075, 145 L. Ed. 2d 1047 (disapproving a rule that would have "extended the limitations period to many decades" because such a rule was "beyond any limit that Congress could have contemplated" and "would have thwarted the basic objective of repose underlying the very notion of a limitations period").

Determining when the Government, as opposed to an individual, knew or reasonably should have known of a fraud presents particular challenges for the courts. Agencies often have hundreds of employees, dozens of offices, and several levels of leadership. In such a case, when does "the Government" know of a violation? Who is the relevant actor? Different agencies often have overlapping responsibilities; is the knowledge of one attributed to all?

In determining what a plaintiff should have known, we ask what facts "a reasonably diligent plaintiff would have discovered." *Merck & Co.*, 559 U.S., at 644, 130 S. Ct. 1784 176 L. Ed. 2d 582. It is unclear whether and how courts should consider agency priorities and resource constraints in applying that test to Government enforcement actions. See *3M Co.* v. *Browner*, 17 F.3d 1453, 1461, 305 U.S. App. D.C. 100 (CADC 1994) ("An agency may experience problems in detecting statutory violations because its enforcement effort is not sufficiently funded; or because the agency has not devoted an adequate number of trained personnel to the task; or because the agency's enforcement program is ill-designed or inefficient; or because the nature of the statute makes it difficult to uncover violations; or because of some combination of these factors and others"). And in the midst of any inquiry as to what it knew when, the Government can be expected to assert various privileges, such as law enforcement, attorney-client, work product, or deliberative process, further complicating judicial attempts to apply the discovery rule. See, *e.g.,* App. in No. 10-3581 (CA2), p. 147 (Government invoking such privileges in this case, in response to a request for documents relating to the SEC's investigation of Headstart); see also *Rotella, supra,* at 559, 120 S. Ct. 1075, 145 L. Ed. 2d 1047 (rejecting a rule in part due to "the controversy inherent in divining when a plaintiff should have discovered" a wrong).

To be sure, Congress has expressly required such inquiries in some statutes. But in many of those instances, the Government is itself an injured victim looking for recompense, not a prosecutor seeking penalties. See, *e.g.,* 28 U.S.C. §§2415, 2416(c) (Government suits for money damages founded on contracts or torts). Moreover, statutes applying a discovery rule in the context of Government suits often couple that rule with an absolute provision for repose, which a judicially imposed discovery rule would lack. See, *e.g.,* 21 U.S.C. §335b(b)(3) (limiting certain Government civil penalty actions to "6 years after the date when facts material to the act are known or reasonably should have been known by the Secretary but in no event more than 10 years after the date the act took place"). And several statutes applying a discovery rule to the Government make some effort to identify the official whose knowledge is relevant. See 31 U.S.C. §3731(b)(2) (relevant knowledge is that of "the official of the United States charged with responsibility to act in the circumstances").

Applying a discovery rule to Government penalty actions is far more challenging than applying the rule to suits by defrauded victims, and we have no mandate from Congress to undertake that challenge here.

* * *

As we held long ago, the cases in which "a statute of limitation may be suspended by causes not mentioned in the statute itself . . . are very limited in character, and are to be admitted with great caution; otherwise the court would make the law instead of administering it." *Amy* v. *Watertown (No. 2)*, 130 U.S. 320, 324, 9 S. Ct. 537, 32 L. Ed. 953 (1889) (internal quotation marks omitted). Given the lack of textual, historical, or equitable reasons to graft a discovery rule onto the statute of limitations of §2462, we decline to do so.

The judgment of the United States Court of Appeals for the Second Circuit is reversed, and the case is remanded for further proceedings consistent with this opinion.

It is so ordered.

LOUIS B. BULLARD, Petitioner
v.
BLUE HILLS BANK,
fka HYDE PARK SAVINGS BANK

14-116
SUPREME COURT
OF THE UNITED STATES

135 S. Ct. 1686

April 1, 2015, Argued
May 4, 2015, Decided

ON WRIT OF CERTIORARI TO THE UNITED STATES COURT OF APPEALS FOR THE FIRST CIRCUIT

Chief Justice Roberts delivered the opinion of the Court.

Chapter 13 of the Bankruptcy Code affords individuals receiving regular income an opportunity to obtain some relief from their debts while retaining their property. To proceed under Chapter 13, a debtor must propose a plan to use future income to repay a portion (or in the rare case all) of his debts over the next three to five years. If the bankruptcy court confirms the plan and the debtor successfully carries it out, he receives a discharge of his debts according to the plan.

The bankruptcy court may, however, decline to confirm a proposed repayment plan because it is inconsistent with the Code. Although the debtor is usually given an opportunity to submit a revised plan, he may be convinced that the original plan complied with the Code and that the bankruptcy court was wrong to deny confirmation. The question presented is whether such an order denying confirmation is a "final" order that the debtor can immediately appeal. We hold that it is not.

I

In December 2010, Louis Bullard filed a petition for Chapter 13 bankruptcy in Federal Bankruptcy Court in Massachusetts. A week later he filed a proposed repayment plan listing the various claims he anticipated creditors would file and the monthly amounts he planned to pay on each claim over the five-year life of his plan. See 11 U. S. C. §§1321, 1322. Chief among Bullard's debts was the roughly $346,000 he owed to Blue Hills Bank, which held a mortgage on a multifamily house Bullard owned. Bullard's plan indicated that the mortgage was significantly "underwater": that is, the house was worth substantially less than the amount Bullard owed the Bank.

Before submitting his plan for court approval, Bullard amended it three times over the course of a year to more accurately reflect the value of the house, the terms of the mortgage, the amounts of creditors' claims, and his proposed payments. See §1323 (allowing preconfirmation modification). Bullard's third amended plan--the one at issue here--proposed a "hybrid" treatment of his debt to the Bank. He proposed splitting the debt into a secured claim in the amount of the house's then-current value (which he estimated at $245,000), and an unsecured claim for the remainder (roughly $101,000). Under the plan, Bullard would continue making his regular mortgage payments toward the secured claim, which he would eventually repay in full, long after the conclusion of his bankruptcy case. He would treat the unsecured claim, however, the same as any other unsecured debt, paying only as much on it as his income would allow over the course of his five-year plan. At the end of this period the remaining balance on the unsecured portion of the loan would be discharged. In total, Bullard's plan called for him to pay only about $5,000 of the $101,000 unsecured claim.

The Bank (no surprise) objected to the plan and, after a hearing, the Bankruptcy Court declined to confirm it. *In re Bullard*, 475 B. R. 304 (Bkrtcy. Ct. Mass. 2012). The court concluded that Chapter 13 did not allow Bullard to split the Bank's claim as he proposed unless he paid the secured portion in full during the plan period. *Id.,* at 314. The court acknowledged, however, that other Bankruptcy Courts in the First Circuit had approved such arrangements. *Id.,* at 309. The Bankruptcy Court ordered Bullard to submit a new plan within 30 days. *Id.,* at 314.

Bullard appealed to the Bankruptcy Appellate Panel (BAP) of the First Circuit. The BAP first addressed its jurisdiction under the bankruptcy appeals statute, noting that a party can immediately appeal only "final" orders of a bankruptcy court. *In re Bullard*, 494 B. R. 92, 95 (2013) (citing 28 U. S. C. §158(a)(1)). The BAP concluded that the order denying plan confirmation was not final because Bullard was "free to propose an alternate plan." 494 B. R., at 95. The BAP nonetheless exercised its discretion to hear the appeal under a provision that allows interlocutory appeals "with leave of the court." §158(a)(3). The BAP granted such leave because the confirmation dispute involved a "controlling question of law . . . as to which there is substantial ground for difference of opinion," and "an immediate appeal [would] materially advance the ultimate termination of the litigation." 494 B. R., at 95, and n. 5. On the merits, the BAP agreed with the Bankruptcy Court that Bullard's proposed treatment of the Bank's claim was not allowed. *Id.,* at 96-101.

Bullard sought review in the Court of Appeals for the First Circuit, but that court dismissed his appeal for lack of jurisdiction. *In re Bullard*, 752 F. 3d 483 (2014). The First Circuit noted that because the BAP had not certified the appeal under §158(d)(2), the only possible source of Court of Appeals jurisdiction was §158(d)(1), which allowed appeal of only a final order of the BAP. *Id.,* at 485, and n. 3. And under First Circuit precedent "an order of the BAP cannot be final unless the underlying bankruptcy court order is final." *Id.,* at 485. The Court of Appeals accordingly examined whether a bankruptcy court's denial of plan confirmation is a final order, a question that it recognized had divided the Circuits. Adopting the majority view, the First Circuit concluded that an order denying confirmation is not final so long as the debtor remains free to propose another plan. *Id.,* at 486-490.

We granted certiorari. 574 U. S. _, 135 S. Ct. 781, 190 L. Ed. 2d 649 (2014).

II

In ordinary civil litigation, a case in federal district court culminates in a "final decisio[n]," 28 U. S. C. §1291, a ruling "by which a district court disassociates itself from a case," *Swint* v. *Chambers County Comm'n*, 514 U. S. 35, 42, 115 S. Ct. 1203, 131 L. Ed. 2d 60 (1995). A party can typically appeal as of right only from that final decision. This rule reflects the conclusion that "[p]ermitting piecemeal, prejudgment appeals . . . undermines 'efficient judicial administration' and encroaches upon the prerogatives of district court judges, who play a 'special role' in managing ongoing litigation." *Mohawk Industries, Inc.* v. *Carpenter*, 558 U. S. 100, 106, 130 S. Ct. 599, 175 L. Ed. 2d 458 (2009) (quoting *Firestone Tire & Rubber Co.* v. *Risjord*, 449 U. S. 368, 374, 101 S. Ct. 669, 66 L. Ed. 2d 571 (1981)).

The rules are different in bankruptcy. A bankruptcy case involves "an aggregation of individual controversies," many of which would exist as stand-alone lawsuits but for the bankrupt status of the debtor. 1 Collier on Bankruptcy ¶5.08[1][b], p. 5-42 (16th ed. 2014). Accordingly, "Congress has long provided that orders in bankruptcy cases may be immediately appealed if they finally dispose of discrete disputes within the larger case." *Howard Delivery Service, Inc.* v. *Zurich American Ins. Co.*, 547 U. S. 651, 657, n. 3, 126 S. Ct. 2105, 165 L. Ed. 2d 110 (2006) (internal quotation marks and emphasis omitted). The current bankruptcy appeals statute reflects this approach: It authorizes appeals as of right not only from final judgments in cases but from "final judgments, orders, and decrees . . . in cases and proceedings." §158(a).

The present dispute is about how to define the immediately appealable "proceeding" in the context of the consideration of Chapter 13 plans. Bullard argues for a plan-by-plan approach. Each time the bankruptcy court reviews a proposed plan, he says, it conducts a separate proceeding. On this view, an order denying confirmation and an order granting confirmation both terminate that proceeding, and both are therefore final and appealable.

In the Bank's view Bullard is slicing the case too thin. The relevant "proceeding," it argues, is the entire process of considering plans, which terminates only when a plan is confirmed or--if the debtor fails to offer any confirmable plan--when the case is dismissed. An order denying confirmation is not final, so long as it leaves the debtor free to propose another plan.

We agree with the Bank: The relevant proceeding is the process of attempting to arrive at an approved plan that would allow the bankruptcy to move forward. This is so, first and foremost, because only plan confirmation--or case dismissal--alters the status quo and fixes the rights and obligations of the parties. When the bankruptcy court confirms a plan, its terms become binding on debtor and creditor alike. 11 U. S. C. §1327(a). Confirmation has preclusive effect, foreclosing relitigation of "any issue actually litigated by the parties and any issue necessarily determined by the confirmation order." 8 Collier ¶1327.02[1][c], at 1327-6; see also *United Student Aid Funds, Inc.* v. *Espinosa*, 559 U. S. 260, 275, 130 S. Ct. 1367, 176 L. Ed. 2d 158 (2010) (finding a confirmation order "enforceable and binding" on a creditor notwithstanding legal error when the creditor "had notice of the error and failed to object or timely appeal"). Subject to certain exceptions, confirmation "vests all of the property of the [bankruptcy] estate in the debtor," and renders that property "free and clear of any claim or interest of any creditor provided for by the plan." §§1327(b), (c). Confirmation also triggers the Chapter 13 trustee's duty to distribute to creditors those funds already received from the debtor. §1326(a)(2).

When confirmation is denied *and the case is dismissed as a result*, the consequences are similarly significant. Dismissal of course dooms the possibility of a discharge and the other benefits available to a debtor under Chapter 13. Dismissal lifts the automatic stay entered at the start of bankruptcy, exposing the debtor to creditors' legal actions and collection efforts. §362(c)(2). And it can limit the availability of an automatic stay in a subsequent bankruptcy case. §362(c)(3).

Denial of confirmation with leave to amend, by contrast, changes little. The automatic stay persists. The parties' rights and obligations remain unsettled. The trustee continues to collect funds from the debtor in anticipation of a different plan's eventual confirmation. The possibility of discharge lives on. "Final" does not describe this state of affairs. An order denying confirmation does rule out the specific arrangement of relief embodied in a particular plan. But that alone does not make the denial final any more than, say, a car buyer's declining to pay the sticker price is viewed as a "final" purchasing decision by either the buyer or seller. "It ain't over till it's over."

Several additional considerations bolster our conclusion that the relevant "proceeding" is the entire process culminating in confirmation or dismissal. First is a textual clue. Among the list of "core proceedings" statutorily entrusted to bankruptcy judges are "confirmations of plans." 28 U. S. C. §157(b)(2)(L). Although this item hardly clinches the matter for the Bank--the provision's purpose is not to explain appealability--it does cut in the Bank's favor. The presence of the phrase "confirmations of plans," combined with the absence of any reference to denials, suggests that Congress viewed the larger confirmation process as the "proceeding," not the ruling on each specific plan.

In Bullard's view the debtor can appeal the denial of the first plan he submits to the bankruptcy court. If the court of appeals affirms the denial, the debtor can then revise the plan. If the new plan is also denied confirmation, another appeal can ensue. And so on. As Bullard's case shows, each climb up the appellate ladder and slide down the chute can take more than a year. Avoiding such delays and inefficiencies is precisely the reason for a rule of finality. It does not make much sense to define the pertinent proceeding so narrowly that the requirement of finality would do little work as a meaningful constraint on the availability of appellate review.

Bullard responds that concerns about frequent piecemeal appeals are misplaced in this context. Debtors do not typically have the money or incentives to take appeals over small beer issues. They will only appeal the relatively rare denials based on significant legal rulings--precisely the cases that should proceed promptly to the courts of appeals. Brief for Petitioner 43-46.

Bullard's assurance notwithstanding, debtors may often view, in good faith or bad, the prospect of appeals as important leverage in dealing with creditors. An appeal extends the automatic stay that comes with bankruptcy, which can cost creditors money and allow a debtor to retain property he might lose if the Chapter 13 proceeding turns out not to be viable. These concerns are heightened if the same rule applies in Chapter 11, as the parties assume. Chapter 11 debtors, often business entities, are more likely to have the resources to appeal and may do so on narrow issues. See Tr. of Oral Arg. 51. But even if Bullard is correct that such appeals will be rare, that does not much support his broader point that an appeal of right should be allowed in every case. It is odd, after all, to argue in favor of allowing more appeals by emphasizing that almost nobody will take them.

We think that in the ordinary case treating only confirmation or dismissal as final will not unfairly burden a debtor. He retains the valuable exclusive right to propose plans, which he can modify freely. 11 U. S. C. §§1321, 1323. The knowledge that he will have no guaranteed appeal from a denial should encourage the debtor to work with creditors and the trustee to develop a confirmable plan as promptly as possible. And expedition is always an important consideration in bankruptcy.

III

Bullard and the Solicitor General present several arguments for treating each plan denial as final, but we are not persuaded.

The Solicitor General notes that disputes in bankruptcy are generally classified as either "adversary proceedings," essentially full civil lawsuits carried out under the umbrella of the bankruptcy case, or "contested matters," an undefined catchall for other issues the parties dispute. See Fed. Rule Bkrtcy. Proc. 7001 (listing ten adversary proceedings); Rule 9014 (addressing "contested matter[s] not otherwise governed by these rules"). An objection to a plan initiates a contested matter. See Rule 3015(f). Everyone agrees that an order resolving that matter by overruling the objection and confirming the plan is final. As the Solicitor General sees it, an order denying confirmation would also resolve that contested matter, so such an order should also be considered final. Brief for United States as *Amicus Curiae* 19-22.

The scope of the Solicitor General's argument is unclear. At points his brief appears to argue that an order resolving *any* contested matter is final and immediately appealable. That version of the argument has the virtue of resting on a general principle--but the vice of being implausible. As a leading treatise notes, the list of contested matters is "endless" and covers all sorts of minor disagreements. 10 Collier ¶9014.01, at 9014-3. The concept of finality cannot stretch to cover, for example, an order resolving a disputed request for an extension of time.

At other points, the Solicitor General appears to argue that because one possible resolution of this particular contested matter (confirmation) is final, the other (denial) must be as well. But this argument begs the question. It simply assumes that confirmation is appealable because it resolves a contested matter, and that therefore anything else that resolves the contested matter must also be appealable. But one can just as easily contend that confirmation is appealable because it resolves the entire plan consideration process, and that therefore the entire process is the "proceeding." A decision that does not resolve the entire plan consideration process--denial--is therefore not appealable.

Perhaps the Solicitor General's suggestion is that a separately appealable "proceeding" must coincide precisely with a particular "adversary proceeding" or "contested matter" under the Bankruptcy Rules. He does not, however, provide any support for such a suggestion. More broadly, it is of course quite common for the finality of a decision to depend on which way the decision goes. An order granting a motion for summary judgment is final; an order denying such a motion is not.

Bullard and the Solicitor General also contend that our rule creates an unfair asymmetry: If the bankruptcy court sustains an objection and denies confirmation, the debtor (always the plan proponent in Chapter 13) must go back to the drafting table and try again; but if the bankruptcy court overrules an objection and grants confirmation, a creditor can appeal without delay. But any asymmetry in this regard simply reflects the fact that confirmation allows the bankruptcy to go forward and alters the legal relationships among the parties, while denial does not have such significant consequences.

Moreover, it is not clear that this asymmetry will always advantage creditors. Consider a creditor who strongly supports a proposed plan because it treats him well. If the bankruptcy court sustains an objection from another creditor--perhaps because the plan treats the first creditor too well--the first creditor might have as keen an interest in a prompt appeal as the debtor. And yet, under the rule we adopt, that creditor too would have to await further developments.

Bullard also raises a more practical objection. If denial orders are not final, he says, there will be no effective means of obtaining appellate review of the denied proposal. The debtor's only two options would be to seek or accept dismissal of his case and then appeal, or to propose an amended plan and appeal its confirmation.

The first option is not realistic, Bullard contends, because dismissal means the end of the automatic stay against creditors' collection efforts. Without the stay, the debtor might lose the very property at issue in the rejected plan. Even if a bankruptcy court agrees to maintain the stay pending appeal, the debtor is still risking his entire bankruptcy case on the appeal.

The second option is no better, says Bullard. An acceptable, confirmable alternative may not exist. Even if one does, its confirmation might have immediate and irreversible effects--such as the sale or transfer of property--and a court is unlikely to stay its execution. Moreover, it simply wastes time and money to place the debtor in the position of seeking approval of a plan he does not want.

All good points. We do not doubt that in many cases these options may be, as the court below put it, "unappealing." 752 F. 3d, at 487. But our litigation system has long accepted that certain burdensome rulings will be "only imperfectly reparable" by the appellate process. *Digital Equipment Corp.* v. *Desktop Direct, Inc.*, 511 U. S. 863, 872, 114 S. Ct. 1992, 128 L. Ed. 2d 842 (1994). This prospect is made tolerable in part by our confidence that bankruptcy courts, like trial courts in ordinary litigation, rule correctly most of the time. And even when they slip, many of their errors--wrongly concluding, say, that a debtor should pay unsecured creditors $400 a month rather than $300--will not be of a sort that justifies the costs entailed by a system of universal immediate appeals.

Sometimes, of course, a question will be important enough that it should be addressed immediately. Bullard's case could well fit the bill: The confirmability of his hybrid plan presented a pure question of law that had divided bankruptcy courts in the First Circuit and would make a substantial financial difference to the parties. But there are several mechanisms for interlocutory review to address such cases. First, a district court or BAP can (as the BAP did in this case) grant leave to hear such an appeal. 28 U. S. C. §158(a)(3). A debtor who appeals to the district court and loses there can seek certification to the court of appeals under the general interlocutory appeals statute, §1292(b). See *Connecticut Nat. Bank* v. *Germain*, 503 U. S. 249, 112 S. Ct. 1146, 117 L. Ed. 2d 391 (1992).

Another interlocutory mechanism is provided in §158(d)(2). That provision allows a bankruptcy court, district court, BAP, or the parties acting jointly to certify a bankruptcy court's order to the court of appeals, which then has discretion to hear the matter. Unlike §1292(b), which permits certification only when three enumerated factors suggesting importance are all present, §158(d)(2) permits certification when any one of several such factors exists, a distinction that allows a broader range of interlocutory decisions to make their way to the courts of appeals. While discretionary review mechanisms such as these "do not provide relief in every case, they serve as useful safety valves for promptly correcting serious errors" and addressing important legal questions. *Mohawk Industries*, 558 U. S., at 111, 130 S. Ct. 599, 175 L. Ed. 2d 458 (internal quotation marks and brackets omitted).

Bullard maintains that interlocutory appeals are ineffective because lower courts have been too reticent in granting them. But Bullard did, after all, obtain one layer of interlocutory review when the BAP granted him leave to appeal under §158(a)(3). He also sought certification to the Court of Appeals under §158(d)(2), but the BAP denied his request for reasons that are not entirely clear. See App. to Pet. for Cert. 17a. The fact that Bullard was not able to obtain further merits review in the First Circuit in this particular instance does not undermine our expectation that lower courts will certify and accept interlocutory appeals from plan denials in appropriate cases.

* * *

Because the Court of Appeals correctly held that the order denying confirmation was not final, its judgment is

Affirmed.

JOHN STURGEON, Petitioner
v.
BERT FROST, in his official capacity as ALASKA REGIONAL DIRECTOR OF THE NATIONAL PARK SERVICE, et al.

14-1209

SUPREME COURT OF THE UNITED STATES

136 S. Ct. 1061

January 20, 2016, Argued
March 22, 2016, Decided

ON WRIT OF CERTIORARI TO THE UNITED STATES COURT OF APPEALS FOR THE NINTH CIRCUIT

Chief Justice Roberts delivered the opinion of the Court.

For almost 40 years, John Sturgeon has hunted moose along the Nation River in Alaska. Because parts of the river are shallow and difficult to navigate, Sturgeon travels by hovercraft, an amphibious vehicle capable of gliding over land and water. To reach his preferred hunting grounds, Sturgeon must pilot his hovercraft over a stretch of the Nation River that flows through the Yukon-Charley Rivers National Preserve, a 1.7 million acre federal preservation area managed by the National Park Service. 16 U.S.C. §410hh(10).

Alaska law permits the use of hovercraft. National Park Service regulations do not. See 36 CFR §2.17(e) (2015). After Park Service rangers informed Sturgeon that he was prohibited from using his hovercraft within the boundaries of the preserve, Sturgeon filed suit, seeking declaratory and injunctive relief. He argues that the Nation River is owned by the State, and that the Alaska National Interest Lands Conservation Act (ANILCA) prohibits the Park Service from enforcing its regulations on state-owned land in Alaska. The Park Service disagrees, contending that it has authority to regulate waters flowing through federally managed preservation areas. The District Court and the Court of Appeals ruled in favor of the Park Service. We granted certiorari.

I

In 1867, Secretary of State William Seward, serving under President Andrew Johnson, negotiated a treaty to purchase Alaska from Russia for $7.2 million. Treaty Concerning the Cession of the Russian Possessions in North America, Mar. 30, 1867, 15 Stat. 539. In a single stroke, the United States gained 365 million acres of land--an area more than twice the size of Texas. Despite the bargain price of two cents an acre, however, the purchase was mocked by contemporaries as "Seward's Folly" and President Johnson's "Polar Bear Garden." See C. Naske & H. Slotnick, Alaska: A History 92-94 (2011) (Naske & Slotnick); S. Rep. No. 1163, 85th Cong., 1st Sess., 2 (1957).

The monikers didn't stick. In 1898, the "Three Lucky Swedes"--Jafet Lindeberg, Eric Lindblom, and Jon Brynteson--struck gold in Nome, Alaska. As word of their discovery spread, thousands traveled to Alaska to try their hand at mining. Once the gold rush subsided, settlers turned to other types of mining, fishing, and trapping, fueling an emerging export economy. See Naske & Slotnick 128-129, 155, 249-251; D. Wharton, The Alaska Gold Rush 186-187 (1972).

Despite newfound recognition of Alaska's economic potential, however, it was not until the 1950's that Congress seriously considered admitting Alaska as a State. By that time, it was clear that Alaska was strategically important both in the Pacific and Arctic, and that the Territory was rich in natural resources, including oil. Moreover, the people of Alaska favored statehood. See Naske & Slotnick 201, 224-235. But there was a problem: Out of the 365 million acres of land in Alaska, 98 percent were owned by the Federal Government. As a result, absent a land grant from the Federal Government to the State, there would be little land available to drive private economic activity and contribute to the state tax base. See S. Rep. No. 1163, at 2, 12 ("The expenses of the State of Alaska will be comparatively high, partially due to the vast land areas within the State; but the State would be able to realize revenues from only 2 percent of this vast area unless some provision were made to modify the present land-ownership conditions").

A solution was struck. The 1958 Alaska Statehood Act permitted Alaska to select 103 million acres of "vacant, unappropriated, and unreserved" federal land--just over a quarter of all land in Alaska--for state ownership. §§6(a)-(b), 72 Stat. 340. That land grant included "mineral deposits," which were "subject to lease by the State as the State legislature may direct." §6(i), *id.*, at 342. Upon statehood, Alaska also gained "title to and ownership of the lands beneath navigable waters" within the State, in addition to "the natural resources within such lands and waters," including "the right and power to manage, administer, lease, develop, and use the said lands and natural resources." §3(a), 67 Stat. 30, 43 U.S.C. §1311(a); §6(m), 72 Stat. 343. With over 100 million acres of land now available to the new State, Alaska could begin to fulfill its state policy "to encourage the settlement of its land and the development of its resources by making them available for maximum use consistent with the public interest." Alaska Const., Art. VIII, §1 (2014).

The Statehood Act did not, however, determine the rights of the Alaska Natives, who asserted aboriginal title to much of the same land now claimed by the State. Naske & Slotnick 287-289. To resolve the dispute, Congress in 1971 passed the Alaska Native Claims Settlement Act (ANCSA), which extinguished aboriginal land claims in Alaska. 85 Stat. 688, as amended, 43 U.S.C. §1601 *et seq.* In exchange, Congress provided for a $960 million settlement and permitted corporations organized by groups of Alaska Natives to select 40 million acres of federal land to manage within the State. §§1605, 1610-1615; Naske & Slotnick 296-297. Congress sought to implement the settlement "rapidly, with certainty, in conformity with the real economic and social needs" of Alaska Natives. §1601(b).

In addition to settling the claims of the Alaska Natives, ANCSA directed the Secretary of the Interior to select up to 80 million acres of unreserved federal land in Alaska for addition to the National Park, Forest, Wildlife Refuge, and Wild and Scenic Rivers Systems, subject to congressional approval. §1616(d)(2). When Congress failed to approve the Secretary's selections, however, President Carter unilaterally designated 56 million acres of federal land in Alaska as national monuments. See Presidential Proclamation Nos. 4611-4627, 3 CFR 69-104 (1978 Comp.).

President Carter's actions were unpopular among many Alaskans, who were concerned that the new monuments would be subject to restrictive federal regulations. Protesters demonstrated in Fairbanks, and more than 2,500 Alaskans participated in the "Great Denali-McKinley Trespass." The goal of the trespass was to break over 25 Park Service rules in a two-day period-- including by camping, hunting, snowmobiling, setting campfires, shooting guns, and unleashing dogs. During the event, a "rider on horseback, acting the part of Paul Revere, galloped through the crowd yelling, 'The Feds are coming! The Feds are coming!'" N. Y. Times, Jan. 15, 1979, p. A8; Anchorage Daily News, Jan. 15, 1979, pp. 1-2.

Congress once again stepped in to settle the controversy, passing the Alaska National Interest Lands Conservation Act. 94 Stat. 2371, 16 U.S.C. §3101 *et seq.* ANILCA had two stated goals: First, to provide "sufficient protection for the national interest in the scenic, natural, cultural and environmental values on the public lands in Alaska." §3101(d). And second, to provide "adequate opportunity for satisfaction of the economic and social needs of the State of Alaska and its people." *Ibid.*

ANILCA set aside 104 million acres of land in Alaska for preservation purposes, in the process creating ten new national parks, preserves, and monuments--including the Yukon-Charley Rivers National Preserve--and tripling the number of acres set aside in the United States for federal wilderness preservation. See §410hh; Naske & Slotnick 315-316. At the same time, ANILCA specified that the Park Service could not prohibit on those lands certain activities of particular importance to Alaskans. See, *e.g.*, §3170(a) (Secretary must permit reasonable use of vehicles "for travel to and from villages and homesites"); §3201 (Secretary must permit "the taking of fish and wildlife for sport purposes and subsistence uses" within National Preserves in Alaska, subject to regulation and certain exceptions). President Carter's earlier land designations were rescinded. See §3209(a).

Under ANILCA, federal preservation lands in Alaska were placed into "conservation system units," which were defined to include "any unit in Alaska of the National Park System, National Wildlife Refuge System, National Wild and Scenic Rivers Systems, National Trails System, National Wilderness Preservation System, or a National Forest Monument." §3102(4). Congress drew the boundaries of those units to "follow hydrographic divides or embrace other topographic or natural features," however, rather than to map the Federal Government's landholdings. §3103(b). As a consequence, in addition to federal land, over 18 million acres of state, Native Corporation, and private land ended up inside the boundaries of conservation system units. See Brief for Petitioner 6.

This brings us back to Sturgeon and his hovercraft.

II

A

One fall day in 2007, Sturgeon was piloting his hovercraft on the Nation River, which rises in the Ogilvie Mountains in Canada and joins the Yukon River within the boundaries of the Yukon-Charley Rivers National Preserve conservation system unit (Yukon-Charley). Sturgeon was headed to a hunting ground upstream from the preserve, just shy of the Canadian border. To reach that hunting ground, dubbed "moose meadows," Sturgeon had to travel on a portion of the river that flows through the preserve.

About two miles into his trip on the Nation River, Sturgeon stopped on a gravel bar to repair the steering cable of his hovercraft. As he was performing the repairs, Sturgeon was approached by three Park Service rangers. The rangers informed him that hovercraft were prohibited under Park Service regulations, and that he was committing a crime by operating his hovercraft within the boundaries of the Yukon-Charley. Despite Sturgeon's protests that

Park Service regulations did not apply because the river was owned by the State of Alaska, the rangers ordered Sturgeon to remove his hovercraft from the preserve. Sturgeon complied, heading home without a moose.

Sturgeon now fears that he will be criminally prosecuted if he returns to hunt along the Nation River in his hovercraft. To avoid prosecution, Sturgeon sued the Park Service and several federal officials in the United States District Court for the District of Alaska. He seeks declaratory and injunctive relief permitting him to operate his hovercraft within the boundaries of the Yukon-Charley. Alaska intervened in support of Sturgeon, and the Park Service opposed the suit.

The District Court granted summary judgment to the Park Service. *Sturgeon* v. *Masica*, 2013 U.S. Dist. LEXIS 157078, 2013 WL 5888230 (Oct. 30, 2013). The Court of Appeals for the Ninth Circuit affirmed in pertinent part. *Sturgeon* v. *Masica*, 768 F. 3d 1066 (2014).

We granted certiorari. 576 U.S. _, 136 S. Ct. 27, 192 L. Ed. 2d 997 (2015).

B

The Secretary of the Interior has authority to "prescribe regulations" concerning "boating and other activities on or relating to water located within System units, including water subject to the jurisdiction of the United States." 54 U.S.C. §100751(b) (2012 ed., Supp. II). "System units" are in turn defined as "any area of land and water administered by the Secretary, acting through the Director [of the Park Service], for park, monument, historic, parkway, recreational, or other purposes." §§100102, 100501.

The Park Service's hovercraft regulation was adopted pursuant to Section 100751(b). The hovercraft ban applies not only within "[t]he boundaries of federally owned lands and waters administered by the National Park Service," but also to "[w]aters subject to the jurisdiction of the United States located within the boundaries of the National Park System, including navigable waters . . . without regard to the ownership of submerged lands." 36 CFR §1.2(a). The hovercraft ban is not limited to Alaska, but instead has effect in federally managed preservation areas across the country.

Section 103(c) of ANILCA, in contrast, addresses the scope of the Park Service's authority over lands within the boundaries of conservation system units in Alaska. The first sentence of Section 103(c) specifies the property included as a portion of those units. It states: "Only those lands within the boundaries of any conservation system unit which are public lands (as such term is defined in this Act) shall be deemed to be included as a portion of such unit." 16 U.S.C. §3103(c). ANILCA defines the word "land" to include "lands, waters, and interests therein," and the term "public lands" to include "lands the title to which is in the United States after December 2, 1980," with certain exceptions. §3102. In sum, only "lands, waters, and interests therein" to which the United States has "title" are considered "public" land "included as a portion" of the conservation system units in Alaska.

The second sentence of Section 103(c) concerns the Park Service's authority to regulate "non-public" lands in Alaska, which include state, Native Corporation, and private property. It provides: "No lands which, before, on, or after December 2, 1980, are conveyed to the State, to any Native Corporation, or to any private party shall be subject to the regulations applicable solely to public lands within such units." §3103(c).

The third sentence of Section 103(c) explains how new lands become part of conservation system units: "If the State, a Native Corporation, or other owner desires to convey any such lands, the Secretary may acquire such lands in accordance with applicable law (including this Act), and any such lands shall become part of the unit, and be administered accordingly." *Ibid.*

C

The parties dispute whether Section 103(c) of ANILCA created an Alaska-specific exception to the Park Service's general authority over boating and related activities in federally managed preservation areas. Sturgeon, the Park Service, and the Ninth Circuit each adopt a different reading of Section 103(c), reaching different conclusions about the scope of the Park Service's powers.

Sturgeon, joined by the State, understands Section 103(c) to stand for a simple proposition: The Park Service is prohibited from regulating "non-public" land in Alaska as if that land were owned by the Federal Government. He contends that his reading is consistent with the history of federal land management in Alaska, beginning with the Alaska Statehood Act and culminating in ANILCA.

Sturgeon's argument proceeds in two steps. First, he asserts that the Nation River is not "public land" for purposes of ANILCA and is therefore not part of the Yukon-Charley. As discussed, ANILCA defines "public lands" as lands to which the United States has "title." 16 U.S.C. §3102. And Section 103(c) provides that "[o]nly those lands within the boundaries of any conservation system unit which are public lands (as such term is defined in this Act) shall be deemed to be included as a portion of such unit." §3103(c).

Sturgeon argues that the Nation River is not "public land" because it is owned by the State and not by the Federal Government. To support his argument, Sturgeon relies on the Alaska Statehood Act, which granted ownership of the submerged lands beneath the navigable waters in Alaska, and the resources within those waters, to the State. See §6(m), 72 Stat. 343; 43 U.S.C. §1311(a). He also cites this Court's decision in *United States* v. *California*, 436 U.S. 32, 98 S. Ct. 1662, 56 L. Ed. 2d 94 (1978), which stated that "the Submerged Lands Act transferred title to and ownership of the submerged lands and waters" to the States. *Id.*, at 40, 98 S. Ct. 1662, 56 L. Ed. 2d 94 (internal quotation marks omitted). Because the State and not the Federal Government owns the Nation River, Sturgeon urges, it is not "public" land under ANILCA and is therefore not part of the Yukon-Charley.

Second, Sturgeon asserts that because the Nation River is not part of the Yukon-Charley, the Park Service lacks authority to regulate it. His argument rests on the second sentence of Section 103(c), which states that "[n]o lands which, before, on, or after December 2, 1980, are conveyed to the State, to any Native Corporation, or to any private party shall be subject to the regulations applicable solely to public lands within such units." 16 U.S.C. §3103(c).

Sturgeon argues that the phrase "regulations applicable solely to public lands within such units" refers to those regulations that apply "solely" by virtue of the Park Service's "authority to manage national parks." Brief for Petitioner 18, 26-27. The word "solely," Sturgeon contends, simply ensures that "non-public" lands within the boundaries of those units remain subject to laws generally "applicable to both public and private lands (such as the Clean Air Act and Clean Water Act)." *Id.*, at 19. Because the hovercraft regulation was adopted pursuant to the Park Service's authority over federally managed preservation areas, and is not a law of general applicability like the Clean Air Act or the Clean Water Act, Sturgeon concludes that Section 103(c) bars enforcement of the regulation.

The Park Service, in contrast, reads Section 103(c) more narrowly. In its brief in this Court, the Park Service, while defending the reasoning of the Ninth Circuit, relies primarily on very different arguments. The agency stresses that it has longstanding authority to regulate waters within federally managed preservation areas, and that Section 103(c) does not take any of that authority away. In reaching its conclusion, the Park Service disagrees with Sturgeon at each step.

First, the Park Service contends that the Nation River is part of the Yukon-Charley. To support that contention, the agency cites ANILCA's definition of "public lands," which--as noted--includes "lands, waters, and interests therein" to which the United States has "title." 16 U.S.C. §3102. The Park Service argues that the United States has "title" to an "interest" in the water within the boundaries of the Yukon-Charley under the reserved water rights doctrine.

The reserved water rights doctrine specifies that "when the Federal Government withdraws its land from the public domain and reserves it for a federal purpose, the Government, by implication, reserves appurtenant water then unappropriated to the extent needed to accomplish the purpose of the reservation." *Cappaert* v. *United States*, 426 U.S. 128, 138, 96 S. Ct. 2062, 48 L. Ed. 2d 523 (1976). By creating the Yukon-Charley, the Park Service urges, the Federal Government reserved the water within the boundaries of the conservation system unit to achieve the Government's conservation goals. As a result, the Federal Government has "title" to an "interest" in the Nation River, making it "public" land subject to Park Service regulations.

Second, the Park Service contends that even if the Nation River is not "public" land, the agency still has authority to regulate it. According to the Park Service, the second sentence of Section 103(c) imposes only a limited restriction on the agency's power, prohibiting it from enforcing on "non-public" lands only those regulations that explicitly apply "solely to public lands." The hovercraft regulation applies both within "[t]he boundaries of federally owned lands and waters administered by the National Park Service" *and* to "[w]aters subject to the jurisdiction of the United States located within the boundaries of the National Park System, including navigable waters . . . without regard to the ownership of submerged lands." 36 CFR §1.2(a). Accordingly, the Park Service asserts, the hovercraft regulation does not apply "solely to public lands," and Section 103(c) therefore does not prevent enforcement of the regulation. See Brief for Respondents 56-58.

The Ninth Circuit, for its part, adopted a reading of Section 103(c) different from the primary argument advanced by the Park Service in this Court. The Court of Appeals did not reach the question whether the Nation River counts as "public" land for purposes of ANILCA. Instead, it held that the phrase "regulations applicable solely to public lands within such units" distinguishes between Park Service regulations that apply solely to "public" lands *in Alaska*, and Park Service regulations that apply to federally managed preservation areas across the country. In the Ninth Circuit's view, the Park Service may enforce nationally applicable regulations on both "public" and "non-public" property within the boundaries of conservation system units in Alaska, because such regulations do not apply "solely to public lands within such units." The Park Service may not, however, apply Alaska-specific regulations to "non-public" lands within the boundaries of those units.

According to the Ninth Circuit, because the hovercraft regulation "applies to all federal-owned lands and waters administered by [the Park Service] nationwide, as well as all navigable waters lying within national parks," the hovercraft ban does not apply "solely" within conservation system units in Alaska. 768 F. 3d, at 1077. The Ninth Circuit concluded that the Park Service therefore has authority to enforce its hovercraft regulation on the Nation River. *Id.*, at 1078. The Ninth Circuit's holding is subject to some interpretation, but Sturgeon, the State, the Alaska Native Corporations, and the Park Service (at least at times) concur in our understanding of the decision below. See Brief for Petitioner 25; Brief for State of Alaska as *Amicus Curiae* 23; Brief for Arctic Slope Regional Corporation et al. as *Amici Curiae* 12-13; Brief for Doyon, Ltd., et al. as *Amici Curiae* 31-32; Brief for Respondents 20; Tr. of Oral Arg. 61; 80 Fed. Reg. 65573 (2015).

III

We reject the interpretation of Section 103(c) adopted by the Ninth Circuit. The court's reading of the phrase "regulations applicable solely to public lands within such units" may be plausible in the abstract, but it is ultimately inconsistent with both the text and context of the statute as a whole. Statutory language "cannot be construed in a vacuum. It is a fundamental canon of statutory construction that the words of a statute must be read in their context and with a view to their place in the overall statutory scheme." *Roberts* v. *Sea-Land Services, Inc.*, 566 U.S. _, _, 132 S. Ct. 1350, 1357, 182 L. Ed. 2d 341, 355 (2012) (internal quotation marks omitted).

Under the reading of the statute adopted below, the Park Service may apply nationally applicable regulations to "non-public" lands within the boundaries of conservation system units in Alaska, but it may not apply Alaska-specific regulations to those lands. That is a surprising conclusion. ANILCA repeatedly recognizes that Alaska is different--from its "unrivaled scenic and geological values," to the "unique" situation of its "rural residents dependent on subsistence uses," to "the need for development and use of Arctic resources with appropriate recognition and consideration given to the unique nature of the Arctic environment." 16 U.S.C. §§3101(b), 3111(2), 3147(b)(5).

ANILCA itself accordingly carves out numerous Alaska-specific exceptions to the Park Service's general authority over federally managed preservation areas. For example, ANILCA requires the Secretary of the Interior to permit "the exercise of valid commercial fishing rights or privileges" within the National Wildlife Refuge System in Alaska, including the use of "campsites, cabins, motorized vehicles, and aircraft landings directly incident to the exercise of such rights or privileges," with certain exceptions. 94 Stat. 2393. ANILCA also requires the Secretary to "permit on the public lands appropriate use for subsistence purposes of snowmobiles, motorboats, and other means of surface transportation traditionally employed for such purposes by local residents, subject to reasonable regulation." 16 U.S.C. §3121(b). And it provides that National Preserves "in Alaska shall be administered and managed as a unit of the National Park System in the same manner as a national park *except* as otherwise provided in this Act and *except* that the taking of fish and wildlife for sport purposes and subsistence uses, and trapping shall be allowed" pursuant to applicable law. §3201 (emphasis added).

Many similar examples are woven throughout ANILCA. See, *e.g.*, 94 Stat. 2393 (Secretary must administer wildlife refuge "so as to not impede the passage of navigation and access by boat on the Yukon and Kuskokwim Rivers," subject to reasonable regulation); *id.*, at 2388 (Secretary must allow reindeer grazing uses in certain areas, including construction of necessary facilities); 16 U.S.C. §3203(a) (Alaska-specific rules for wilderness management apply "in recognition of the unique conditions in Alaska"); §3170(a) (Secretary must permit reasonable use of snowmachines, motorboats, and airplanes within conservation system units "for travel to and from villages and homesites").

All those Alaska-specific provisions reflect the simple truth that Alaska is often the exception, not the rule. Yet the reading below would prevent the Park Service from recognizing Alaska's unique conditions. Under that reading, the Park Service could regulate "non-public" lands in Alaska only through rules applicable *outside* Alaska as well. Thus, for example, if the Park Service elected to allow hovercraft during hunting season in Alaska--in a departure from its nationwide rule--the more relaxed regulation would apply only to the "public" land within the boundaries of the unit. Hovercraft would still be banned from the "non-public" land, even during hunting season. Whatever the reach of the Park Service's authority under ANILCA, we cannot conclude that Section 103(c) adopted such a topsy-turvy approach.

Moreover, it is clear that Section 103(c) draws a distinction between "public" and "non-public" lands within the boundaries of conservation system units in Alaska. See §3103(c) ("Only those lands within the boundaries of any conservation system unit which are public lands . . . shall be deemed to be included as a portion of such unit"); *ibid.* (No lands "conveyed to the State, to any Native Corporation, or to any private party shall be subject to the regulations applicable solely to public lands within such units"). And yet, according to the court below, if the Park Service wanted to differentiate between that "public" and "non-public" land in an Alaska-specific way, it would have to regulate the "non-public" land pursuant to rules applicable outside Alaska, and the "public" land pursuant to Alaska-specific provisions. Assuming the Park Service has authority over "non-public" land in Alaska (an issue we do not decide), that strikes us as an implausible reading of the statute.

Looking at ANILCA both as a whole and with respect to Section 103(c), the Act contemplates the possibility that all the land within the boundaries of conservation system units in Alaska may be treated differently from federally managed preservation areas across the country, and that "non-public" lands within the boundaries of those units may be treated differently from "public" lands within the unit. Under the Ninth Circuit's reading of Section 103(c), however, the former is not an option, and the latter would require contorted and counterintuitive measures.

We therefore reject the interpretation of Section 103(c) adopted by the court below. That reading of the statute was the sole basis for the disposition of this case by the Court of Appeals. We accordingly vacate the judgment of that court and remand for further proceedings.

We do not reach the remainder of the parties' arguments. In particular, we do not decide whether the Nation River qualifies as "public land" for purposes of ANILCA. Sturgeon claims that it does not; the Park Service that it does. The parties' arguments in this respect touch on vital issues of state sovereignty, on the one hand, and federal authority, on the other. We find that in this case those issues should be addressed by the lower courts in the first instance.

Given this determination, we also do not decide whether the Park Service has authority under Section 100751(b) to regulate Sturgeon's activities on the Nation River, even if the river is not "public" land, or whether--as Sturgeon argues--any such authority is limited by ANILCA. Finally, we do not consider the Park Service's alternative argument that it has authority under ANILCA over both "public" and "non-public" lands within the boundaries of conservation system units in Alaska, to the extent a regulation is written to apply specifically to both types of land. We leave those arguments to the lower courts for consideration as necessary.

The judgment of the Court of Appeals for the Ninth Circuit is vacated, and the case is remanded for further proceedings consistent with this opinion.

It is so ordered.

ENDREW F., a minor, by and through his
parents and next friends,
JOSEPH F. AND JENNIFER F., Petitioner
v.
DOUGLAS COUNTY
SCHOOL DISTRICT RE-1.

15-827.
SUPREME COURT
OF THE UNITED STATES

137 S. Ct. 988

January 11, 2017, Argued
March 22, 2017, Decided

ON WRIT OF CERTIORARI TO THE UNITED STATES COURT OF APPEALS FOR THE TENTH CIRCUIT

Chief Justice Roberts delivered the opinion of the Court.

Thirty-five years ago, this Court held that the Individuals with Disabilities Education Act establishes a substantive right to a "free appropriate public education" for certain children with disabilities. *Board of Ed. of Hendrick Hudson Central School Dist., Westchester Cty.* v. *Rowley*, 458 U. S. 176, 102 S. Ct. 3034, 73 L. Ed. 2d 690 (1982). We declined, however, to endorse any one standard for determining "when handicapped children are receiving sufficient educational benefits to satisfy the requirements of the Act." *Id.*, at 202, 102 S. Ct. 3034, 73 L. Ed. 2d 690. That "more difficult problem" is before us today. *Ibid.*

I

A

The Individuals with Disabilities Education Act (IDEA or Act) offers States federal funds to assist in educating children with disabilities. 84 Stat. 175, as amended, 20 U. S. C. §1400 *et seq.*; see *Arlington Central School Dist. Bd. of Ed.* v. *Murphy*, 548 U. S. 291, 295, 126 S. Ct. 2455, 165 L. Ed. 2d 526 (2006). In exchange for the funds, a State pledges to comply with a number of statutory conditions. Among them, the State must provide a free appropriate public education--a FAPE, for short--to all eligible children. §1412(a)(1).

A FAPE, as the Act defines it, includes both "special education" and "related services." §1401(9). "Special education" is "specially designed instruction . . . to meet the unique needs of a child with a disability"; "related services" are the support services "required to assist a child . . . to benefit from" that instruction. §§1401(26), (29). A State covered by the IDEA must provide a disabled child with such special education and related services "in conformity with the [child's] individualized education program," or IEP. §1401(9)(D).

The IEP is "the centerpiece of the statute's education delivery system for disabled children." *Honig* v. *Doe*, 484 U. S. 305, 311, 108 S. Ct. 592, 98 L. Ed. 2d 686 (1988). A comprehensive plan prepared by a child's "IEP Team" (which includes teachers, school officials, and the child's parents), an IEP must be drafted in compliance with a detailed set of procedures. §1414(d)(1)(B) (internal quotation marks omitted). These procedures emphasize collaboration among parents and educators and require careful consideration of the child's individual circumstances. §1414. The IEP is the means by which special education and related services are "tailored to the unique needs" of a particular child. *Rowley*, 458 U. S., at 181, 102 S. Ct. 3034, 73 L. Ed. 2d 690.

The IDEA requires that every IEP include "a statement of the child's present levels of academic achievement and functional performance," describe "how the child's disability affects the child's involvement and progress in the general education curriculum," and set out "measurable annual goals, including academic and functional goals," along with a "description of how the child's progress toward meeting" those goals will be gauged. §§1414(d)(1)(A)(i)(I)-(III). The IEP must also describe the "special education and related services . . . that will be provided" so that the child may "advance appropriately toward attaining the annual goals" and, when possible, "be involved in and make progress in the general education curriculum." §1414(d)(1)(A)(i)(IV).

Parents and educators often agree about what a child's IEP should contain. But not always. When disagreement arises, parents may turn to dispute resolution procedures established by the IDEA. The parties may resolve their differences informally, through a "[p]reliminary meeting," or, somewhat more formally, through mediation. §§1415(e), (f)(1)(B)(i). If these measures fail to produce accord, the parties may proceed to what the Act calls a "due process hearing" before a state or local educational agency. §§1415(f)(1)(A), (g). And at the conclusion of the administrative process, the losing party may seek redress in state or federal court. §1415(i)(2)(A).

B

This Court first addressed the FAPE requirement in *Rowley*.[1] Plaintiff Amy Rowley was a first grader with impaired hearing. Her school district offered an

IEP under which Amy would receive instruction in the regular classroom and spend time each week with a special tutor and a speech therapist. The district proposed that Amy's classroom teacher speak into a wireless transmitter and that Amy use an FM hearing aid designed to amplify her teacher's words; the district offered to supply both components of this system. But Amy's parents argued that the IEP should go further and provide a sign-language interpreter in all of her classes. Contending that the school district's refusal to furnish an interpreter denied Amy a FAPE, Amy's parents initiated administrative proceedings, then filed a lawsuit under the Act. *Rowley*, 458 U. S., at 184-185, 102 S. Ct. 3034, 73 L. Ed. 2d 690.

> 1 The requirement was initially set out in the Education of the Handicapped Act, which was later amended and renamed the IDEA. See Pub. L. 101-476, §901(a), 104 Stat. 1141. For simplicity's sake--and to avoid "acronym overload"--we use the latter title throughout this opinion. *Fry* v. *Napoleon Community Schools*, 580 U. S. _, _, n. 1, 137 S. Ct. 743, 197 L. Ed. 2d 46, 56 (2017).

The District Court agreed that Amy had been denied a FAPE. The court acknowledged that Amy was making excellent progress in school: She was "perform[ing] better than the average child in her class" and "advancing easily from grade to grade." *Id.*, at 185, 102 S. Ct. 3034, 73 L. Ed. 2d 690 (internal quotation marks omitted). At the same time, Amy "under[stood] considerably less of what goes on in class than she could if she were not deaf." *Ibid.* (internal quotation marks omitted). Concluding that "it has been left entirely to the courts and the hearings officers to give content to the requirement of an 'appropriate education,'" 483 F. Supp. 528, 533 (SDNY 1980), the District Court ruled that Amy's education was not "appropriate" unless it provided her "an opportunity to achieve [her] full potential commensurate with the opportunity provided to other children." *Rowley*, 458 U. S., at 185-186, 102 S. Ct. 3034, 73 L. Ed. 2d 690 (internal quotation marks omitted). The Second Circuit agreed with this analysis and affirmed.

In this Court, the parties advanced starkly different understandings of the FAPE requirement. Amy's parents defended the approach of the lower courts, arguing that the school district was required to provide instruction and services that would provide Amy an "equal educational opportunity" relative to children without disabilities. *Id.*, at 198, 102 S. Ct. 3034, 73 L. Ed. 2d 690 (internal quotation marks omitted). The school district, for its part, contended that the IDEA "did not create substantive individual rights"; the FAPE provision was instead merely aspirational. Brief for Petitioners in *Rowley*, O. T. 1981, No. 80-1002, pp. 28, 41.

Neither position carried the day. On the one hand, this Court rejected the view that the IDEA gives "courts *carte blanche* to impose upon the States whatever burden their various judgments indicate should be imposed." *Rowley*, 458 U. S., at 190, n. 11, 102 S. Ct. 3034, 73 L. Ed. 2d 690. After all, the statutory phrase "free appropriate public education" was expressly defined in the Act, even if the definition "tend[ed] toward the cryptic rather than the comprehensive." *Id.*, at 188, 102 S. Ct. 3034, 73 L. Ed. 2d 690. This Court went on to reject the "equal opportunity" standard adopted by the lower courts, concluding that "free appropriate public education" was a phrase "too complex to be captured by the word 'equal' whether one is speaking of opportunities or services." *Id.*, at 199, 102 S. Ct. 3034, 73 L. Ed. 2d 690. The Court also viewed the standard as "entirely unworkable," apt to require "impossible measurements and comparisons" that courts were ill suited to make. *Id.*, at 198, 102 S. Ct. 3034, 73 L. Ed. 2d 690.

On the other hand, the Court also rejected the school district's argument that the FAPE requirement was actually no requirement at all. *Id.*, at 200, 102 S. Ct. 3034, 73 L. Ed. 2d 690. Instead, the Court carefully charted a middle path. Even though "Congress was rather sketchy in establishing substantive requirements" under the Act, *id.*, at 206, 102 S. Ct. 3034, 73 L. Ed. 2d 690, the Court nonetheless made clear that the Act guarantees a substantively adequate program of education to all eligible children, *id.*, at 200-202, 207, 102 S. Ct. 3034, 73 L. Ed. 2d 690; see *id.*, at 193, n. 15, 102 S. Ct. 3034, 73 L. Ed. 2d 690 (describing the "substantive standard . . . implicit in the Act"). We explained that this requirement is satisfied, and a child has received a FAPE, if the child's IEP sets out an educational program that is "reasonably calculated to enable the child to receive educational benefits." *Id.*, at 207, 102 S. Ct. 3034, 73 L. Ed. 2d 690. For children receiving instruction in the regular classroom, this would generally require an IEP "reasonably calculated to enable the child to achieve passing marks and advance from grade to grade." *Id.*, at 204, 102 S. Ct. 3034, 73 L. Ed. 2d 690; see also *id.*, at 203, n. 25, 102 S. Ct. 3034, 73 L. Ed. 2d 690.

In view of Amy Rowley's excellent progress and the "substantial" suite of specialized instruction and services offered in her IEP, we concluded that her program satisfied the FAPE requirement. *Id.*, at 202, 102 S. Ct. 3034, 73 L. Ed. 2d 690. But we went no further. Instead, we expressly "confine[d] our analysis" to the facts of the case before us. *Ibid.* Observing that the Act requires States to "educate a wide spectrum" of children with disabilities and that "the benefits obtainable by children at one end of the spectrum will differ dramatically from those obtainable by children at the other end," we declined "to establish any one test for determining the adequacy of educational benefits conferred upon all children covered by the Act." *Ibid.*

C

Petitioner Endrew F. was diagnosed with autism at age two. Autism is a neurodevelopmental disorder generally marked by impaired social and communicative skills, "engagement in repetitive activities and stereotyped movements, resistance to environmental change or change in daily routines, and unusual responses to sensory experiences." 34 CFR §300.8(c)(1)(i) (2016); see Brief for Petitioner 8. A child with autism qualifies as a "[c]hild with a disability" under the IDEA, and Colorado (where Endrew resides) accepts IDEA funding. §1401(3)(A). Endrew is therefore entitled to the benefits of the Act, including a FAPE provided by the State.

Endrew attended school in respondent Douglas County School District from preschool through fourth grade. Each year, his IEP Team drafted an IEP addressed to his educational and functional needs. By Endrew's fourth grade year, however, his parents had become dissatisfied with his progress. Although Endrew displayed a number of strengths--his teachers described him as a humorous child with a "sweet disposition" who "show[ed] concern[ ] for friends"--he still "exhibited multiple behaviors that inhibited his ability to access learning in the classroom." Supp. App. 182a; 798 F. 3d 1329, 1336 (CA10 2015). Endrew would scream in class, climb over furniture and other students, and occasionally run away from school. *Id.*, at 1336. He was afflicted by severe fears of commonplace things like flies, spills, and public restrooms. As Endrew's parents saw it, his academic and functional progress had essentially stalled: Endrew's IEPs largely carried over the same basic goals and objectives from one year to the next, indicating that he was failing to make meaningful progress toward his aims. His parents believed that only a thorough overhaul of the school district's approach to Endrew's behavioral problems could reverse the trend. But in April 2010, the school district presented Endrew's parents with a proposed fifth grade IEP that was, in their view, pretty much the same as his past ones. So his parents removed Endrew from public school and enrolled him at Firefly Autism House, a private school that specializes in educating children with autism.

Endrew did much better at Firefly. The school developed a "behavioral intervention plan" that identified Endrew's most problematic behaviors and set out particular strategies for addressing them. See Supp. App. 198a-201a. Firefly also added heft to Endrew's academic goals. Within months, Endrew's behavior improved significantly, permitting him to make a degree of academic progress that had eluded him in public school.

In November 2010, some six months after Endrew started classes at Firefly, his parents again met with representatives of the Douglas County School District. The district presented a new IEP. Endrew's parents considered the IEP no more adequate than the one proposed in April, and rejected it. They were particularly concerned that the stated plan for addressing Endrew's behavior did not differ meaningfully from the plan in his fourth grade IEP, despite the fact that his experience at Firefly suggested that he would benefit from a different approach.

In February 2012, Endrew's parents filed a complaint with the Colorado Department of Education seeking reimbursement for Endrew's tuition at Firefly. To qualify for such relief, they were required to show that the school district had not provided Endrew a FAPE in a timely manner prior to his enrollment at the private school. See §1412(a)(10)(C)(ii). Endrew's parents contended that the final IEP proposed by the school district was not "reasonably calculated to enable [Endrew] to receive educational benefits" and that Endrew had therefore been denied a FAPE. *Rowley*, 458 U. S., at 207, 102 S. Ct. 3034, 73 L. Ed. 2d 690. An Administrative Law Judge (ALJ) disagreed and denied relief.

Endrew's parents sought review in Federal District Court. Giving "due weight" to the decision of the ALJ, the District Court affirmed. 2014 U.S. Dist. LEXIS 128659, 2014 WL 4548439, *5 (D Colo., Sept. 15, 2014) (quoting *Rowley*, 458 U. S., at 206, 102 S. Ct. 3034, 73 L. Ed. 2d 690). The court acknowledged that Endrew's performance under past IEPs "did not reveal immense educational growth." 2014 U.S. Dist. LEXIS 128659, 2014 WL 4548439, at *9. But it concluded that annual modifications to Endrew's IEP objectives were "sufficient to show a pattern of, at the least, minimal progress." *Ibid.* Because Endrew's previous IEPs had enabled him to make this sort of progress, the court reasoned, his latest, similar IEP was reasonably calculated to do the same thing. In the court's view, that was all *Rowley* demanded. 2014 U.S. Dist. LEXIS 128659, 2014 WL 4548439, at *9.

The Tenth Circuit affirmed. The Court of Appeals recited language from *Rowley* stating that the instruction and services furnished to children with disabilities must be calculated to confer "*some* educational benefit." 798 F. 3d, at 1338 (quoting *Rowley*, 458 U. S., at 200, 102 S. Ct. 3034, 73 L. Ed. 2d 690; emphasis added by Tenth Circuit). The court noted that it had long interpreted this language to mean that a child's IEP is adequate as long as it is calculated to confer an "educational benefit [that is] merely ... more than *de minimis*." 798 F. 3d, at 1338 (internal quotation marks omitted). Applying this standard, the Tenth Circuit held that Endrew's IEP had been "reasonably calculated to enable [him] to make *some* progress." *Id.*, at 1342 (internal quotation marks omitted). Accordingly, he had not been denied a FAPE.

We granted certiorari. 579 U. S. _, 137 S. Ct. 29, 195 L. Ed. 2d 901(2016).

II

A

The Court in *Rowley* declined "to establish any one test for determining the adequacy of educational benefits conferred upon all children covered by the Act." 458 U. S., at 202, 102 S. Ct. 3034, 73 L. Ed. 2d 690. The school district, however, contends that *Rowley* nonetheless established that "an IEP need not promise any particular *level* of benefit," so long as it is "' reasonably calculated' to provide *some* benefit, as opposed to *none*." Brief for Respondent 15.

The district relies on several passages from *Rowley* to make its case. It points to our observation that "any substantive standard prescribing the level of education to be accorded" children with disabilities was "[n]oticeably absent from the language of the statute." 458 U. S., at 189, 102 S. Ct. 3034, 73 L. Ed. 2d 690; see Brief for Respondent 14. The district also emphasizes the Court's statement that the Act requires States to provide access to instruction "sufficient to confer *some* educational benefit," reasoning that any benefit, however minimal, satisfies this mandate. Brief for Respondent 15 (quoting *Rowley*, 458 U. S., at 200, 102 S. Ct. 3034, 73 L. Ed. 2d 690). Finally, the district urges that the Court conclusively adopted a "some educational benefit" standard when it wrote that "the intent of the Act was more to open the door of public education to handicapped children . . . than to guarantee any particular level of education." *Id.*, at 192, 102 S. Ct. 3034, 73 L. Ed. 2d 690; see Brief for Respondent 14.

These statements in isolation do support the school district's argument. But the district makes too much of them. Our statement that the face of the IDEA imposed no explicit substantive standard must be evaluated alongside our statement that a substantive standard was "implicit in the Act." *Rowley*, 458 U. S., at 193, n. 15, 102 S. Ct. 3034, 73 L. Ed. 2d 690. Similarly, we find little significance in the Court's language concerning the requirement that States provide instruction calculated to "confer some educational benefit." *Id.*, at 200, 102 S. Ct. 3034, 73 L. Ed. 2d 690. The Court had no need to say anything more particular, since the case before it involved a child whose progress plainly demonstrated that her IEP was designed to deliver more than adequate educational benefits. See *id.*, at 202, 209-210, 102 S. Ct. 3034, 73 L. Ed. 2d 690. The Court's principal concern was to correct what it viewed as the surprising rulings below: that the IDEA effectively empowers judges to elaborate a federal common law of public education, and that a child performing *better* than most in her class had been denied a FAPE. The Court was not concerned with precisely articulating a governing standard for closer cases. See *id.*, at 202, 102 S. Ct. 3034, 73 L. Ed. 2d 690. And the statement that the Act did not "guarantee any particular level of education" simply reflects the unobjectionable proposition that the IDEA cannot and does not promise "any particular [educational] outcome." *Id.*, at 192, 102 S. Ct. 3034, 73 L. Ed. 2d 690 (internal quotation marks omitted). No law could do that--for any child.

More important, the school district's reading of these isolated statements runs headlong into several points on which *Rowley* is crystal clear. For instance--just after saying that the Act requires instruction that is "sufficient to confer some educational benefit"--we noted that "[t]he determination of when handicapped children are receiving *sufficient* educational benefits . . . presents a . . . difficult problem." *Id.*, at 200, 202, 102 S. Ct. 3034, 73 L. Ed. 2d 690 (emphasis added). And then we expressly declined "to establish any one test for determining the *adequacy* of educational benefits" under the Act. *Id.*, at 202, 102 S. Ct. 3034, 73 L. Ed. 2d 690 (emphasis added). It would not have been "difficult" for us to say when educational benefits are sufficient if we had just said that *any* educational benefit was enough. And it would have been strange to refuse to set out a test for the adequacy of educational benefits if we had just done exactly that. We cannot accept the school district's reading of *Rowley*.

B

While *Rowley* declined to articulate an overarching standard to evaluate the adequacy of the education provided under the Act, the decision and the statutory language point to a general approach: To meet its substantive obligation under the IDEA, a school must offer an IEP reasonably calculated to enable a child to make progress appropriate in light of the child's circumstances.

The "reasonably calculated" qualification reflects a recognition that crafting an appropriate program of education requires a prospective judgment by school officials. *Id.*, at 207, 102 S. Ct. 3034, 73 L. Ed. 2d 690. The Act contemplates that this fact-intensive exercise will be informed not only by the expertise of school officials, but also by the input of the child's parents or guardians. *Id.*, at 208-209, 102 S. Ct. 3034, 73 L. Ed. 2d 690. Any review of an IEP must appreciate that the question is whether the IEP is *reasonable*, not whether the court regards it as ideal. *Id.*, at 206-207, 102 S. Ct. 3034, 73 L. Ed. 2d 690.

The IEP must aim to enable the child to make progress. After all, the essential function of an IEP is to set out a plan for pursuing academic and functional advancement. See §§1414(d)(1)(A)(i)(I)-(IV). This reflects the broad purpose of the IDEA, an "ambitious" piece of legislation enacted "in response to Congress' perception that a majority of handicapped children in the United States 'were either totally excluded from schools or [were] sitting idly in regular classrooms awaiting the time when they were old enough to "drop out."'" *Rowley*, 458 U. S., at 179, 102 S. Ct. 3034, 73 L. Ed. 2d 690 (quoting H. R. Rep. No. 94-332, p. 2 (1975)). A substantive standard not focused on student progress would do little to remedy the pervasive and tragic academic stagnation that prompted Congress to act.

That the progress contemplated by the IEP must be appropriate in light of the child's circumstances should come as no surprise. A focus on the particular child is at the core of the IDEA. The instruction offered must be "*specially* designed" to meet a child's "*unique* needs" through an "[*i*]*ndividualized* education program." §§1401(29), (14) (emphasis added). An IEP is not a form document. It is constructed only after careful consideration of the child's present levels of achievement, disability, and potential for growth. §§1414(d)(1)(A)(i)(I)-(IV), (d)(3)(A)(i)-(iv). As we observed in *Rowley*, the IDEA "requires participating States to educate a wide spectrum of handicapped children," and "the benefits obtainable by children at one end of the spectrum will differ dramatically from those obtainable by children at the other end, with infinite variations in between." 458 U. S., at 202, 102 S. Ct. 3034, 73 L. Ed. 2d 690.

Rowley sheds light on what appropriate progress will look like in many cases. There, the Court recognized that the IDEA requires that children with disabilities receive education in the regular classroom "whenever possible." *Ibid.* (citing §1412(a)(5)). When this preference is met, "the system itself monitors the educational progress of the child." *Id.*, at 202-203, 102 S. Ct. 3034, 73 L. Ed. 2d 690. "Regular examinations are administered, grades are awarded, and yearly advancement to higher grade levels is permitted for those children who attain an adequate knowledge of the course material." *Id.*, at 203, 102 S. Ct. 3034, 73 L. Ed. 2d 690. Progress through this system is what our society generally means by an "education." And access to an "education" is what the IDEA promises. *Ibid.* Accordingly, for a child fully integrated in the regular classroom, an IEP typically should, as *Rowley* put it, be "reasonably calculated to enable the child to achieve passing marks and advance from grade to grade." *Id.*, at 203-204, 102 S. Ct. 3034, 73 L. Ed. 2d 690.

This guidance is grounded in the statutory definition of a FAPE. One of the components of a FAPE is "special education," defined as "specially designed instruction . . . to meet the unique needs of a child with a disability." §§1401(9), (29). In determining what it means to "meet the unique needs" of a child with a disability, the provisions governing the IEP development process are a natural source of guidance: It is through the IEP that "[t]he 'free appropriate public education' required by the Act is tailored to the unique needs of" a particular child. *Id.*, at 181, 102 S. Ct. 3034, 73 L. Ed. 2d 690.

The IEP provisions reflect *Rowley*'s expectation that, for most children, a FAPE will involve integration in the regular classroom and individualized special education calculated to achieve advancement from grade to grade. Every IEP begins by describing a child's present level of achievement, including explaining "how the child's disability affects the child's involvement and progress in the general education curriculum." §1414(d)(1)(A)(i)(I)(aa). It then sets out "a statement of measurable annual goals . . . designed to . . . enable the child to be involved in and make progress in the general education curriculum," along with a description of specialized instruction and services that the child will receive. §§1414(d)(1)(A)(i)(II), (IV). The instruction and services must likewise be provided with an eye toward "progress in the general education curriculum." §1414(d)(1)(A)(i)(IV)(bb). Similar IEP requirements have been in place since the time the States began accepting funding under the IDEA.

The school district protests that these provisions impose only procedural requirements--a checklist of items the IEP must address--not a substantive standard enforceable in court. Tr. of Oral Arg. 50-51. But the procedures are there for a reason, and their focus provides insight into what it means, for purposes of the FAPE definition, to "meet the unique needs" of a child with a disability. §§1401(9), (29). When a child is fully integrated in the regular classroom, as the Act prefers, what that typically means is providing a level of instruction reasonably calculated to permit advancement through the general curriculum. 2

> 2 This guidance should not be interpreted as an inflexible rule. We declined to hold in *Rowley*, and do not hold today, that "every handicapped child who is advancing from grade to grade . . . is automatically receiving a [FAPE]." *Board of Ed. of Hendrick Hudson Central School Dist., Westchester Cty.* v. *Rowley*, 458 U. S. 176, 203, n. 25, 102 S. Ct. 3034, 73 L. Ed. 2d 690 (1982).

Rowley had no need to provide concrete guidance with respect to a child who is not fully integrated in the regular classroom and not able to achieve on grade level. That case concerned a young girl who was progressing smoothly through the regular curriculum. If that is not a reasonable prospect for a child, his IEP need not aim for grade-level advancement. But his educational program must be appropriately ambitious in light of his circumstances, just as advancement from grade to grade is appropriately ambitious for most children in the regular classroom. The goals may differ, but every child should have the chance to meet challenging objectives.

Of course this describes a general standard, not a formula. But whatever else can be said about it, this standard is markedly more demanding than the "merely more than *de minimis*" test applied by the Tenth Circuit. It cannot be the case that the Act typically aims for grade-level advancement for children with disabilities who can be educated in the regular classroom, but is satisfied with barely more than *de minimis* progress for those who cannot.

When all is said and done, a student offered an educational program providing "merely more than *de minimis*" progress from year to year can hardly be said to have been offered an education at all. For children with disabilities, receiving instruction that aims so low would be tantamount to "sitting idly . . . awaiting the time when they were old enough to 'drop out.'" *Rowley*, 458 U. S., at 179, 102 S. Ct. 3034, 73 L. Ed. 2d 690 (some internal quotation marks omitted). The IDEA demands more. It requires an educational program reasonably calculated to enable a child to make progress appropriate in light of the child's circumstances.

C

Endrew's parents argue that the Act goes even further. In their view, a FAPE is "an education that aims to provide a child with a disability opportunities to achieve academic success, attain self-sufficiency, and contribute to society that are substantially equal to the opportunities afforded children without disabilities." Brief for Petitioner 40.

This standard is strikingly similar to the one the lower courts adopted in *Rowley*, and it is virtually identical to the formulation advanced by Justice Blackmun in his separate writing in that case. See 458 U. S., at 185-186, 102 S. Ct. 3034, 73 L. Ed. 2d 690; *id.*, at 211, 102 S. Ct. 3034, 73 L. Ed. 2d 690 (opinion concurring in judgment) ("[T]he question is whether Amy's program . . . offered her an opportunity to understand and participate in the classroom that was substantially equal to that given her non-handicapped classmates"). But the majority rejected any such standard in clear terms. *Id.*, at 198, 102 S. Ct. 3034, 73 L. Ed. 2d 690 ("The requirement that States provide 'equal' educational opportunities would . . . seem to present an entirely unworkable standard requiring impossible measurements and comparisons"). Mindful that Congress (despite several intervening amendments to the IDEA) has not materially changed the statutory definition of a FAPE since *Rowley* was decided, we decline to interpret the FAPE provision in a manner so plainly at odds with the Court's analysis in that case. Compare §1401(18) (1976 ed.) with §1401(9) (2012 ed.).

D

We will not attempt to elaborate on what "appropriate" progress will look like from case to case. It is in the nature of the Act and the standard we adopt to resist such an effort: The adequacy of a given IEP turns on the unique circumstances of the child for whom it was created. This absence of a bright-line rule, however, should not be mistaken for "an invitation to the courts to substitute their own notions of sound educational policy for those of the school authorities which they review." *Rowley*, 458 U. S., at 206, 102 S. Ct. 3034, 73 L. Ed. 2d 690.

At the same time, deference is based on the application of expertise and the exercise of judgment by school authorities. The Act vests these officials with responsibility for decisions of critical importance to the life of a disabled child. The nature of the IEP process, from the initial consultation through state administrative proceedings, ensures that parents and school representatives will fully air their respective opinions on the degree of progress a child's IEP should pursue. See §§1414, 1415; *id.*, at 208-209, 102 S. Ct. 3034, 73 L. Ed. 2d 690. By the time any dispute reaches court, school authorities will have had a complete opportunity to bring their expertise and judgment to bear on areas of disagreement. A reviewing court may fairly expect those authorities to be able to offer a cogent and responsive explanation for their decisions that shows the IEP is reasonably calculated to enable the child to make progress appropriate in light of his circumstances.

The judgment of the United States Court of Appeals for the Tenth Circuit is vacated, and the case is remanded for further proceedings consistent with this opinion.

It is so ordered.

LEVON DEAN, Jr., Petitioner
v.
UNITED STATES

15-9260
SUPREME COURT
OF THE UNITED STATES

137 S. Ct. 1170

February 28, 2017, Argued
April 3, 2017, Decided

ON WRIT OF CERTIORARI TO THE UNITED STATES COURT OF APPEALS FOR THE EIGHTH CIRCUIT

Chief Justice Roberts delivered the opinion of the Court.

Congress has made it a separate offense to use or possess a firearm in connection with a violent or drug trafficking crime. 18 U.S.C. §924(c). That separate firearm offense carries a mandatory minimum sentence of five years for the first conviction and 25 years for a second. Those sentences must be in addition to and consecutive to the sentence for the underlying predicate offense. The question presented is whether, in calculating the sentence for the predicate offense, a judge must ignore the fact that the defendant will serve the mandatory minimums imposed under §924(c).

I

Levon Dean, Jr., and his brother robbed a methamphetamine dealer in a Sioux City motel room. Less than two weeks later, they robbed another drug dealer at his home. During each robbery, Dean's brother threatened the victim with a modified semiautomatic rifle, later using that rifle to club the victim on the head. Dean, meanwhile, ransacked the area for drugs, money, and other valuables.

A federal grand jury returned a multicount indictment charging Dean and his brother with a host of crimes related to the two robberies. Following a joint trial, a jury convicted Dean of one count of conspiracy to commit robbery, two counts of robbery, and one count of possessing a firearm as a convicted felon. He was also convicted of two counts of possessing and aiding and abetting the possession of a firearm in furtherance of a crime of violence, in violation of 18 U.S.C. §§2 and 924(c). Section 924(c) criminalizes using or carrying a firearm during and in relation to a crime of violence or drug trafficking crime, or possessing a firearm in furtherance of such an underlying crime. There is no dispute that Dean's two robbery convictions qualified as predicate crimes of violence for purposes of §924(c).

Section 924(c) does more than create a distinct offense. It also mandates a distinct penalty, one that must be imposed "*in addition to* the punishment provided for [the predicate] crime of violence or drug trafficking crime." §924(c)(1)(A) (emphasis added). A first-time offender under §924(c) receives a five-year mandatory minimum. A "second or subsequent conviction" under §924(c) carries an additional 25-year mandatory minimum. §§924(c)(1)(A)(i), (C)(i).

A sentence imposed under §924(c) must run consecutively to "any other term of imprisonment imposed on the person," including any sentence for the predicate crime "during which the firearm was used, carried, or possessed." §924(c)(1)(D)(ii). For Dean, this meant a 30-year mandatory minimum, to be served after and in addition to any sentence he received for his other counts of conviction.

At sentencing Dean did not dispute that each of his four other counts resulted in a sentencing range of 84-105 months under the Sentencing Guidelines. He argued, however, that the court should consider his lengthy mandatory minimum sentences when calculating the sentences for his other counts, and impose concurrent one-day sentences for those counts.

Finding that Dean was "clearly the follower" and that he lacked "any significant history of any violence," the District Judge agreed that 30 years plus one day was "more than sufficient for a sentence in this case." App. 26. Yet the judge understood §924(c) to preclude such a sentence. In his view, he was required to disregard Dean's 30-year mandatory minimum when determining the appropriate sentences for Dean's other counts of conviction. Viewed on their own--and not as part of a combined package--those counts plainly warranted sentences longer than one day. In the end, the judge still granted a significant downward variance from the 84-105 month Guidelines range. Dean received concurrent sentences of 40 months for each non-§924(c) conviction, which, when added to his 360-month mandatory minimum, yielded a total sentence of 400 months. Dean appealed.

Before the Eighth Circuit, Dean argued that the District Court had erred in concluding that it could not vary from the Guidelines range based on the mandatory minimum sentences he would receive under §924(c). The Court of Appeals disagreed, ruling that Dean's argument was foreclosed by Circuit precedent and that his sentence was otherwise substantively reasonable. 810 F. 3d 521 (2015). We granted certiorari. 580 U.S. _, 137 S. Ct. 368, 196 L. Ed. 2d 283 (2016).

II

Sentencing courts have long enjoyed discretion in the sort of information they may consider when setting an appropriate sentence. *Pepper* v. *United States*, 562 U.S. 476, 487-489, 131 S. Ct. 1229, 179 L. Ed. 2d 196 (2011). This durable tradition remains, even as federal laws have required sentencing courts to evaluate certain factors when exercising their discretion. *Ibid.*

A

Section 3553(a) of Title 18 specifies the factors courts are to consider in imposing a sentence. The list of factors is preceded by what is known as the parsimony principle, a broad command that instructs courts to "impose a sentence sufficient, but not greater than necessary, to comply with" the four identified purposes of sentencing: just punishment, deterrence, protection of the public, and rehabilitation. *Ibid.* A sentencing court is then directed to take into account "the nature and circumstances of the offense and the history and characteristics of the defendant," as well as "the need for the sentence imposed" to serve the four overarching aims of sentencing. §§3553(a)(1), (2)(A)-(D); see *Gall* v. *United States*, 552 U.S. 38, 50, n. 6, 128 S. Ct. 586, 169 L. Ed. 2d 445 (2007). The court must also consider the pertinent guidelines and policies adopted by the Sentencing Commission. §§3553(a)(4), (5); see *id.*, at 50, n. 6, 128 S. Ct. 586, 169 L. Ed. 2d 445.

The §3553(a) factors are used to set both the length of separate prison terms and an aggregate prison term comprising separate sentences for multiple counts of conviction. Under §3582 a court, "in determining whether to impose a term of imprisonment, and, if a term of imprisonment is to be imposed, in determining the length of the term, shall consider the factors set forth in section 3553(a)." §3582(a). And §3584 provides: "[I]n determining whether the terms imposed are to be ordered to run concurrently or consecutively, [the court] shall consider, as to each offense for which a term of imprisonment is being imposed, the factors set forth in section 3553(a)." §3584(b).

As a general matter, the foregoing provisions permit a court imposing a sentence on one count of conviction to consider sentences imposed on other counts. Take the directive that a court assess "the need for the sentence imposed . . . to protect the public from further crimes of the defendant." §3553(a)(2)(C). Dean committed the two robberies at issue here when he was 23 years old. That he will not be released from prison until well after his fiftieth birthday because of the §924(c) convictions surely bears on whether-- in connection with his predicate crimes--still more incarceration is necessary to protect the public. Likewise, in considering "the need for the sentence imposed . . . to afford adequate deterrence," §3553(a)(2)(B), the District Court could not reasonably ignore the deterrent effect of Dean's 30-year mandatory minimum.

According to the Government, this is not how sentencing is meant to work. Rather, district courts should calculate the appropriate term of imprisonment for each individual offense. That determination, insists the Government, disregards whatever sentences the defendant may also face on other counts. Not until deciding whether to run sentences consecutively or concurrently-- *i.e.*, not until applying §3584--should a district court consider the effect of those other sentences. Brief for United States 21-26.

Nothing in the law requires such an approach. The Government states that the §3553(a) factors are "normally relevant in determining the total length of imprisonment" under §3584. *Id.*, at 28. No doubt they are. But there is no reason they may not also be considered at the front end, when determining a prison sentence for each individual offense in a multicount case.

At odds with the text, the Government's interpretation is also at odds with its own practice in "sentencing package cases." *Greenlaw* v. *United States*, 554 U.S. 237, 253, 128 S. Ct. 2559, 171 L. Ed. 2d 399 (2008). "Those cases typically involve multicount indictments and a successful attack by a defendant on some but not all of the counts of conviction." *Ibid.* In those cases--including ones where §924(c) convictions are invalidated--the Government routinely argues that an appellate court should vacate the entire sentence so that the district court may increase the sentences for any remaining counts up to the limit set by the original aggregate sentence. See *United States* v. *Smith*, 756 F. 3d 1179, 1188-1189, and n. 5 (CA10 2014) (collecting cases). And appellate courts routinely agree. *Id.*, at 1189, and n. 6 (same). As we understand it, the Government's theory in those cases is that the district court may have relied on a now-vacated conviction when imposing sentences for the other counts. But that theory of course directly contradicts the position the Government now advances--that district courts must determine sentences independently of one another, accounting for multiple sentences only when deciding whether to stack them or run them concurrently.

B

Nothing in §924(c) restricts the authority conferred on sentencing courts by §3553(a) and the related provisions to consider a sentence imposed under §924(c) when calculating a just sentence for the predicate count.

The Government points to two limitations in §924(c). First, the Government notes, a mandatory sentence under §924(c) must be imposed "*in addition to* the punishment provided" for the predicate crime. §924(c)(1)(A) (emphasis added). This limitation says nothing about the length of a non-§924(c) sentence, much less about what information a court may consider in determining that sentence. Whether the sentence for the predicate offense is one day or one decade, a district court does not violate the terms of §924(c) so long as it imposes the mandatory minimum "in addition to" the sentence for the violent or drug trafficking crime.

Second, §924(c) states that "no term of imprisonment imposed on a person under this subsection shall run concurrently with any other term of imprisonment imposed on the person, including any term of imprisonment imposed for the [predicate] crime during which the firearm was used, carried, or possessed." §924(c)(1)(D)(ii). Nothing in that language prevents a district court from imposing a 30-year mandatory minimum sentence under §924(c) and a one-day sentence for the predicate violent or drug trafficking crime, provided those terms run one after the other. The Government emphasizes that the requirement of consecutive sentences removes the discretion to run sentences concurrently that district courts exercise under §3584. We agree. So does Dean, for that matter. But we fail to see the significance of the point. The bar on imposing concurrent sentences does not affect a court's discretion to consider a mandatory minimum when calculating each individual sentence.

The Government would, in effect, have us read an additional limitation into §924(c): Where §924(c) says "in addition to the punishment provided for [the predicate] crime of violence," what the statute *really* means is "in addition to the punishment provided for [the predicate] crime of violence *in the absence of a Section 924(c) conviction*." See Reply Brief 2. We have said that "[d]rawing meaning from silence is particularly inappropriate" where "Congress has shown that it knows how to direct sentencing practices in express terms." *Kimbrough* v. *United States*, 552 U.S. 85, 103, 128 S. Ct. 558, 169 L. Ed. 2d 481 (2007). Congress has shown just that in another statute, 18 U.S.C. §1028A. That section, which criminalizes the commission of identity theft "during and in relation to" certain predicate felonies, imposes a mandatory minimum sentence "in addition to the punishment provided for" the underlying offense. §1028A(a)(1). It also says that the mandatory minimum must be consecutive to the sentence for the underlying offense. §1028A(b)(2). So far, §1028A tracks §924(c) in relevant respects. But §1028A goes further: It provides that in determining the appropriate length of imprisonment for the predicate felony "a court shall not in any way reduce the term to be imposed for such crime so as to compensate for, or otherwise take into account, any separate term of imprisonment imposed or to be imposed for a violation of this section." §1028A(b)(3). Section 1028A says just what the Government reads §924(c) to say--of course, without *actually* saying it.

The Government responds that §1028A was passed in 2004, long after Congress enacted the 1984 amendments creating the current sentencing regime in §924(c). Brief for United States 46. True. But §1028A confirms that it would have been easy enough to make explicit what the Government argues is implicit in §924(c). It also underscores that for over a decade Congress has been aware of a clear way to bar consideration of a mandatory minimum, but never during that time changed the language of §924(c) to mirror that of §1028A, even as it has amended other aspects of §924(c).

* * *

The Government speaks of Congress's intent to prevent district courts from bottoming out sentences for predicate §924(c) offenses whenever they think a mandatory minimum under §924(c) is already punishment enough. But no such intent finds expression in the language of §924(c). That language simply requires any mandatory minimum under §924(c) to be imposed "in addition to" the sentence for the predicate offense, and to run consecutively to that sentence. Nothing in those requirements prevents a sentencing court from considering a mandatory minimum under §924(c) when calculating an appropriate sentence for the predicate offense.

The judgment of the United States Court of Appeals for the Eighth Circuit is reversed, and the case is remanded for further proceedings consistent with this opinion.

It is so ordered.

HALL, as personal representative of the
ESTATE OF HALL and as successor
trustee of the ETHLYN LOUISE HALL
FAMILY TRUST

v.

HALL et al.

16–1150
SUPREME COURT
OF THE UNITED STATES

January 16, 2018, Argued
March 27, 2018, Decided

ON WRIT OF CERTIORARI TO THE UNITED STATES COURT OF APPEALS FOR THE THIRD CIRCUIT

Chief Justice Roberts delivered the opinion of the Court.

Three Terms ago, we held that one of multiple cases consolidated for multidistrict litigation under 28 U. S. C. §1407 is immediately appealable upon an order disposing of that case, regardless of whether any of the others remain pending. Gelboim v. Bank of America Corp., 574 U. S. _ (2015). We left open, however, the question whether the same is true with respect to cases consolidated under Rule 42(a) of the Federal Rules of Civil Procedure. Id., at _, n. 4 (slip op., at 7, n. 4). This case presents that question.

I

Petitioner Elsa Hall and respondent Samuel Hall are siblings enmeshed in a long-running family feud. Their mother, Ethlyn Hall, lived and owned property in the United States Virgin Islands. Samuel, a lawyer in the Virgin Islands, served as Ethlyn's caretaker and provided her with legal assistance. But trouble eventually came to paradise, and Samuel and Ethlyn fell out over Samuel's management of Ethlyn's real estate holdings. During a visit from Elsa, Ethlyn established an inter vivos trust, transferred all of her property into the trust, and designated Elsa as her successor trustee. Ethlyn then moved to Miami—under circumstances disputed by the parties—to live with her daughter.

The family squabble made its way to court in May 2011. Ethlyn, acting in her individual capacity and as trustee of her inter vivos trust, sued Samuel and his law firm in Federal District Court (the "trust case"). Ethlyn's claims—for breach of fiduciary duty, legal malpractice, conversion, fraud, and unjust enrichment—concerned the handling of her affairs by Samuel and his law firm before she left for Florida.

Then Ethlyn died, and Elsa stepped into her shoes as trustee and accordingly as plaintiff in the trust case. Samuel promptly filed counterclaims in that case against Elsa—in both her individual and representative capacities—for intentional infliction of emotional distress, fraud, breach of fiduciary duty, conversion, and tortious interference. Samuel contended that Elsa had turned their mother against him by taking advantage of Ethlyn's alleged mental frailty. But Samuel ran into an obstacle: Elsa was not a party to the trust case in her individual capacity (only Ethlyn had been). So Samuel filed a new complaint against Elsa in her individual capacity in the same District Court (the "individual case"), raising the same claims that he had asserted as counterclaims in the trust case.

The trust and individual cases initially proceeded along separate tracks. Eventually, on Samuel's motion, the District Court consolidated the cases under Rule 42(a) of the Federal Rules of Civil Procedure, ordering that "[a]ll submissions in the consolidated case shall be filed in" the docket assigned to the trust case. App. to Pet. for Cert. A–15.

Just before the trial commenced, the District Court dismissed from the trust case Samuel's counterclaims against Elsa. Those claims remained in the individual case. The parties then tried the consolidated cases together before a jury.

In the individual case, the jury returned a verdict for Samuel on his intentional infliction of emotional distress claim against Elsa, awarding him $500,000 in compensatory damages and $1.5 million in punitive damages. The clerk entered judgment in that case, but the District Court granted Elsa a new trial, which had the effect of reopening the judgment. The individual case remains pending before the District Court.

In the trust case, the jury returned a verdict against Elsa, in her representative capacity, on her claims against Samuel and his law firm. The clerk entered judgment in that case directing that Elsa "recover nothing" and that "the action be dismissed on the merits." Id., at A–12.

Elsa filed a notice of appeal from the District Court's judgment in the trust case. Samuel and his law firm moved to dismiss the appeal on jurisdictional grounds, arguing that the judgment was not final and appealable because his claims against Elsa remained unresolved in the individual case. The Court of Appeals for the Third Circuit agreed. When two cases have been consolidated for all purposes, the court reasoned, a final decision on one set of claims is generally not appealable while the second set remains pending. The court explained that it considers "whether a less-than-complete judgment is appealable" on a "case-by-case basis." 679 Fed. Appx. 142, 145 (2017). Here, the fact that the claims in the trust and individual cases had been "scheduled together and tried before a single jury" "counsel[ed] in favor of keeping the claims together on appeal." Ibid. The court dismissed Elsa's appeal for lack of jurisdiction.

We granted certiorari, 582 U. S. _ (2017), and now reverse.

II

A

Had the District Court never consolidated the trust and individual cases, there would be no question that Elsa could immediately appeal from the judgment in the trust case. Title 28 U. S. C. §1291 vests the courts of appeals with jurisdiction over "appeals from all final decisions of the district courts," except those directly appealable to this Court. A final decision "ends the litigation on the merits and leaves nothing for the court to do but execute the judgment." Ray Haluch Gravel Co. v. Central Pension Fund of Operating Engineers and Participating Employers, 571 U. S. 177, 183 (2014) . The archetypal final decision is "one[ ] that trigger[s] the entry of judgment." Mohawk Industries, Inc. v. Carpenter, 558 U. S. 100, 103 (2009) . Appeal from such a final decision is a "matter of right." Gelboim, 574 U. S., at _ (slip op., at 1). Under §1291, "any litigant armed with a final judgment from a lower federal court is entitled to take an appeal," Arizona v. Manypenny, 451 U. S. 232, 244 (1981) , which generally must be filed within 30 days, 28 U. S. C. §2107(a).

Here the jury's verdict against Elsa resolved all of the claims in the trust case, and the clerk accordingly entered judgment in that case providing that "the action be dismissed on the merits." App. to Pet. for Cert. A–12. With the entry of judgment, the District Court "completed its adjudication of [Elsa's] complaint and terminated [her] action." Gelboim, 574 U. S., at _ (slip op., at 7). An appeal would normally lie from that judgment.

But, Samuel contends, there is more to the litigation than the suit Elsa pursued against him in her representative capacity. There is also his suit against her in her individual capacity, which has not yet been decided. Because the District Court consolidated the trust and individual cases under Rule 42(a)(2), he argues, they merged and should be regarded as one case. Viewed that way, the judgment in the trust case was merely interlocutory, and more remains to be done in the individual case before the consolidated cases in the aggregate are finally resolved and subject to appeal.

B

Rule 42(a)—entitled "[c]onsolidation"—provides that if "actions before the court involve a common question of law or fact, the court may" take one of three measures. First, the court may "join for hearing or trial any or all matters at issue in the actions." Fed. Rule Civ. Proc. 42(a)(1). Second, the court may "consolidate the actions." Rule 42(a)(2). Third, the court may "issue any other orders to avoid unnecessary cost or delay." Rule 42(a)(3). Whether the judgment entered in the trust case is an immediately appealable final decision turns on the effect of consolidation under Rule 42(a).

Samuel, looking to dictionary definitions, asserts that the "plain meaning of the phrase 'consolidate the actions' is . . . to unite two or more actions into one whole—that is, to join them into a single case." Brief for Respondents 23 (citing Black's Law Dictionary (10th ed. 2014); some internal quotation marks and alterations omitted). But the meaning of "consolidate" in the present context is ambiguous. When Rule 42(a) was adopted, the term was generally defined, as it is now, as meaning to "unite, as various particulars, into one mass or body; to bring together in close union; to combine." Webster's New International Dictionary 570 (2d ed. 1942). Consolidation can thus sometimes signify the complete merger of discrete units: "The company consolidated two branches." But the term can also mean joining together discrete units without causing them to lose their independent character. The United States, for example, is composed of States "unite[d], as various particulars, into one mass or body," "br[ought] together in close union," or "combine[d]." Yet all agree that entry into our Union "by no means implies the loss of distinct and individual existence . . . by the States." Texas v. White, 7 Wall. 700, 725 (1869). "She consolidated her books" hardly suggests that the "books" became "book." The very metaphor Samuel offers—that consolidation "make[s] two one, like marriage"—highlights this point. Tr. of Oral Arg. 56. However dear to each other, spouses would be surprised to hear that their union extends beyond the metaphysical. This is not a plain meaning case.

It is instead about a term—consolidate—with a legal lineage stretching back at least to the first federal consolidation statute, enacted by Congress in 1813. Act of July 22, 1813, §3, 3Stat. 21 (later codified as Rev. Stat. §921 and 28 U. S. C. §734 (1934 ed.)). Over 125 years, this Court, along with the courts of appeals and leading treatises, interpreted that term to mean the joining together—but not the complete merger—of constituent cases. Those authorities particularly emphasized that constituent cases remained independent when it came to judgments and appeals. Rule 42(a), promulgated in 1938, was expressly based on the 1813 statute. The history against which Rule 42(a) was adopted resolves any ambiguity regarding the meaning of "consolidate" in subsection (a)(2). It makes clear that one of multiple cases consolidated under the Rule retains its independent character, at least to the extent it is appealable when finally resolved, regardless of any ongoing proceedings in the other cases.

C

Lord Mansfield pioneered the consolidation of related cases in England, and the practice quickly took root in American courts. See Mutual Life Ins. Co. v. Hillmon, 145 U. S. 285, 292 (1892) . In 1813, Congress authorized the newly formed federal courts, when confronted with "causes of like nature, or relative to the same question," to "make such orders and rules concerning proceedings therein as may be conformable to the principles and usages belonging to courts for avoiding unnecessary costs or delay in the administration of justice" and to "consolidate[ ]" the causes when it "shall appear reasonable." §3, 3Stat. 21. This consolidation statute applied at law, equity, and admiralty, see 1 W. Rose, A Code of Federal Procedure §823(a) (1907) (Rose), and remained in force for 125 years, until its replacement by Rule 42(a).

From the outset, we understood consolidation not as completely merging the constituent cases into one, but instead as enabling more efficient case management while preserving the distinct identities of the cases and the rights of the separate parties in them. In Rich v. Lambert, 12 How. 347 (1852), for example, we considered an appeal from several consolidated cases in admiralty. The appellees, the owners of cargo damaged during shipment, raised a challenge to our jurisdiction that turned on the nature of the consolidation. At the time, we could exercise appellate jurisdiction only over cases involving at least $2,000 in controversy. The damages awarded to the cargo owners in the consolidated cases surpassed $2,000 in the aggregate, but most of the constituent cases did not individually clear that jurisdictional hurdle. Id., at 352–353.

We declined to view the consolidated cases as one for purposes of appeal, concluding that we had jurisdiction only over those constituent cases that individually involved damages exceeding $2,000. Ibid. As we explained, "although [a consolidated] proceeding assumes the form of a joint suit, it is in reality a mere joinder of distinct causes of action by distinct parties, arising out of a common injury, and which are heard and determined, so far as the merits are concerned, the same as in the case of separate libels for each cause of action." Id., at 353. Consolidation was "allowed by the practice of the court for its convenience, and the saving of time and expense to the parties." Ibid.

The trial court's decree, we noted, had the effect of individually resolving each constituent case. Ibid. ("The same decree . . . is entered as in the case of separate suits."); see Black's Law Dictionary 532 (3d ed. 1933) ("decree" is a "judgment of a court of equity or admiralty, answering for most purposes to the judgment of a court of common law"). Accordingly, we did "not perceive . . . any ground for a distinction as to the right of appeal from a decree as entered in these cases from that which exists where the proceedings have been distinct and separate throughout." Rich, 12 How., at 353; see Hanover Fire Ins. Co. v. Kinneard, 129 U. S. 176, 177 (1889) (evaluating appellate jurisdiction over a writ of error in one of several consolidated cases without reference to the others).

We elaborated on the principles underlying consolidation in Mutual Life Insurance Co. v. Hillmon, 145 U. S. 285 . Hillmon, a staple of law school courses on evidence, involved three separate actions instituted against different life insurance companies by one Sallie Hillmon, the beneficiary on policies purchased by her husband John. Sallie claimed she was entitled to the sizable proceeds of the policies because John had died while journeying through southern Kansas with two companions in search of a site for a cattle ranch. The three companies countered that John was in fact still alive, having conspired with one of the companions to murder the other and pass his corpse off as John's, all as part of an insurance fraud scheme. The trial court consolidated the cases and tried them together. Id., at 285–287.

The court, for purposes of determining the number of peremptory juror challenges to which each defendant was entitled, treated the three cases as though they had merged into one. Ibid. On appeal we disagreed, holding that each defendant should receive the full complement of peremptory challenges. Id., at 293. That was because, "although the defendants might lawfully be compelled, at the discretion of the court, to try the cases together, the causes of action remained distinct, and required separate verdicts and judgments; and no defendant could be deprived, without its consent, of any right material to its defence . . . to which it would have been entitled if the cases had been tried separately." Ibid. On remand, one case settled, and a consolidated trial of the others "result[ed] in separate judgments" for Sallie. Connecticut Mut. Life Ins. Co. v. Hillmon, 188 U. S. 208, 209 (1903) .

In Stone v. United States, 167 U. S. 178, 189 (1897) , we held that a party appealing from the judgment in one of two cases consolidated for trial could not also raise claims with respect to the other case. John Stone was the sole defendant in one case and one of three defendants in the other. Id., at 179–181. After a consolidated trial, the jury returned a verdict in the case against Stone alone; its verdict in the multidefendant case was set aside. Id., at 181. Stone appealed from the judgment in his case, arguing that the failure to grant a peremptory challenge in the multidefendant case affected the jury's verdict in his. Id., at 189. We rejected that claim, punctiliously respecting the distinction between the constituent cases. There was "no merit in the objection," we said, because in the case before us Stone had "had the benefit of the three peremptory challenges" to which he was entitled in that case. Ibid.; see Stone v. United States, 64 F. 667, 672 (CA9 1894) ("The two cases, although consolidated, were separate and distinct. Defendant had exercised all the rights and privileges he was entitled to in this case.").

And just five years before Rule 42(a) became law, we reiterated that, under the consolidation statute, consolidation did not result in the merger of constituent cases. Johnson v. Manhattan R. Co., 289 U. S. 479 –497 (1933). A major case of its day, Johnson arose from the "financial embarrassment" during the Great Depression of two companies involved in operating the New York subway system. Johnson v. Manhattan R. Co., 61 F. 2d 934, 936 (CA2 1932). In the resulting litigation, the District Court consolidated two suits, apparently with the intent to "effect an intervention of the parties to the [first suit] in the [second] suit"—in other words, to make the two suits one. Id., at 940. Judge Learned Hand, writing for the Second Circuit on appeal, would have none of it: "consolidation does not merge the suits; it is a mere matter of convenience in administration, to keep them in step. They remain as independent as before." Ibid. We affirmed, relying on Hillmon and several lower court cases reflecting the same understanding of consolidation. Johnson, 289 U. S., at 497, n. 8. We explained once more that "consolidation is permitted as a matter of convenience and economy in administration, but does not merge the suits into a single cause, or change the rights of the parties, or make those who are parties in one suit parties in another." Id., at 496–497.

Decisions by the Courts of Appeals, with isolated departures,[1]* reflected the same understanding in cases involving all manners of consolidation. See, e.g., Baltimore S. S. Co., Inc. v. Koppel Indus. Car & Equip. Co., 299 F. 158, 160 (CA4 1924) ("the consolidation for convenience of trial did not merge the two causes of action" or "deprive either party of any right or relieve it of any burden incident to the libel or cross-libel as a separate proceeding"); Taylor v. Logan Trust Co., 289 F. 51, 53 (CA8 1923) (parties to one constituent case could not appeal orders in the other because "consolidation did not make the parties to one suit parties to the other"; cited in Johnson); Toledo, St. L. & K. C. R. Co. v. Continental Trust Co., 95 F. 497, 506 (CA6 1899) (consolidation "operates as a mere carrying on together of two separate suits supposed to involve identical issues" and "does not avoid the necessity of separate decrees in each case"; cited in Johnson).

One frequently cited case illustrates the point. In Adler v. Seaman, 266 F. 828, 831 (CA8 1920), the District Court "sought to employ consolidation as a medium of getting the two independent suits united," but the Court of Appeals made clear that the consolidation statute did not authorize such action. The court explained that constituent cases sometimes "assume certain natural attitudes toward each other, such as 'in the nature of' a cross-bill or intervention." Id., at 838. Be that as it may, the court continued, "this is purely a rule of convenience, and does not result in actually making such parties defendants or interveners in the other suit." Ibid. The court described "the result of consolidation" as instead "merely to try cases together, necessitating separate verdicts and judgments or separate decrees," and to "leave" the constituent cases "separate, independent action[s]." Id., at 838, 840.

Treatises summarizing federal precedent applying the consolidation statute also concluded that consolidated cases "remain distinct." 1 Rose §823(c), at 758. They recognized that consolidated cases should "remain separate as to parties, pleadings, and judgment," W. Simkins, Federal Practice 63 (rev. ed. 1923), and that "[t]here must be separate verdicts, judgments or decrees, even although the consolidating party wished for one verdict," 1 Rose §823(c), at 758; see also G. Virden, Consolidation Under Rule 42 of the Federal Rules of Civil Procedure, in 141 F. R. D. 169, 173–174 (1992) (Virden) ("as of 1933 and the Johnson case of that year, it was well settled that consolidation in the federal courts did not merge the separate cases into a single action").

Several aspects of this body of law support the inference that, prior to Rule 42(a), a judgment completely resolving one of several consolidated cases was an immediately appealable final decision. We made clear, for example, that each constituent case must be analyzed individually on appeal to ascertain jurisdiction and to decide its disposition—a compartmentalized analysis that would be gratuitous if the cases had merged into a single case subject to a single appeal. We emphasized that constituent cases should end in separate decrees or judgments—the traditional trigger for the right to appeal, for which there would be no need if an appeal could arise only from the resolution of the consolidated cases as a whole. We explained that the parties to one case did not become parties to the other by virtue of consolidation—indicating that the right of each to pursue his individual case on appeal should not be compromised by the litigation conduct of the other. And, finally, we held that consolidation could not prejudice rights to which the parties would have been due had consolidation never occurred. Forcing an aggrieved party to wait for other cases to conclude would substantially impair his ability to appeal from a final decision fully resolving his own case—a "matter of right," Gelboim, 574 U. S., at _ (slip op., at 1), to which he was "entitled," Manypenny, 451 U. S., at 244.

D

Against this background, two years after Johnson, the Rules Advisory Committee began discussion of what was to become Rule 42(a). The Rule, which became effective in 1938, was expressly modeled on its statutory predecessor, the Act of July 22, 1813. See Advisory Committee's Notes on 1937 Adoption of Fed. Rule Civ. Proc. 42(a), 28 U. S. C. App., p. 887. The Rule contained no definition of "consolidate," so the term presumably carried forward the same meaning we had ascribed to it under the consolidation statute for 125 years, and had just recently reaffirmed in Johnson. See Frankfurter, Some Reflections on the Reading of Statutes, 47 Colum. L. Rev. 527, 537 (1947) ("if a word is obviously transplanted from another legal source, whether the common law or other legislation, it brings the old soil with it"); cf. Class v. United States, 583 U. S. _, _ (2018) (slip op., at 10)

(Federal Rule of Criminal Procedure 11(a)(2) did not silently alter existing doctrine established by this Court's past decisions).

Samuel nonetheless asserts that there is a significant distinction between the original consolidation statute and Rule 42(a). The statute authorized district courts to "consolidate" related "causes when it appears reasonable to do so" or to "make such orders and rules . . . as may be conformable to the usages of courts for avoiding unnecessary costs or delay in the administration of justice." 28 U. S. C. §734 (1934 ed.). Rule 42(a) permits district courts not only to "consolidate the actions" (subsection (a)(2)) and "issue any other orders to avoid unnecessary cost or delay" (subsection (a)(3)), but also to "join for hearing or trial any or all matters at issue in the actions" (subsection (a)(1)).

Whatever "consolidate" meant under the statute, Samuel posits, it took on a different meaning under Rule 42(a) with the addition of subsection (a)(1). Samuel describes the Rule as "permit[ting] two forms of consolidation": consolidation that "extend[s] only to certain proceedings," such as discovery, and consolidation "for all purposes." Brief for Respondents 4–5. He locates textual authority for the former in subsection (a)(1), which he says empowers courts to "join[ ] multiple actions for procedural purposes." Id., at 23. In light of this broad grant of authority, he contends, subsection (a)(2) must provide for something more if it is not to be superfluous. And Samuel sees that something more as the ability to merge cases that have been consolidated for "all purposes" into a single, undifferentiated case—one appealable only when all issues in each formerly distinct case have been decided. See id., at 22–24 (to "consolidate" separate actions is "to join them into a single case" or "meld [them] into a single unit" (alterations omitted)).

We disagree. It is only by substantially overreading subsection (a)(1) that Samuel can argue that its addition compels a radical reinterpretation of the familiar term "consolidate" in subsection (a)(2). The text of subsection (a)(1) permits the joining of cases only for "hearing or trial." That narrow grant of authority cannot fairly be read as the exclusive source of a district court's power to "join[ ] multiple actions for procedural purposes." Brief for Respondents 23. There is, after all, much more to litigation than hearings or trials—such as motions practice or discovery. A district court's undisputed ability to consolidate cases for such limited purposes must therefore stem from subsection (a)(2). That defeats Samuel's argument that interpreting subsection (a)(2) to adopt the traditional understanding of consolidation would render it "wholly duplicative of [subsection] (a)(1)," and that subsection (a)(2) "therefore must permit courts . . . to 'consolidate' the actions themselves into a single unit." Id., at 23–24. Samuel's reinterpretation of "consolidate" is, in other words, a solution in search of a problem.

We think, moreover, that if Rule 42(a) were meant to transform consolidation into something sharply contrary to what it had been, we would have heard about it. Congress, we have held, "does not alter the fundamental details" of an existing scheme with "vague terms" and "subtle device[s]." Whitman v. American Trucking Assns., Inc., 531 U. S. 457, 468 (2001) ; cf. Class, 583 U. S., at _ (slip op., at 10). That is true in spades when it comes to the work of the Federal Rules Advisory Committees. Their laborious drafting process requires years of effort and many layers of careful review before a proposed Rule is presented to this Court for possible submission to Congress. See Report of Advisory Committee on Rules for Civil Procedure (Apr. 1937) (describing the exhaustive process undertaken to draft the first Federal Rules of Civil Procedure). No sensible draftsman, let alone a Federal Rules Advisory Committee, would take a term that had meant, for more than a century, that separate actions do not merge into one, and silently and abruptly reimagine the same term to mean that they do.

Similarly, nothing in the pertinent proceedings of the Rules Advisory Committee supports the notion that Rule 42(a) was meant to overturn the settled understanding of consolidation. See United States v. Vonn, 535 U. S. 55 , n. 6 (2002) (Advisory Committee Notes are "a reliable source of insight into the meaning of a rule"). In this instance, the Committee simply commented that Rule 42(a) "is based upon" its statutory predecessor, "but insofar as the statute differs from this rule, it is modified." Advisory Committee's Notes on 1937 Adoption of Fed. Rule Civ. Proc. 42(a), 28 U. S. C. App., at 887. The Committee did not identify any specific instance in which Rule 42(a) changed the statute, let alone the dramatic transformation Samuel would have us recognize. See Virden 174–181 (evaluating the history of the development of Rule 42(a) and finding no evidence that the Committee intended a shift in meaning along the lines proposed by Samuel). This is significant because when the Committee intended a new rule to change existing federal practice, it typically explained the departure. See, e.g., Advisory Committee's Notes on 1937 Adoption of Fed. Rule Civ. Proc. 4, 28 U. S. C. App., p. 747 (a predecessor statute "is substantially continued insofar as it applies to a summons, but its requirements as to teste of process are superseded"); Advisory Committee's Notes on 1937 Adoption of Fed. Rule Civ. Proc. 18, 28 U. S. C. App., p. 802 ("In respect to fraudulent conveyances the rule changes the former rule requiring a prior judgment against the owner . . . to conform to the provisions of the Uniform Fraudulent Conveyance Act, §§ 9 and 10.").

As a leading treatise explained at the time, through consolidation under Rule 42(a) "one or many or all of the phases of the several actions may be merged. But merger is never so complete in consolidation as to deprive any party of any substantial rights which he may have possessed had the actions proceeded separately." 3 J. Moore & J. Friedman, Moore's Federal Practice §42.01, pp. 3050–3051 (1938). Thus, "separate verdicts and judgments are normally necessary." Id., at 3051, n. 12.

The limited extent to which this Court has addressed consolidation since adoption of Rule 42(a) confirms the traditional understanding. Just recently in Bank Markazi v. Peterson, 578 U. S. _, _–_ (2016) (slip op., at 19–20), for example, the Court determined that cases "consolidated for administrative purposes at the execution stage . . . were not independent of the original actions for damages and each claim retained its separate character." The Court quoted as authority a treatise explaining that "actions do not lose their separate identity because of consolidation." Id., at _ (slip op., at 20) (quoting 9A C. Wright & A. Miller, Federal Practice and Procedure §2382, p. 10 (3d ed. 2008) (Wright & Miller)).

In Butler v. Dexter, 425 U. S. 262 –267 (1976) (per curiam), we dismissed an appeal because the constitutional question that supplied our jurisdiction had been raised not in the case before us, but instead only in other cases with which it had been consolidated. We explained that "[e]ach case . . . must be considered separately to determine whether or not this Court has jurisdiction to consider its merits". Id., at 267, n. 12; see Rich, 12 How., at 352–353. And in Alfred Dunhill of London, Inc. v. Republic of Cuba, 425 U.S. 682 , and n. 22 (1976) (Marshall, J., dissenting), four dissenting Justices—reaching an issue not addressed by the majority—cited Johnson for the proposition that actions are "not merged" and do "not lose their separate identities because of . . . consolidation" under Rule 42(a).

In the face of all the foregoing, we cannot accept Samuel's contention that "consolidate" in Rule 42(a) carried a very different meaning—with very different consequences—than it had in Johnson, just five years before the Rule was adopted.

None of this means that district courts may not consolidate cases for "all purposes" in appropriate circumstances. District courts enjoy substantial discretion in deciding whether and to what extent to consolidate cases. See 9A Wright & Miller §2383 (collecting cases). What our decision does mean is that constituent cases retain their separate identities at least to the extent that a final decision in one is immediately appealable by the losing party. That is, after all, the point at which, by definition, a "district court disassociates itself from a case." Swint v. Chambers County Comm'n, 514 U. S. 35, 42 (1995) . We thus express no view on any issue arising prior to that time.

* * *

The normal rule is that a "final decision" confers upon the losing party the immediate right to appeal. That rule provides clear guidance to litigants. Creating exceptions to such a critical step in litigation should not be undertaken lightly. Congress has granted us the authority to prescribe rules "defin[ing] when a ruling of a district court is final for the purposes of appeal under" §1291, 28 U. S. C. §2072(c), and we have explained that changes with respect to the meaning of final decision "are to come from rulemaking, . . . not judicial decisions in particular controversies," Microsoft Corp. v. Baker, 582 U. S. _, _ (2017) (slip op., at 15). If, as Samuel fears, our holding in this case were to give rise to practical problems for district courts and litigants, the appropriate Federal Rules Advisory Committees would certainly remain free to take the matter up and recommend revisions accordingly.

Rule 42(a) did not purport to alter the settled understanding of the consequences of consolidation. That understanding makes clear that when one of several consolidated cases is finally decided, a disappointed litigant is free to seek review of that decision in the court of appeals.

We reverse the judgment of the Court of Appeals for the Third Circuit and remand the case for further proceedings consistent with this opinion.

It is so ordered.

UNITED STATES, Petitioner
v.
RENE SANCHEZ-GOMEZ, et al.

17-312
SUPREME COURT
OF THE UNITED STATES

March 26, 2018, Argued
May 14, 2018, Decided

ON WRIT OF CERTIORARI TO THE UNITED STATES COURT OF APPEALS FOR THE NINTH CIRCUIT

Chief Justice Roberts delivered the opinion of the Court.

Four criminal defendants objected to being bound by full restraints during pretrial proceedings in their cases, but the District Court denied relief. On appeal, the Court of Appeals for the Ninth Circuit held that the use of such restraints was unconstitutional, even though each of the four criminal cases had ended prior to its decision. The question presented is whether the appeals were saved from mootness either because the defendants sought "class-like relief" in a "functional class action," or because the challenged practice was "capable of repetition, yet evading review."

I

It is the responsibility of the United States Marshals Service to "provide for the security . . . of the United States District Courts." 28 U. S. C. §566(a). To fulfill that duty, the United States Marshal for the Southern District of California requested that the judges of that district permit the use of full restraints on all in-custody defendants during nonjury proceedings. When "full restraints" are applied, "a defendant's hands are closely handcuffed together, these handcuffs are connected by chain to another chain running around the defendant's waist, and the defendant's feet are shackled and chained together." 859 F. 3d 649, 653 (CA9 2017) (en banc). In support of his proposal, the Marshal cited safety concerns arising from understaffing, past incidents of violence, and the high volume of in-custody defendants produced in the Southern District. The judges agreed to the Marshal's request, with modifications providing that a district or magistrate judge may require a defendant to be produced without restraints, and that a defendant can request that this be done. See App. 78–79.

Respondents Jasmin Morales, Rene Sanchez-Gomez, Moises Patricio-Guzman, and Mark Ring were among the defendants produced by the Marshals Service for pretrial proceedings in full restraints. They raised constitutional objections to the use of such restraints in their respective cases, and to the restraint policy as a whole. They noted that the policy had resulted in the imposition of full restraints on, for example, a woman with a fractured wrist, a man with a severe leg injury, a blind man, and a wheelchair-bound woman. The District Court denied their challenges.

Respondents appealed to the Court of Appeals for the Ninth Circuit, but before the court could issue a decision, their underlying criminal cases came to an end. Morales, Sanchez-Gomez, and Patricio-Guzman each pled guilty to the offense for which they were charged: Morales, to felony importation of a controlled substance, in violation of 21 U. S. C. §§952 and 960; Sanchez-Gomez, to felony misuse of a passport, in violation of 18 U. S. C. §1544; and Patricio-Guzman, to misdemeanor illegal entry into the United States, in violation of 8 U. S. C. §1325. The charges against Ring—for making an interstate threat in violation of 18 U. S. C. §875(c)—were dismissed pursuant to a deferred-prosecution agreement.

A panel of the Court of Appeals nonetheless concluded that respondents' claims were not moot, and went on to strike down the restraint policy as violating the Due Process Clause of the Fifth Amendment. 798 F. 3d 1204 (CA9 2015). Those rulings were reaffirmed on rehearing en banc. 859 F. 3d 649. The en banc court understood the "main dispute" before it to be a challenge to the policy itself, not just to the application of that policy to respondents. Id., at 655. The court then construed respondents' notices of appeal as petitions for mandamus, which invoked the court's supervisory authority over the Southern District. Id., at 657. The case was, in the court's view, a "functional class action" involving "class-like claims" seeking "class-like relief." Id., at 655, 657–658. In light of that understanding, the Court of Appeals held that this Court's civil class action precedents kept the case alive, even though respondents were no longer subject to the restraint policy. Id., at 657–659 (citing Gerstein v. Pugh, 420 U. S. 103, 110–111, n. 11 (1975)). On the merits, the Court of Appeals concluded that the restraint policy violated the Constitution. 859 F. 3d, at 666.

Judge Ikuta, writing in dissent for herself and four colleagues, rejected the majority's application of class action precedents to the individual criminal cases before the court and would have held the case moot. Id., at 675. She also disagreed with the majority on the merits, concluding that the restraint policy did not violate the Constitution. Id., at 683.

We granted certiorari. 583 U. S. _ (2017).

II

To invoke federal jurisdiction, a plaintiff must show a "personal stake" in the outcome of the action. Genesis HealthCare Corp. v. Symczyk, 569 U. S. 66, 71 (2013). "This requirement ensures that the Federal Judiciary confines itself to its constitutionally limited role of adjudicating actual and concrete disputes, the resolutions of which have direct consequences on the parties involved." Ibid. Such a dispute "must be extant at all stages of review, not merely at the time the complaint is filed." Preiser v. Newkirk, 422 U. S. 395, 401 (1975). A case that becomes moot at any point during the proceedings is "no longer a 'Case' or 'Controversy' for purposes of Article III," and is outside the jurisdiction of the federal courts. Already, LLC v. Nike, Inc., 568 U. S. 85, 91 (2013).

A

In concluding that this case was not moot, the Court of Appeals relied upon our class action precedents, most prominently Gerstein v. Pugh. That reliance was misplaced. 1 *

Gerstein, a class action brought under Federal Rule of Civil Procedure 23, involved a certified class of detainees raising claims concerning their pretrial detention. 420 U. S., at 106–107. By the time this Court heard the case, the named representatives' claims were moot, and the record suggested that their interest might have lapsed even before the District Court certified the class. See id., at 110–111, n. 11. Normally a class action would be moot if no named class representative with an unexpired claim remained at the time of class certification. See ibid. (citing Sosna v. Iowa, 419 U. S. 393, 402, n. 11 (1975)). The Court nevertheless held that the case remained live. As we explained, pretrial custody was inherently temporary and of uncertain length, such that we could not determine "that any given individual, named as plaintiff, would be in pretrial custody long enough for a district judge to certify the class." Gerstein, 420 U. S., at 110–111, n. 11. At the same time, it was certain that there would always be some group of detainees subject to the challenged practice. Ibid. Given these circumstances, the Court determined that the class action could proceed. Ibid.; see Swisher v. Brady, 438 U. S. 204, 213–214, n. 11 (1978) (employing same analysis in a class action challenging juvenile court procedures).

The Court of Appeals interpreted Gerstein to cover all "cases sufficiently similar to class actions" in which, "because of the inherently transitory nature of the claims," the claimant's "interests would expire before litigation could be completed." 859 F. 3d, at 658. Gerstein was an action brought under Federal Rule of Civil Procedure 23, but the Court of Appeals decided that such "a procedural mechanism to aggregate the claims" was not a "necessary prerequisite" for application of the Gerstein rule. 859 F. 3d, at 659 (alteration omitted). Respondents, the court noted, sought "relief [from the restraint policy] not merely for themselves, but for all in-custody defendants in the district." Id., at 655. Those "class-like claims" seeking "class-like relief" were sufficient to trigger the application of Gerstein and save the case from mootness, despite the termination of respondents' criminal cases. 859 F. 3d, at 655.

We reject the notion that Gerstein supports a freestanding exception to mootness outside the class action context. The class action is a creature of the Federal Rules of Civil Procedure. See generally 7A C. Wright, A. Miller & M. Kane, Federal Practice and Procedure §1751 et seq. (3d ed. 2005). It is an "exception to the usual rule that litigation is conducted by and on behalf of the individual named parties only," and "provides a procedure by which the court may exercise . . . jurisdiction over the various individual claims in a single proceeding." Califano v. Yamasaki, 442 U. S. 682, 700–701 (1979). "The certification of a suit as a class action has important consequences for the unnamed members of the class." Sosna, 419 U. S., at 399, n. 8. Those class members may be "bound by the judgment" and are considered parties to the litigation in many important respects. Devlin v. Scardelletti, 536 U. S. 1, 7, 9–10 (2002). A certified class thus "acquires a legal status separate from the interest asserted by the named plaintiff." Genesis HealthCare, 569 U. S., at 74 (quoting Sosna, 419 U. S., at 399; alterations omitted).

Gerstein belongs to a line of cases that we have described as turning on the particular traits of civil class actions. The first case in this line, Sosna v. Iowa, held that when the claim of the named plaintiff becomes moot after class certification, a "live controversy may continue to exist" based on the ongoing interests of the remaining unnamed class members. Genesis HealthCare, 569 U. S., at 74 (citing Sosna, 419 U. S., at 399–402); see Franks v. Bowman Transp. Co., 424 U. S. 747, 755–756 (1976). The "fact that a putative class acquires an independent legal status once it is certified" was, we later explained, "essential to our decision[ ] in Sosna." Genesis HealthCare, 569 U. S., at 75; see Kremens v. Bartley, 431 U. S. 119, 131–133 (1977) (explaining that, under Sosna's rule, "only a 'properly certified' class . . . may succeed to the adversary position of a named representative whose claim becomes moot"); Alvarez v. Smith, 558 U. S. 87, 92–93 (2009) (same).

Gerstein, announced one month after Sosna, provides a limited exception to Sosna's requirement that a named plaintiff with a live claim exist at the time of class certification. The exception applies when the pace of litigation and the inherently transitory nature of the claims at issue conspire to make that requirement difficult to fulfill. See Sosna, 419 U. S., at 402, n. 11 (anticipating the Gerstein rule as an exception); Gerstein, 420 U. S., at 110–111, n. 11 (describing its holding as "a suitable exception" to Sosna). We have repeatedly tied Gerstein's rule to the class action setting from which it emerged. See, e.g., Genesis HealthCare, 569 U. S., at 71, n. 2 (describing Gerstein's rule as "developed in the context of class actions under Rule 23 to address the circumstance in which a named plaintiff's claim becomes moot prior to certification of the class"); United States Parole Comm'n v. Geraghty, 445 U. S. 388, 397–399 (1980) (highlighting Gerstein as an example of the Court "consider[ing] the application of the 'personal stake' requirement in the class-action context").

In concluding that Gerstein reaches further, the Court of Appeals looked to our recent decision in Genesis HealthCare Corp. v. Symczyk. But in that case the Court refused to extend Gerstein beyond the class action context, even with respect to a procedural device bearing many features similar to a class action. Genesis HealthCare addressed whether a "collective action" brought under the Fair Labor Standards Act (FLSA) by a plaintiff on behalf of herself "and other 'similarly situated' employees" remained "justiciable when the lone plaintiff's individual claim bec[ame] moot." 569 U. S., at 69. In an effort to continue her case on behalf of others, the plaintiff turned to Sosna and its progeny, including Gerstein. But those cases, we explained, were "inapposite," not least because "Rule 23 actions are fundamentally different from collective actions under the FLSA." Genesis HealthCare, 569 U. S., at 74. Such collective actions, we stressed, do not "produce a class with an independent legal status, or join additional parties to the action." Id., at 75.

This case, which does not involve any formal mechanism for aggregating claims, is even further removed from Rule 23 and Gerstein. The Federal Rules of Criminal Procedure establish for criminal cases no vehicle comparable to the FLSA collective action, much less the class action. And we have never permitted criminal defendants to band together to seek prospective relief in their individual criminal cases on behalf of a class. As we said when declining to apply nonparty preclusion outside the formal class action context, courts may not "recognize . . . a common-law kind of class action" or "create de facto class actions at will." Taylor v. Sturgell, 553 U. S. 880, 901 (2008) (alterations omitted); see Smith v. Bayer Corp., 564 U. S. 299, 315–316 (2011) (same); Pasadena City Bd. of Ed. v. Spangler, 427 U. S. 424, 430 (1976) (rejecting in mootness context the idea that "the failure to obtain the class certification required under Rule 23 is merely the absence of a meaningless 'verbal recital' ").

The court below designated respondents' case a "functional class action" because respondents were pursuing relief "not merely for themselves, but for all in-custody defendants in the district." 859 F. 3d, at 655, 657–658. But as explained in Genesis HealthCare, the "mere presence of . . . allegations" that might, if resolved in respondents' favor, benefit other similarly situated individuals cannot "save [respondents'] suit from mootness once the[ir] individual claim[s]" have dissipated. 569 U. S., at 73.

Our conclusion is unaffected by the decision of the court below to recast respondents' appeals as petitions for "supervisory mandamus." See 859 F. 3d, at 659 (viewing such a petition, like the civil class action, as a procedural vehicle to which the Gerstein rule applies). Supervisory mandamus refers to the authority of the Courts of Appeals to exercise "supervisory control of the District Courts" through their "discretionary power to issue writs of mandamus." La Buy v. Howes Leather Co., 352 U. S. 249, 259–260 (1957). There is no sign in our scant supervisory mandamus precedents that such cases are exempt from the normal mootness rules. See generally Will v. United States, 389 U. S. 90 (1967); Schlagenhauf v. Holder, 379 U. S. 104 (1964); La Buy, 352 U. S. 249. Indeed, as the court below acknowledged, "[s]upervisory mandamus cases require live controversies." 859 F. 3d, at 657.

B

Respondents do not defend the reasoning of the Court of Appeals. See Brief for Respondents 58 (arguing that this Court need not reach the functional class action issue and should "discard[ ]" that label); Tr. of Oral Arg. 43 (respondents' counsel agreeing that they "have not made any effort to defend" the functional class action approach). In respondents' view, functional class actions and Gerstein's rule are beside the point because two respondents—Sanchez-Gomez and Patricio-Guzman—retain a personal stake in the outcome of their appeals.

Sanchez-Gomez and Patricio-Guzman are no longer in pretrial custody. Their criminal cases, arising from their illegal entry into the United States, ended in guilty pleas well before the Court of Appeals issued its decision. Respondents contend, however, that the claims brought by Sanchez-Gomez and Patricio-Guzman fall within the "exception to the mootness doctrine for a controversy that is capable of repetition, yet evading review." Kingdomware Technologies, Inc. v. United States, 579 U. S. _, _ (2016) (slip op., at 7) (internal quotation marks omitted). A dispute qualifies for that exception only "if (1) the challenged action is in its duration too short to be fully liti-gated prior to its cessation or expiration, and (2) there is a reasonable expectation that the same complaining party will be subjected to the same action again." Turner v. Rogers, 564 U. S. 431, 439–440 (2011) (alterations and internal quotation marks omitted). The parties do not contest that the claims at issue satisfy the first prong of that test, but they sharply disagree as to the second.

Respondents argue that Sanchez-Gomez and Patricio-Guzman meet the second prong because they will again violate the law, be apprehended, and be returned to pretrial custody. But we have consistently refused to "conclude that the case-or-controversy requirement is satisfied by" the possibility that a party "will be prosecuted for violating valid criminal laws." O'Shea v. Littleton, 414 U. S. 488, 497 (1974). We have instead "assume[d] that [litigants] will conduct their activities within the law and so avoid prosecution and conviction as well as exposure to the challenged course of conduct." Ibid.;

see, e.g., Spencer v. Kemna, 523 U. S. 1, 15 (1998) (reasoning that a claim regarding a parole revocation order was moot following release from custody because any continuing consequences of the order were "contingent upon [the claimant] violating the law, getting caught, and being convicted"); Honig v. Doe, 484 U. S. 305, 320 (1988) ("[W]e generally have been unwilling to assume that the party seeking relief will repeat the type of misconduct that would once again place him or her at risk of that injury."); Lane v. Williams, 455 U. S. 624, 632–633, n. 13 (1982) (concluding that case was moot where the challenged parole revocation could not "affect a subsequent parole determination unless respondents again violate state law, are returned to prison, and become eligible for parole").

Respondents argue that this usual refusal to assume future criminal conduct is unwarranted here given the particular circumstances of Sanchez-Gomez's and Patricio-Guzman's offenses. They cite two civil cases—Honig v. Doe and Turner v. Rogers—in which this Court concluded that the expectation that a litigant would repeat the misconduct that gave rise to his claims rendered those claims capable of repetition. Neither case, however, supports a departure from the settled rule.

Honig involved a disabled student's challenge to his suspension from school for disruptive behavior. We found that given his "inability to conform his conduct to socially acceptable norms" or "govern his aggressive, impulsive behavior," it was "reasonable to expect that [the student would] again engage in the type of misconduct that precipitated this suit" and "be subjected to the same unilateral school action for which he initially sought relief." 484 U. S., at 320–321. In Turner, we determined that an indigent person repeatedly held in civil contempt for failing to make child support payments, who was at the time over $13,000 in arrears, and whose next hearing was only five months away, was destined to find himself in civil contempt proceedings again. The challenged denial of appointed counsel at his contempt hearing was thus capable of repetition. See 564 U. S., at 440.

Respondents contend that Sanchez-Gomez and Patricio-Guzman, like the challengers in Honig and Turner, are likely to find themselves right back where they started if we dismiss their case as moot. Respondents cite a Sentencing Commission report finding that in 2013 thirty-eight percent of those convicted and sentenced for an illegal entry or illegal reentry offense "were deported and subsequently illegally reentered at least one time." United States Sentencing Commission, Illegal Reentry Offenses 15 (2015) (cited by Brief for Respondents 51). Respondents emphasize the economic and familial pressures that often compel individuals such as Sanchez-Gomez and Patricio-Guzman to repeatedly attempt to enter the United States. And respondents note that both men, after their release, actually did cross the border into the United States, were apprehended again, and were charged with new illegal entry offenses. All this, respondents say, adds up to a sufficient showing that

Sanchez-Gomez and Patricio-Guzman satisfy the "capable of repetition" requirement. Because the Court of Appeals was not aware that Sanchez-Gomez and Patricio-Guzman had subsequently reentered the United States illegally, respondents invite us to remand this case for further proceedings.

We decline to do so because Honig and Turner are inapposite. Our decisions in those civil cases rested on the litigants' inability, for reasons beyond their control, to prevent themselves from transgressing and avoid recurrence of the challenged conduct. In Honig, such incapacity was the very reason the school sought to expel the student. And in Turner, the indigent individual's large outstanding debt made him effectively incapable of satisfying his imminent support obligations. Sanchez-Gomez and Patricio-Guzman, in contrast, are "able—and indeed required by law"—to refrain from further criminal conduct. Lane, 455 U. S., at 633, n. 13. Their personal incentives to return to the United States, plus the elevated rate of recidivism associated with illegal entry offenses, do not amount to an inability to obey the law. We have consistently refused to find the case or controversy requirement satisfied where, as here, the litigants simply "anticipate violating lawful criminal statutes." O'Shea, 414 U. S., at 496.

III

None of this is to say that those who wish to challenge the use of full physical restraints in the Southern District lack any avenue for relief. In the course of this litigation the parties have touched upon several possible options. See, e.g., Tr. of Oral Arg. 12 (indicating circumstances under which detainees could bring a civil suit). Because we hold this case moot, we take no position on the question.

* * *

We vacate the judgment of the Court of Appeals for the Ninth Circuit and remand the case to that court with instructions to dismiss as moot.

It is so ordered.

Conclusion

This book is a collection of unanimous opinions authored by Chief Justice John Roberts for the Supreme Court of the United States.

Reading these decisions can reveal a portrait of the jurisprudential thought of the Court under Chief Justice Roberts and of the aesthetics of modern American law. These writings are amongst the master works of the highest American legal function. They are presented in this book collection as a sort of coffee-table conversation starter, but they are all serious legal texts with serious legal purpose.

Readers should use the internet to read more about any of the cases in this book. If you enjoyed the writings of Chief Justice Roberts there are many more opinions that he's authored; many are more controversial issues. And if you enjoyed reading unanimous opinions there are also many more of those written by each of the justices every year.

Despite the passionate and bitter ideological differences that separate the justices on some of the most highly publicized cases, there is also a deep consensus that belies these forceful characters who hold such monumental influence on American law; toward a more perfect union.

ROBERTS

UNANIMOUS

ABOUT THE EDITOR

Joshua Warren is an artist, educator, scientist and practicing attorney with an interest in politics, language and creativity.

<u>case law collections by this editor include:</u>

Alito Dissents
Nino's Last
Thomas Concurs
Roberts Unanimous

Cocker Spaniel in the Federal Courts
Dachshund in the Federal Courts
Labrador Retriever in the Federal Courts

Mad Scientist in the Federal Courts
Undead in the Federal Courts
Werewolf in the Federal Courts
Zombie in the Federal Courts

Creativity in the Supreme Court
Catch-22 in the Supreme Court
Red Herring in the Supreme Court

and more…

Other artwork by Joshua Warren can be found at: **warrbo**.com

www.ingramcontent.com/pod-product-compliance
Lightning Source LLC
Chambersburg PA
CBHW031632210526
45464CB00004B/1864